Study Guide

to accompany

Human Development

Ninth Edition

Diane E. Papalia
Sally Wendkos Olds
Ruth Duskin Feldman
in consultation with
Dana Gross

Prepared by
Dr. Saundra K. Ciccarelli
Gulf Coast Community College

Boston Burr Ridge, IL Dubuque, IA Madison, WI New York
San Francisco St. Louis Bangkok Bogotá Caracas Kuala Lumpur
Lisbon London Madrid Mexico City Milan Montreal New Delhi
Santiago Seoul Singapore Sydney Taipei Toronto

The **McGraw·Hill** Companies

Study Guide to accompany
Human Development, Ninth Edition
Diane E. Papalia/Sally Wendkos Olds/Ruth Duskin Feldman

Published by McGraw-Hill Higher Education, an imprint of The McGraw-Hill Companies, Inc., 1221 Avenue of the Americas, New York, NY 10020. Copyright © The McGraw-Hill Companies, Inc., 2004. All rights reserved.

This book is printed on acid-free paper.

1 2 3 4 5 6 7 8 9 0 QPD QPD 0 3

ISBN 0-07-282034-9

www.mhhe.com

HUMAN DEVELOPMENT
STUDY GUIDE
Table of Contents

Preface

This Study Guide is developed for use with *Human Development,* Ninth Edition, by Diane E. Papalia, Sally Wendkos Olds, Ruth Duskin Feldman, and in consultation with Dana Gross. It is intended to assist you with your understanding of the concepts and information in the chapters and to help you synthesize the information, ideas, theories, and concepts in ways that will be of further benefit in your future career.

How to Use the Study Guide

This study guide has been written to help you navigate through the text chapters, explore key concepts and information, synthesize this information into an easily recalled form, and put information to practical use. As you use the study guide, keep your text handy, along with pencils, markers, and pens. It is helpful to many students to keep notes, to study with fellow students, and to be consistent in working with the study guide. Many students find it helpful to use the study guide *before* the instructor's discussion of the chapter material.

Guideposts for Study open each chapter, followed by a **Detailed Chapter Outline** of the entire chapter, with all headings and subheadings included as well as key terms and their definitions. The outline is designed to help you see how material flows within the chapter and how topics relate to each other. Use it as a roadmap to navigate through the material. Additionally, use the guideposts provided when you're reviewing the material before a test.

True/False and Multiple-Choice Self-Tests are exercises that clarify conceptual information in your memory. Refer to the chapter summary, tables, and focus boxes for information needed to complete these exercises. You may find it useful to make a copy of each of these tests and take them twice. It may be helpful to time yourself both times. Shorter times are often correlated with higher scores.

Organize It! is an exercise that organizes conceptual information into an easily recalled list form. After you have made your lists, use them! The brain is a wonderful organ; by singing or dancing information into it, you are using pathways that are not heavily used in everyday academic work. The information may be more easily retrieved this way. You may also want to memorize the lists and verbalize them to yourself as you are driving or jogging.

The **Short Essay Questions** exercise is designed to hone your skills at writing short essays. Many of these questions are based on the Checkpoints section of each chapter. Choose your words carefully!

Critical Thinking Questions are included at the end of every study guide chapter. These questions are loosely based on the "What's Your View" questions within the text. They may be used as extra-credit assignments or may stimulate discussions in small groups in class.

A Note to Professors

The enjoyment of any course in human development greatly depends on the presentation and organization of the information in the text so that students are able to use it in practical ways and remember it long after they have left the course. This study guide is designed to benefit professors as well as students by organizing information in a variety of ways and putting concepts to use in class and during study time. The self-tests and exercises in each chapter may also be used as quiz material to assess the students' grasp of concepts in the chapters.

A Note To Students

The enjoyment of a human life-span course greatly depends on your ability to keep up with the reading in the main text. Most professors realize that a semester is a short time to present a large volume of material, and they pace the course to correspond to reading about one chapter per week in the text. It is to your benefit to read the chapter *before* the lecture/discussion, so that your questions may be answered at the optimal time. You will find that if you read the chapter before the lecture or discussion, you will understand the concepts better when the professor begins the discussion. By keeping ahead of the reading, your anxiety level will go down, and at test time, you will be able to think more clearly and feel more confident.

Take Good Care of Yourself
Many students, and especially students in their first year of college, do not get enough sleep and do not eat a good diet. Taking good care of yourself involves three key activities: time management, exercise, and good diet. These three components interact to reduce detrimental stress, enhance brain activity, and generally keep your grades up rather than down.

Guilt-free Free Time
Time management involves making a schedule on paper, so that you always know where you are supposed to be and what time you are supposed to be there. Just as important, a written schedule lets you know when you have *free time*. Planning for your free time keeps you from feeling that your whole time is taken up with class attendance and study, and allows you to get enough sleep and to enjoy your free time without guilt.

A Walk in the Park
Exercise has been shown to be beneficial in keeping a positive outlook, and it may also be a factor in enhancing brain activity. Exercise gets you up on your feet, outside your dorm room, and into the sunshine. Thirty minutes of walking, biking, or jogging in the fresh air will boost your energy level and give you a fresh look at your assignments. Most college campuses are designed with a parklike atmosphere specifically for this purpose. Enjoy!

An Apple in Your Pocket
Diet can make the difference in your general feeling of well-being, your test performance, and your overall health. If you had to choose one meal to skip, which would it be? For many students, breakfast is the meal that is skipped, but breakfast is the most important meal of the day. Studies have shown that students do better on tests if they have eaten breakfast. A piece of toast, a glass of milk or juice, and a piece of fruit is an easy way to eat breakfast in a hurry. *Always* eat breakfast

on the day of an exam, even if it means sticking an apple in your pocket on the way out the door and eating it on the walk to class.

The Big Picture and A Few Survival Skills

It is easy to live life from one assignment or one exam to the next when you are a college student. It helps reduce anxiety, frustration, and stress to look at the whole semester, rather than living from stress point to stress point. Drawing a picture or graphic of the semester may improve your performance and reduce stress simply by allowing you to see how every course and every event in the courses fit together in a unified whole. Be creative when you make your drawing; include some wishes and hopes for the semester, too.

Separating the parts of this unified whole into manageable pieces is easiest when you organize separate courses into separate notebooks. Keep handouts in the notebook in a folder. Put dates on your handouts or number them. Keep your syllabus and a copy of your schedule, along with a schedule of the library hours and school holidays in sheet protectors in the front of *each notebook*, so that you are never "lost" in a course. If you miss class, catch up right away. Make friends with your lab partner and share notes and information in your classes. These survival skills have a positive effect on your life as a college student.

Read the next section, written by Anita Rosenfield of Yavapai College, for some more in-depth tips and suggestions on how to succeed in this and other courses.

Being An Excellent Student

Anita Rosenfield, Yavapai College

Most students who are in college want to be good students, and most students have some particular goal in mind, which is probably why they chose the particular college or university they are attending. As you chose your college or university, and perhaps even an area of major interest or concentration, you had certain goals in mind, which likely included doing well in school, earning good grades, and graduating. Unfortunately, many students do not do as well in college as they had hoped and expected. Let's examine some of the reasons for this disappointing outcome to see how to avoid them and to learn, instead, how to be a good student and guide your behavior to improve your chances of achieving your goals.

A common definition of *education* is that it is "how people learn stuff." For most of our history, educators have focused on the "stuff." Teachers were required to be masters of their respective academic fields. Even today, some states have requirements that speak only to the need to be qualified in the subject matter one teaches, not in the teaching methods themselves. In the 1960s, we became more interested in the "people" part of the definition, which was evidenced by moving to strategies like open classrooms and free universities. The idea was that, given the opportunity to do so, people will naturally learn. Although these experiments were dismal failures, they taught us something.

The key to the definition of *education* is the word *how*. Today, thanks to a wealth of research on the principles that guide the phenomenon of learning, and on the nature of learning and memory, we know much more about how learning occurs and how we can make it better. By using these principles, we can become better students.

Formulating the Plan

Anything worth having is worth planning for. Whether you hope to learn to teach, to fly, to write for profit, or to change diapers correctly, you have in mind a goal. An everyday question from the first days in elementary school is: "What do you want to be when you grow up?" The answer to this question is one way of formulating a goal. Now that you are a college student, many people will expect you to know what you want to do for a profession or career. Yet you may not have the foggiest notion, or you might have an idea that is still slightly foggy. That's okay. What is clear, however, is that you want to succeed in your college courses. This is a relatively long-range goal, and as such can serve a purpose in keeping you on track.

But our day-to-day behavior is often hard to connect to our long-range goals. We need short-term goals to keep us organized and to be sure that the flow of our activities is in the direction we want to be going. To accomplish our long-range goals, we need to focus on three types of short-term goals: (1) goals for the day, (2) goals for the week, and (3) goals for the semester or term. Let's look at each of these separately.

Goals for Today

It is helpful to keep a daily checklist, diary, or schedule as a reminder of what must be done each day. Check off the things as you accomplish them. A pocket calendar is particularly helpful for this task.

Goals for the Week

Students who are successful in college also schedule their time weekly. Sometime during the course of registration, you made up a schedule showing your classes for the whole week. If you have a job, you must allow time for that, too. Also, many college or university students have family obligations that need to be considered as well. Finally, everyone needs some time for relaxing, eating, sleeping, and playing (even in graduate school we were advised that we needed to find some time to have fun in order to keep our balance). With all these things in mind, it is no wonder many students find little time to study.

But good students do all these things, too, yet they study. Do they have more time? No, we all have the same amount of time. But successful students schedule their time carefully. So, make up a weekly schedule and block off time for all these necessary events: classes, work, relaxation, eating, sleeping, playing, family, and studying. Students who actually schedule their time and keep to their schedules are amazed at how much time they find they have!

As you make up your weekly schedule, you may find your study time in a large block. If this is true, please remember to take a short break every 20 to 30 minutes. This is called *distributed practice* and is far more efficient than studying for hours on end. After the first 20 or 30 minutes, most of us become much less efficient anyway. When you take that break, reward yourself somehow; then get back to your studying. Something I always tell my students is never to try to read a whole chapter in one sitting. In fact, when I am preparing for a new class, or have changed texts in a class I have been teaching, I take that advice myself!

Goals for the Semester

At the beginning of each semester, we find ourselves immersed in many new courses. Often, you will be confronted by several new professors with whom you have never worked before. It is difficult to sort out the expectations and demands of these several courses; however, it is important to organize the information that will be needed for completing all of the course requirements in order to be successful in the courses.

If you can, obtain a large wall calendar, and mark on it all the dates of tests, exams, and term paper due dates, being sure to write on the calendar the course for which each date applies. Now estimate how long it will take you to make final preparations for those exams, and mark those dates as warning or alert dates. Look over the dates on which papers are due, and see if they are bunched together. If your college is typical, they will probably be close. You can help yourself to avoid pulling last-minute all-nighters if you simply determine a spread of due dates for yourself, and mark those on the calendar too. As you do this step, please be sure to avoid any days that have personal significance for you, such as birthdays, anniversaries, and so on. This calendar gives you an overview of major dates in your semester.

If you have followed this plan carefully, you now have a large semester calendar plastered on your wall, a weekly schedule of major life events, classes, and study times taped over your desk, and a daily checklist of must-do items in your pocket or purse. So, your scheduling is on its way. Let's look now at other important strategies.

Attending Classes

Many students believe that, because they are in college, they can decide whether to go to class at all. This is true. Some students also believe that attendance in class is not important to their grade. This is *not* true! Some colleges or universities have attendance requirements, so that if students miss a given number of classes it will either lower their grade a full letter grade or the instructor may drop the student from the course; some instructors have in-class activities that count toward students' grades, so if students are not in class, they do not get credit for participating. Even without such strategies, students who do not attend class sessions almost always do more poorly on tests and exams. Perhaps they were absent when a crucial item was discussed or when the instructor lectured on the material this examination requires.

Remember that more often than not, instructors will include information in their lectures that is not in your textbook, and that information (whether from class lecture, videos shown in class, guest lectures, and so on) is fair game for tests. Moreover, if you are not there, the instructor cannot get to know you, and therefore cannot give you the benefit of the doubt on your answers. It should come as no surprise that in study after research study, the data clearly show that those students who attend class regularly receive the highest grades and actually learn more, too! So, the first rule of being an effective student is to attend classes. Besides, how else can you get your money's worth? Now that you've determined you will go to every class, what will you do?

Benefiting from Lectures

Sometimes students think that if they come to class and "pay attention," they will remember what the instructor talked about; they think that if they take notes, they will miss much of what the instructor says. But sitting and paying attention is difficult. For one thing, most people can think much faster than they can speak. While the instructor lectures at 80 words per minute, the student thinks at about 350 words per minute! If the student is using this extra "thinking capacity" to focus on what the instructor is saying, it is fine, but this rarely lasts more than five minutes at a time. Most of the time, this extra "thinking capacity" is used in daydreaming!

Daydreaming can be helpful in resolving our emotional problems, planning the course of our lives, and avoiding work. Often, it is motivated by the desire to avoid work. For whatever motive, however, daydreaming is not compatible with attending a lecture. Human beings simply cannot attend to more than one stimulus at one time. And you have to admit, your daydreams can be ever so much more interesting than your professor's lectures.

Attending lectures is best done while taking notes. Use plenty of paper, and leave blank lines at regular intervals, or leave wide side margins. You will use these spaces later. If the instructor permits it, be brave and interrupt with questions if you do not understand what is being said. One thing I try to stress to my students is that I may know what I am talking about, but it may be unclear to them—and if it's unclear to one student, it may well be unclear to other students. So, for the sake of the other students who didn't understand what I was talking about, each student should take on the responsibility of asking me to clarify what I said or to expand in a way that will help them understand. Remember that lectures have a way of progressing and building on earlier information. It is important to understand each point, or later points will be lost.

When you take notes, write out the major points, and try to just make simple notes on the supporting minor points. If you miss something, and you cannot ask a question about it, approach the instructor immediately afterward, when it is likely to still be fresh in both your minds. *Do not* try to write down every word, and *do* try to use abbreviations or symbols, or you could do what I did—learn shorthand! (Or make up your own system.)

Often my students will ask if they may tape-record my lectures. Personally, I have no objection to having students do this. In fact, I did this during my first term in college but found it was terribly tedious trying to transcribe the lecture. The students for whom this may be particularly helpful are those who have visual, auditory, or motor impairments; however, do not ever tape-record a lecture without first asking for and obtaining the professor's permission.

Within one or two hours after the lecture, on the same day, go back over your notes, and do two things. First, fill in the rest of the minor points. This often amounts to completing the sentence or other element. Second, write brief summaries and any questions that you now have in the blank spaces (lines or margins) you left earlier. These few minutes spent reviewing and organizing your notes will pay off in greatly improved memory. The questions you have you can ask in class, or during the instructor's office hours, and reap two benefits: (1) you will get the answers, and (2) you will demonstrate that you are a serious student, which will impress your instructor.

One other thing about going to class: While this is not always true, I have found that typically my best students sit in front. And most students seem to have a need to have "their seat," while a few students have a need to move around, sitting in one seat one day and a different seat the next. It wasn't until my graduate school days that I realized why I needed "my seat"—as a student, we are being overwhelmed with new information, which is a stressful experience; we need some structure we can count on to reduce that stress. So, if you are one of those who likes to wander, be considerate of your classmates' needs for stress reduction.

By the way, to get the most out of the lectures, do complete the assigned reading *before* the class begins so you are familiar with the material. This will help you keep up with what the instructor is talking about, will reduce the amount of information you do not understand, but may also bring up important questions for you to ask in class if the instructor does not talk about them.

Reading for Learning

We all know how to read. You are proving it by reading these words. Hopefully, you are also realizing some ideas as a result of reading. If you are only reading words, please *wake up* and *stop daydreaming*! We can read a variety of things: newspapers, movie reviews, novels, magazines, and textbooks. Textbooks are unlike all the others and must be read with a strategy all their own.

There are many reading and studying strategies, and all of them work to an extent. Perhaps you learned one or more in the course of going to high school. Perhaps you even took a how-to-study course when you entered college. If so, you probably learned one or two of these systems. If you have one you like that works for you, keep it. If you are interested in learning a new one, read on.

The PQ4R Method

One of the most successful and most widely used methods of studying written material was the SQ3R method, first developed at Ohio State University. Researchers had noted that students who were more successful were more active readers. More recently, this method has been updated to the PQ4R method, which adds an additional step. This method teaches you the same skills that have made many thousands of students successful. If you use this method when you read and study, you will be more successful, too. I have outlined the steps as follows.

The P stands for PREVIEW. After you have read the overview or chapter outline and the list of learning objectives, you should survey the chapter in the text. This is also called *skimming*. Look at the headings and subheadings, and get the gist of the major points in this chapter. Check off each point in the outline of this Study Guide as you pass it in the pages of the text.

The Q stands for QUESTION. Reading is greatly enhanced if you are searching for answers to questions. For this text, the Student Study Guide provides learning objectives that can serve as questions. For other texts, make up questions for yourself, based on the chapter overview or on your own survey of the chapter. Be sure that you have at least one question for each major unit in the chapter; you will be less efficient at studying those units for which you do not have questions.

The first of the four Rs is for READ. As you read, look for the answers to the questions you posed or to the study or learning objectives furnished for you. When you find material that answers these questions, put a mark (X) or a sticky note in the margin next to that material. This will help now, because you are actively involved, and later, when you review. It is a good idea to wait to underline or highlight lines of text until after you have read the entire chapter at least once, so you will know what is and what is not most important. (In fact, while some "authorities" suggest you underline or highlight no more than 10 percent of what you are reading, I find that when most of us begin to underline or highlight, we wind up doing it to most of the chapter—I suggest not doing it at all because it becomes too passive, which counteracts your attempts to read actively.)

The second R stands for REFLECT. As you are reading, stop every so often and reflect on the material to increase its meaningfulness. This includes analyzing the material, thinking about how to apply it to your own life, interpreting the information, and connecting it with information you already have in your long-term memory.

The third R is for RECITE. One of the oldest classroom techniques in the world (Aristotle used it) is recitation. In the classroom version, the teacher asks the questions and the students answer them. Unless you can get your teacher to study with you regularly, you'll have to play both roles. Periodically stop in your reading and say aloud (if possible) what the author is telling you. Try to put it in your own words, but be sure to use technical terms as you learn them. If you are not in a situation where you can recite out loud, do it in writing. Just thinking it is not enough. When should you pause to recite? A good rule of thumb is that each time you come to the end of a major subheading, you should recite. One professor encourages his students to recite at least one sentence at the end of each paragraph and two or three or more sentences at the end of each subunit (when you come to a new heading).

People who do not use recitation usually forget half of what they read in one hour and another half of the half they remembered by the end of the day. People who use recitation often remember from 75 to 90 percent of what they studied. This technique pays off. By the way, if anyone questions why you are talking to yourself, tell him or her that a psychologist recommended it.

The fourth R is for REVIEW. You should review a chapter soon after you have studied it (using the PQ and first 3Rs). You should review it again the day or evening before a test. It is not usually helpful to cram the night before a test, and particularly not the day of the test! That type of studying does not produce good memory and is likely to make you more anxious during the test itself.

Taking Tests

One of the things students fear most is failure. Failure signifies that things are not going well and alerts us to the possibility that we may not achieve our goals. Unfortunately, many students see tests and exams as opportunities to fail. They prepare by becoming anxious and fearful and by trying to cram as much as possible right before the exam. These students rarely do well on the exam. They often fail, thus accomplishing just what they feared.

Taking tests requires strategy and planning. First, it is helpful to know what type of tests you will have. Your instructor probably told you during the first class meeting, or it may be in the class syllabus or course outline. If you do not know, ask.

If you are going to be taking essay exams, the best way to prepare is by writing essays. Before you do this, it is a good idea to find out what types of questions the instructor asks and what is expected in a response. Again, it is helpful to ask the instructor for this material. Perhaps you can even see some examples of essay questions from previous years—some instructors at some colleges have copies of their exams on file in the department office or in the library. By finding out what is expected, you can formulate a model against which you can evaluate your answers.

Now, using the learning objectives, or some essay questions you wrote, actually sit down and write out the answers. *Hint*: If you usually feel more anxious during a test, it may help you to practice writing your essays in the room in which the test will be given. Simply find a time when the room is vacant, and make yourself at home.

If your instructor gives multiple-choice tests, you should practice taking multiple-choice tests. For each chapter, either use questions provided in the Study Guide or make up your own. You may find it helpful to work out an arrangement to pool questions with other students, thereby reducing the amount of work you have to do, and developing a network of friends. Or, you may ask your professor if he or she would entertain the idea of having students write some of the exam questions—some of my professors did that in my undergraduate classes, and it is something I sometimes have my students do.

Whichever way you do it, the important thing is to prepare for tests and exams. Preparation is about 95 percent of the secret to getting a good grade. (Yes, there is some actual luck or chance involved in test scores, as even your instructor will admit!) Preparation is not only a good study and review technique, but it also helps reduce anxiety.

Dealing with Test Anxiety

Anxiety can be a helpful response when it occurs at low levels. In 1908, Yerkes and Dodson showed that the amount of anxiety that could benefit performance was a function of the difficulty and complexity of the task. As the difficulty of the task rose, anxiety became less helpful and more likely to interfere with performance.

If you have ever been so anxious in a test situation that you were unable to do well, even though you knew the information, you have test anxiety. If you get your exams back and are surprised that you marked wrong answers when you knew the correct answers, or if you can only remember the correct answers after you leave the examination room, you too may have test anxiety.

Strategy 1: Effective Study

Use study habits that promote learning and make the best use of time. Strategies, such as scheduling your time and using the PQ4R system, reduce anxiety by increasing confidence. As you come to realize that you know the material, your confidence rises and anxiety retreats.

Strategy 2: Relaxation

Each of us develops a unique pattern of relaxation. Some people relax by going to a specific place, either in person or mentally. Others relax by playing music, by being with friends, by using autogenic relaxation phrases, or by meditating. Whatever you do, be aware of it, and try to practice relaxation techniques. If you are good at relaxing, try thinking about those situations that make you anxious, and relax while you think of them. To do this, allow yourself to think only briefly (15 to 30 seconds at a time) of the situation that makes you anxious, and then relax again. After several such pairings, you will find that thinking about that situation no longer makes you anxious. At this point, you may be surprised to find that the situation itself also no longer produces anxiety.

You may find it helpful to think about these anxiety-provoking situations in a sequence from those that produce very little anxiety to those that are more anxiety-evoking. Such a list, from low to high anxiety, might look something like this:

1. Your instructor announces that there will be a test in four weeks.
2. Your instructor reminds you of the test next week.
3. As you study, you see on the course outline the word *test* and remember next week's test.
4. One of your friends asks you if you want to study together for the test, which is the day after tomorrow.
5. You choose not to go out with your friends because of the test tomorrow.
6. As you get up in the morning, you remember that today is the day of the test.
7. You are walking down the hall toward the classroom, thinking about what questions might be on the test.
8. The instructor enters the classroom, carrying a sheaf of papers in hand.
9. The instructor distributes the papers, and you see the word *test* or *exam* at the top.
10. After reading the first five questions, you have not been able to think of the answer to any of them.

If you work at it gradually and consistently, pairing these types of thoughts (briefly) with relaxation and remembering to let go and relax after each one, this process will dispel test anxiety and make test taking a more productive and successful experience.

Strategy 3: Thinking Clearly

Most students who have test anxiety think in unclear and unproductive ways. They say to themselves things like: "I can't get these answers correct . . . I don't know this stuff," "I don't know anything at all . . . I'm going to fail this test," "I'm probably going to flunk out of school . . . I'm just a dumb nerd." These thoughts share two unfortunate characteristics: They are negative and they are absolute. They should be replaced. When we tell ourselves negative and absolute thoughts, we find it impossible to focus on the test material. The result is that we miss questions even when we know the answers. Our thinking prevents us from doing well.

A good strategy for replacing these negative and absolute thoughts is to practice thinking positive and honest thoughts, such as: "I may not know all the answers, but I know some of them," "I don't know the answer to that right now, so I will go on to the next one and come back to that," "I don't have to get them all right . . . I studied hard and carefully, and I can get some of them correct," "I am a serious student and have some abilities . . . I am prepared for this test, and know many of the answers," "This test is important, but it is not going to determine the course of my entire life. and if I don't do well, it doesn't mean I'm a horrible person or a dummy."

By thinking clearly, honestly, and positively, we quiet the flood of anxiety and focus on the task at hand. Students who use this technique invariably do better on tests. It takes practice to think clearly, but it is worth the effort. After a while, you will find that it becomes natural and does not take any noticeable effort. And as anxiety is reduced, more energy is available for studying and for doing well on examinations. The eventual outcome is more enjoyment with learning, better learning, more success in college, and the achievement of your goals.

Strategy 4: Guided Imagery

Something I often do with my students before a test is to have them relax (see Strategy 2), close their eyes, and visualize themselves walking into a tall building. They go into the elevator in the building and take it to the top floor, which is 56 stories up. They walk out of the elevator and go to the stairwell, then climb to the top of the building. There is no railing on the top of the building. I direct them to walk over to the very edge of the building and put their toes at the very edge, then look down. I ask them to think about how they are feeling as they are looking down onto the street from the top of this building. I then tell them to back up, have the realization that they can fly—just spread out their arms and they can fly. Then they are directed back to the edge of the building, knowing that they can fly. They put their toes on the edge, look down, then spread their arms and fly, eventually flying down to land safely on the ground below. Next I have them visualize themselves in the classroom; on the desk before them is their test. They look at the test and see themselves reading the questions, saying "I know that answer. Yes, I remember learning that." They visualize themselves being successful, answering all the questions correctly, feeling good about themselves. Then I have them visualize getting their tests back, with a big "A" on the test.

Some students are much better able to visualize than others. You can try combining Strategy 2 with this strategy to help you improve your visualization because it can be an effective success strategy.

Strategy 5: Do the Easy Ones First

One technique I learned while studying for the GRE (Graduate Record Exam) was to read each question and answer the ones I knew, then go back to the harder ones. Two things to watch out for on this strategy: (1) be sure you get the answers in the right place—sometimes when we skip a question or two, we wind up marking the wrong space, so check that your answer to question 10 is in space 10; (2) you may find that you're stumped by the first several questions—don't let that throw you, just keep going because there is bound to be one you jump on and say, "Yes! I know that one." Answer the easy ones first, then go back to the others after you've built up your confidence seeing you *do* know "stuff." Then, always go back over the whole test to be sure you answered every question (the exception here is if you have a professor who takes more than one point off for wrong answers—in that case, it's better not to answer than to answer wrong, but I don't know anyone who does that).

Strategy 6: State-Dependent Learning

Research has found that we remember information best when we are in the same "state" we were in when we first learned the information. So, for example, you might remember a certain song when prompted by a specific stimulus (seeing someone who reminds you of your "first true love"), or we will remember things we learned when we were particularly happy if we are again in that mood. This goes for physical contexts as well—so that we have an advantage if we take an exam in the same room where we learned the information in the first place. But it also goes to physical context in terms of our bodies—if you drink coffee or caffeine-laden sodas when you study, try to do the same before your exam. On the other hand, if you don't consume caffeine when you study, by all means, *do not* suddenly have a cup of coffee before your exam. Because of the power of this phenomenon, you may want to create a particular mental context for yourself when you study so you can put yourself into the same mental context when you take exams.

Strategy 7: Take a Break

If you find yourself getting stressed out during the test, take a break. Put your pencil down, breathe deeply, and you may even want to put your head down on the desk (but please, do not fall asleep!). Use the relaxation techniques or the guided imagery strategy; visualize yourself looking at the test and suddenly realizing that you *do* know the answers to at least most of the questions. Then go back to taking the test.

Remember that with all of these test-taking strategies, if you don't do the first one, none of the others will help! Passing the course requires that you actively study the material.

Memory Techniques

No matter how much you read, it won't help you if you don't remember *what* you read. The most critical factor in remembering is being able to apply what you have learned. Of course, some things such as people's names, or certain dates, or statistical information are not easily applied to your life, so you'll have to use other techniques. But first, let's talk about the "easy way."

Apply It to Your Life

If you can take the material you are learning and use it in your everyday life, you will remember it without any problem. Connect it with what you already know, either from life experience or other courses you have taken. Sometimes what you are learning fits nicely with what you already knew, but sometimes it will contradict what you learned before. This is an opportunity to look at how the new information fits in with the old: Were there new research findings? Or is it merely a difference of opinion? Make these associations—don't keep the information for any class neatly compartmentalized—if you do, you'll have a hard time trying to find it when you need it.

Teach It to Someone Else!

When we start teaching something to someone else, we find we *have to* learn it, and by trying to explain the material to another person, we examine it and think about it differently. So, take the material you are learning in this class (or any class) and teach it to someone else. When the other person asks you questions, you can look them up and find the answers, or think them out together, or ask someone else. As you explain these concepts to someone else (your children, your friends, or even your dog), you will suddenly see them in a totally different light.

Mnemonic Techniques

Some things are just really difficult to apply to your own life. Dates, names, places, statistics, and such may not have a great deal of meaning for you. In that event, use the tricks that memory specialists use—mnemonics. There are many different types. For example, one famous mnemonic is an acronym for remembering the Great Lakes: HOMES = Huron, Ontario, Michigan, Erie, and Superior; or the colors of the rainbow is a man's name: ROY G. BIV = Red, Orange, Yellow, Green, Blue, Indigo, and Violet (if not for this "man," I'd never remember indigo!) You can make up your own acronyms by taking the first initial of any term, person, and so on. It's easiest, though, if it's something that makes sense to you.

Another mnemonic technique is called the "method of loci," and I've been told it's one that medical students use to remember body parts. You list the things you need to remember, then visualize yourself walking around a familiar place (like your living room), putting one item on a particular piece of furniture. Then, when you need to remember that item, you go through your "living room" to see where it is. One other mnemonic technique is the story method. Take the information you need to remember and put it into a story.

Be an "Information Dropper"

This is similar to the suggestion to teach, but less formal. Ask your friends to indulge you by listening to what you learned in your Life-Span Development class (or any other class). Then *tell* them what you are learning. You may, in fact, find that you have managed to help one of your friends by sharing this information!

Rote Memory

If you can remember back to grade school, when you learned to multiply, somehow the only way that seems to happen is by repeating the multiplication tables over and over and over again. Personally, I think this is about the worst way to learn almost anything, but for some things (like multiplication tables) it works. You can try making flashcards as a way to help you learn through repeating the material you don't know until you are able to answer the questions posed without looking at the reverse side of the cards. Hopefully you will then go further and apply the information to other areas of your life.

Most Important

Remember this: Professors don't actually "teach" their students; rather, they facilitate learning so students end up teaching themselves. Although we try really hard to motivate our students, keep them interested, and present information in a way that helps them understand, the ultimate responsibility for learning rests with the students. Some students have learned *despite* their professors, whereas others don't learn even with the very best of professors. So, keep your goals in mind, study hard, ask questions, and aim for success!

Further Resources

Student CD-ROM
Packaged free with the text, this new Student CD-ROM features video and audio clips that expand on the material in the text, as well as interactive exercises. The CD also includes multiple-choice and true/false test preparation questions that provide immediate feedback and scoring. The CD also contains an Internet guide, a guide to doing electronic research, and a study skills primer.

Online Learning Center
www.mhhe.com/papaliah9
This extensive website, designed specifically to accompany *Human Development*, offers a wide variety of resources. The Student Site includes the Guideposts for Study, chapter outlines, chapter summaries, and a variety of self-quizzes. The site also includes a glossary of the key terms in the book and a list of helpful and informative websites. The Online Learning Center also includes PowerWeb, a website that includes current articles, weekly updates, web links, and more.

Multimedia Courseware for Child Development
Charlotte J. Patterson, University of Virginia
This interactive CD-ROM covers central phenomena and classic experiments in the field of child development. Included are hours of video footage of classic and contemporary experiments, detailed viewing guides, challenging follow-up and interactive feedback, graduated developmental charts, a variety of hands-on projects, and related websites and navigation aids. (0-07-254580-1)

Multimedia Courseware for Adult Development
Carolyn Johnson, Pennsylvania State University
This interactive CD-ROM showcases video clips central to phenomena in adult development. The CD-ROM includes hours of video footage of classic and contemporary experiments, detailed viewing guides, challenging follow-up and interactive feedback, graphics, graduated developmental charges, a variety of hands-on projects, and related websites and navigation aids. (0-07-251761-1)

Acknowledgments

I would like to thank Sienne Patch, Developmental Editor for Psychology at McGraw-Hill, for getting me into this mess in the first place. Seriously, her patience and encouragement were phenomenal. Thank you, Sienne! Kudos also go to Maggie Barbieri, freelance supplements coordinator extraordinaire, for her support and empathy throughout moments of hair-pulling (mine), nail-biting (hers), and whining (definitely mine). You were great, Maggie!

Finally, I have to thank Ginjer L. Clarke, freelance editor and copyeditor on this study guide. Ginjer has taken all of my chapters and prettied them up so that the page numbers are all correct and the headings and sections look nice. It's a lovely thing, having a copyeditor, because any mistakes can be blamed on her! Thank you, Ginjer!

Sandy Ciccarelli
Gulf Coast Community College
sciccarelli@gulfcoast.edu
June 2003

PART 1: ABOUT HUMAN DEVELOPMENT

Part I contains Chapters 1 and 2 and is designed as a guide map to the study of human development. The first chapter discusses the routes that investigators have followed in their quest for information about how people grow and develop, why they proceed to develop in certain ways, and what makes it all possible. The main investigative directions of today and the central questions being posed about human development are also presented.

CHAPTER 1: THE STUDY OF HUMAN DEVELOPMENT

Chapter 1 describes how the study of human development has evolved and introduces the basic goals and concepts of the field. The many influences that make each person a unique individual are introduced and discussed in this chapter.

Guideposts for Study

1. What is human development, and how has its study evolved?

2. What are the four goals of the scientific study of human development, and what do developmental scientists study?

3. What are three major domains and eight periods of human development?

4. What kinds of influences make one person different from another?

5. What are the six principles of the life-span developmental approach?

Detailed Chapter Outline with Key Terms

I. HOW THE STUDY OF HUMAN DEVELOPMENT EVOLVED
   Human development: Scientific study of processes of change and stability throughout the human life span.
   A. Early Approaches
      Baby biographies: Journals kept to record the early development of a child; early forerunners of the scientific study of development.
   B. Studying the Life Span
      - **Life-span development**: Concept of development as a lifelong process, which can be studied scientifically.
      - *Interdisciplinary:* Study that draws on many fields, or disciplines. The study of life-span development is interdisciplinary.

II. HUMAN DEVELOPMENT TODAY: AN INTRODUCTION TO THE FIELD
   - *Describe:* Goal in the study of human development in which scientists observe behavior in order to describe what happens in the lives of children and adults.
   - *Explain:* Goal in which scientists attempt to understand, or explain, why observed behavior occurs—the cause of observed behavior.

1

- *Predict:* Goal in which scientists make educated guesses about what might happen in the future to behavior.
- *Modify:* Goal in which scientists use the knowledge of causes of behavior to change or control behavior.

A. Developmental Processes: Change and Stability
- **Quantitative change**: Change in number or amount, such as in height, weight, or size of vocabulary.
- **Qualitative change**: Change in kind, structure, or organization, such as the change from nonverbal to verbal communication.
- *Stability:* Constancy of personality and behavior that most people show.

B. Domains of Development
- *Domain:* A dimension, such as physical, cognitive, or psychosocial.
- **Physical development**: Growth of body and brain and change or stability in sensory capacities, motor skills, and health.
- **Cognitive development**: Change or stability in mental abilities, such as learning, memory, language, thinking, moral reasoning, and creativity.
- **Psychosocial development**: Change and stability in emotions, personality, and social relationships.

C. Periods of the Life Span

Social construction: Concept about the nature of reality, based on societally shared perceptions or assumptions.

III. INFLUENCES ON DEVELOPMENT

Individual differences: Differences in characteristics, influences, or developmental outcomes.

A. Heredity, Environment, and Maturation
- **Heredity**: Inborn characteristics inherited from biological parents at conception.
- **Environment**: Totality of nonhereditary, or experiential, influences on development.
- **Maturation**: Unfolding of a natural sequence of physical and behavioral changes, including readiness to master new abilities.
- *Milestones:* Landmarks of development, or the average ages for the occurrence of certain events such as walking and talking.
- *Environmental:* Experiential factors that affect people, such as socioeconomic status or culture.

B. Major Contextual Influences
1. Family
   - **Nuclear family**: Kinship and household unit made up of one or two parents and their natural, adopted, or stepchildren.
   - **Extended family**: Kinship network of parents, children, and other relatives, sometimes living together in an *extended-family household.*
2. Socioeconomic Status and Neighborhood
   - **Socioeconomic status (SES)**: Combination of economic and social factors describing an individual or family, including income, education, and occupation.
   - **Risk factors**: Conditions that increase the likelihood of a negative developmental outcome.

3. Culture and Race/Ethnicity
  - **Culture**: A society's or group's total way of life, including customs, traditions, beliefs, values, language, and physical products—all learned behavior passed on from parents to children.
  - **Ethnic group**: Group united by ancestry, race, religion, language, and/or national origins, which contribute to a sense of shared identity.
4. The Historical Context
C. Normative and Nonnormative Influences
  - **Normative**: Characteristic of an event that occurs in a similar way for most people in a group.
    - *Normative age-graded influences:* Event or influence that is highly similar for people in a particular age group. Includes biological (puberty, menopause) and social (marriage, retirement) events.
    - *Normative history-graded influences:* Event or influence common to a particular cohort.
  - **Cohort**: Group of people growing up at about the same time.
  - **Nonnormative**: Characteristic of an unusual event that happens to a particular person, or a typical event that happens at an unusual time of life.
D. Timing of Influences: Critical or Sensitive Periods
  - **Imprinting**: Phenomenon in which newly hatched birds will instinctively follow the first moving object they see, the result of the readiness of the nervous system of the organism to acquire certain information during a brief critical period in early life.
  - **Critical period**: Specific time when a given event, or its absence, has the greatest impact on development.
  - **Sensitive periods**: Times in development when a person is particularly open to certain kinds of experiences.

IV. BALTES'S LIFE-SPAN DEVELOPMENTAL APPROACH
1. Development is lifelong.
2. Development involves both gain and loss.
3. Relative influences of biology and culture shift over the life span.
4. Development involves a changing allocation of resources.
5. Development is modifiable.
6. Development is influenced by the historical and cultural context.

True/False Self-Test

Place a T or an F in the appropriate space. These questions are taken from the chapter content, tables, key terms, Guideposts for Study, and Checkpoints.

1. _____ The idea that development continues beyond childhood is relatively new.

2. _____One of the principles of the life-span developmental approach is that development depends on history and context.

3. _____ Qualitative changes include changes in height and weight.

4. ____ Most people show an underlying stability, or constancy, of personality and behavior.

5. ____ All societies recognize eight periods of the life span.

6. ____ All societies recognize differences in the ways people of different ages think, feel, and act.

7. ____ Most people are mentally alert in late adulthood.

8. ____ Socioeconomic status limits people's choices of where to live.

9. ____ Most ethnic groups have no country of origin in their background.

10. ___ Biological events such as puberty and menopause are nonnormative events.

11. ___ People often help create their own nonnormative events.

12. ___ The concept of critical periods is more controversial when applied to cognitive and psychosocial development.

13. ___ The Elder study demonstrates that poverty has no long-term effects on children's development.

14. ___ Many abilities, such as memory, strength, and endurance, can be significantly improved with training and practice, even late in life.

15. ___ Broad dimensions of personality, such as conscientiousness and openness to new experience, are fixed in early childhood.

16. ___ Historically, the nuclear family was the dominant form of family structure in the United States and other Western industrial societies.

17. ___ In Asia and Latin America, and among some minority groups in the United States, the extended family is the basic pattern of societal organization.

18. ___ Poor children are less likely than wealthy children to have emotional or behavioral problems.

Multiple-Choice Self-Test

Circle the letter of the best answer. These questions are based on many aspects of the chapter content, in no particular order.

1. Jean-Marc-Gaspard Itard is best known for his study of
   a. gifted children.
   b. The Farm Crisis.
   c. the children of the Great Depression.
   d. the Wild Boy of Aveyron.

2. The idea that adolescence is a separate period of development began in
   a. 1820.
   b. 1453.
   c. the early twentieth century.
   d. 1989.

3. Life-span studies in the United States grew out of studies
   a. of primates.
   b. in Europe.
   c. designed to follow children through adulthood.
   d. in China.

4. Ideas about the nature of reality based on shared subjective perceptions or assumptions are known as
   a. myth.
   b. religion.
   c. social construction.
   d. realism.

5. According to Elder's studies of families in the Depression era and the Farm Crisis era, depressed parents are more likely to
   a. become more loving.
   b. fight with each other.
   c. become closer to their children.
   d. become more religious.

6. Paul Baltes is best known for
   a. discovering penicillin.
   b. inventing the IQ test.
   c. the life-span developmental approach.
   d. the Oakland Growth Study.

7. One important characteristic of development is plasticity, which refers to
   a. rigidity of ideas.
   b. lack of change.
   c. modifiability of performance.
   d. growing in one direction at a time.

8. If a physical problem interfering with the ability to focus the eyes is not corrected early in life, the brain mechanisms necessary for depth perception will not develop. This demonstrates the concept of
   a. sensitive periods.
   b. critical periods.
   c. normative events.
   d. history-graded events.

9. A change in height, weight, and frequency of communication is an example of
   a. qualitative change.
   b. quantitative change.
   c. interaction.
   d. intervention.

10. The emergence of new phenomena that cannot be easily anticipated on the basis of earlier functioning is an example of
    a. stability.
    b. boldness.
    c. qualitative change.
    d. explanation.

11. Change and stability in personality and social relationships together constitute
a. anxiety.
b. psychosocial development.
c. physical development.
d. puberty.

12. The periods of the life span may vary by culture and society. The Western developed world generally recognizes the life span divided into
a. two periods.
b. eight periods.
c. four periods.
d. twelve periods.

13. Physical growth is most rapid in the developmental period of
a. adolescence.
b. early childhood.
c. late adulthood.
d. conception to birth.

14. Reproductive maturity occurs during
a. middle adulthood.
b. adolescence.
c. infancy.
d. early childhood.

15. In young adulthood, physical condition
a. declines.
b. peaks.
c. peaks, then declines slightly.
d. remains unchanged from adolescence.

16. In middle adulthood, most basic mental abilities
a. decline.
b. remain unchanged.
c. peak.
d. begin to deteriorate.

17. In late adulthood, most people are
a. healthy and active.
b. sedentary.
c. depressed and lonely.
d. divorced.

18. The search for meaning in life assumes central importance in
a. late adulthood.
b. middle age.
c. adolescence.
d. young adulthood.

19. The establishment of independent lifestyles and occupations best describes some of the main tasks of
a. late adulthood.
b. middle age.
c. adolescence.
d. young adulthood.

20. The unfolding of a natural, genetically influenced sequence of physical changes and behavior patterns, including readiness to master new abilities, is
a. growth.
b. maturation.
c. risk taking.
d. independence.

21. A two-generational kinship, economic, and household unit consisting of two parents and their biological children is
a. a nuclear family.
b. a tribe.
c. an extended family.
d. a society.

22. The kinds of homes and neighborhoods people live in, as well as the quality of medical care, and other opportunities available to them are examples of
a. socioeconomic status (SES).
b. stratification.
c. factors associated with socioeconomic status.
d. welfare states.

23. The presence of educated, employed adults who can build the economic base of a community and provide models of achievement is known as
a. wealth.
b. human capital.
c. upper class.
d. middle class.

24. Which of the following statements is FALSE concerning culture?
a. Culture is unchanging.
b. Culture includes tradition.
c. Culture is all of the learned behavior passed on from parents to children.
d. Culture includes art work and tools.

25. Which of the following characteristics of development is incorrect, according to Baltes?
a. lifelong
b. multidimensional
c. nonmodifiable
d. multidirectional

Organize It!

Making lists is a fun and useful way to organize information in your mind. After making each list, think of ways to memorize it so that you have immediate recall. Singing a list, dancing while you recite it, or simply saying it in a rhythmic pattern as you are walking, driving, or jogging allows your brain to store the information in easily retrievable form. Try it!

1. List the eight periods of the life span, according to the chapter information (see Table 1-1).
   1.
   2.
   3.
   4.
   5.
   6.
   7.
   8.

2. List the six principles of the life-span developmental approach according to Baltes.
   1.

   2.

   3.

   4.

   5.

   6.

7

3. List and briefly describe the four goals of the field of human development.
   1.

   2.

   3.

   4.

4. List three types of qualitative change and three types of quantitative change.
   Qualitative change
   1.
   2.
   3.

   Quantitative change
   1.
   2.
   3.

5. List and briefly describe the three major aspects of development.
   1.

   2.

   3.

Short Essay Questions

These short essay questions are based in part on the Checkpoints in the chapter. Answer each question as completely and succinctly as possible.

1. Trace the highlights in the evolution of the study of human development.

2. Summarize the central assumptions of Baltes' life-span developmental approach.

3. Name four goals of the scientific study of human development.

4. Explain why the concept of "critical " periods may more accurately apply to physical than to cognitive development.

5. In view of poverty's long-term effects on children's development, what can and should be done to combat it?

Critical Thinking Questions

These questions can be used in small group discussions or as extra-credit assignments.

1. Do you think there should be more stages in the life span, and if so, how many? How would you describe the extra stages?

2. How might you be different if you had grown up in a culture other than your own?

3. Can you think of a major cultural event within your lifetime that shaped the lives of families and children? How would you go about studying such effects?

Answer Keys

True/False Self-Test

1. T	p. 8	GP 1		10. F	p. 18	GP 4
2. T	p. 13	GP 4		11. T	p. 18	GP 4
3. F	p. 9	GP 2		12. T	p. 19	GP 4
4. T	p. 9	GP 2		13. F	p. 17	GP 4
5. F	p. 10	GP 3		14. T	p. 21	GP 4
6. T	p. 10	GP 3		15. F	p. 9	GP 5
7. T	p. 13	GP 4		16. T	p. 14	GP 2
8. T	p. 15	GP 4		17. T	p. 14	GP 4
9. F	p. 16	GP 4		18. F	p. 15	GP 4

Multiple-Choice Self-Test

1. d	p. 5	GP 1		14. b	p. 13	GP 3
2. c	p. 8	GP 1		15. c	p. 13	GP 3
3. c	p. 8	GP 1		16. c	p. 13	GP 3
4. c	p. 10	GP 3		17. a	p. 13	GP 3
5. b	p. 17	GP 4		18. a	p. 13	GP 3
6. c	p. 19	GP 5		19. d	p. 13	GP 3
7. c	p. 19	GP 4		20. b	p. 12	GP 4
8. b	p. 19	GP 4		21. a.	p. 14	GP 4
9. b	p. 9	GP 2		22. c	p. 15	GP 4
10. c	p. 9	GP 2		23. b	p. 15	GP 4
11. b	p. 10	GP 3		24. a	p. 16	GP 4
12. b	p. 11	GP 3		25. c	p. 19	GP 5
13. d	p. 12	GP 3				

Organize It!

1.	pp. 12-13	GP 3
2.	pp. 19-21	GP 5
3.	p. 8	GP 2
4.	p. 9	GP 2
5.	p. 9	GP 3

Short Essay Questions

1.	pp. 7-8	GP 1
2.	pp. 19-22	GP 5
3.	pp. 8-9	GP 2
4.	pp. 17-19	GP 4
5.	pp. 18-19	GP 4

CHAPTER 2: THEORY AND RESEARCH

This chapter introduces the basic theoretical issues and perspectives in the study of human development. Developmental research designs and the concept of ethics in the study of human development conclude this informative chapter. This annotated outline is helpful as a guide to important issues and concepts discussed in the chapter.

Guideposts for Study

1. What purposes do theories serve?

2. What are three basic theoretical issues on which developmental scientists differ?

3. What are five theoretical perspectives on human development, and what are some theories representative of each?

4. How do developmental scientists study people, and what are some advantages and disadvantages of each research method?

5. What ethical problems may arise in research?

Detailed Chapter Outline with Key Terms

I. BASIC THEORETICAL ISSUES
   - **Theory**: Coherent set of logically related concepts that seeks to organize, explain, and predict data.
   - **Hypotheses**: Possible explanations for phenomena, used to predict the outcome of research.
   A. Issue 1: Which is More Important—Heredity or Environment?
      - *Nature:* The inborn traits and characteristics inherited from the biological parents.
      - *Nurture:* Environmental influences, both before and after birth, including influences of family, peers, schools, neighborhoods, society, and culture.
   B. Issue 2: Is Development Active or Passive?
      - *Tabula rasa:* Literally, a "blank slate"; philosopher John Locke's view that society influences the development of the child.
      - **Mechanistic model**: Model that views development as a passive, predictable response to stimuli.
      - **Organismic model**: Model that views development as internally initiated by an active organism, and as occurring in a sequence of qualitatively different stages.
   C. Issue 3: Is Development Continuous, or Does It Occur in Stages?
      - *Quantitative change:* Changes in number or amount, such as the frequency with which a response is made.
      - *Qualitative change:* Changes in kind or nature, implying that development occurs in a series of distinct stages or steps.

D. An Emerging Consensus
   Bidirectional: Referring to the fact that children change their world even as the world changes them.

II. THEORETICAL PERSPECTIVES
A. Perspective 1: Psychoanalytic
   - **Psychoanalytic perspective**: View of development as shaped by unconscious forces.
   - *Psychoanalysis:* A therapeutic approach aimed at giving patients insight into unconscious emotional conflicts.
   1. Sigmund Freud: Psychosexual Development
      a. In Freudian theory, an unvarying sequence of stages of personality development during infancy, childhood, and adolescence, in which gratification shifts from the mouth to the anus and then to the genitals:
         - *Oral stage:* Stage in psychosexual development in which feeding is the main source of sensual pleasure.
         - *Anal stage:* Stage in psychosexual development in which the chief source of pleasure is moving the bowels.
         - *Phallic stage:* Stage in psychosexual development in which boys develop sexual attachment to their mothers and girls to their fathers, with aggressive urges toward the same-sex parent.
         - *Latency stage:* Stage in psychosexual development in which the child is sexually calm and becomes socialized, develops skills, and learns about self and society.
         - *Genital stage:* Stage in psychosexual development that lasts throughout adulthood, in which repressed sexual urges resurface to flow in socially approved channels.
         - *Fixation:* In psychoanalysis, an arrest in development that can show up in adult personality.
      b. Freud proposed three hypothetical parts of the personality:
         - *Id:* Part of the personality that governs newborns, operating on the pleasure principle. (*Pleasure principle:* The drive to seek immediate satisfaction of needs and desires.)
         - *Ego:* Part of the personality that represents reason, operating on the reality principle. (*Reality principle:* Finding realistic ways to gratify the id.)
         - *Superego:* Part of the personality containing the conscience, incorporating socially approved behavior into the child's own value system.
   2. Erik Erikson: Psychosocial Development
      The socially and culturally influenced process of development of the ego, or self, which Erikson described in eight stages:
      - *Basic trust versus basic mistrust:* Critical theme of infancy, in which hope is developed.
      - *Autonomy versus shame and doubt:* Child develops a balance of independence and will.
      - *Initiative versus guilt:* Early childhood stage in which purposed is derived.
      - *Industry versus inferiority:* Child learns skills of the culture.
      - *Identity versus identity confusion:* Adolescent determines a sense of self.
      - *Intimacy versus isolation:* Young adult makes commitment to others.

- *Generativity versus stagnation:* Mature adult establishes and guides the next generation.
- *Ego integrity versus despair:* Late adulthood stage in which one must come to terms with the way one has lived one's life or succumb to despair.

B. Perspective 2: Learning
  - **Learning perspective**: View of development that holds that changes in behavior result from experience or adaptation to the environment.
  - *Learning:* A long-lasting change in behavior based on experience or adaptation to the environment.

  1. Behaviorism
     - **Behaviorism**: Learning theory that emphasizes the predictable role of environment in causing observable behavior.
     - *Associative learning:* The formation of a mental link between two events.
     a. **Classical Conditioning:** Learning based on association of a stimulus that does not ordinarily elicit a response with another stimulus that does elicit the response.
     b. Operant Conditioning
        - **Operant conditioning**: Learning based on reinforcement or punishment.
        - **Reinforcement**: In operant conditioning, a stimulus that encourages repetition of a desired behavior.
        - **Punishment**: In operant conditioning, a stimulus that discourages repetition of a behavior.
           - *Positive reinforcement:* Giving a reward, such as food, gold stars, or praise.
           - *Negative reinforcement:* Taking away something the individual does not like (an aversive event), such as the removal of a loud, raspy noise.
           - *Extinguished:* Term referring to the return of a behavior to its original, or baseline, level after removal of reinforcement.
           - *Behavior modification:* Also called behavior therapy, it is the use of conditioning to gradually change behavior.

  2. Social Learning (Social Cognitive) Theory
     - **Social learning theory**: Theory that behaviors are learned by observing and imitating models. Also called social cognitive theory.
     - **Observational learning** *(modeling):* Learning through watching others' behavior.
     - *Applied behavior analysis:* A combination of conditioning and modeling that can be used to eliminate undesirable behaviors and encourage socially desirable ones.
     - *Social cognitive theory:* Bandura's newest version of social learning theory, in which the emphasis on cognitive response to perceptions is increased.
     - *Self-efficacy:* A confidence that a person has the characteristics needed to succeed.

C. Perspective 3: Cognitive
  Cognitive perspective: View that thought processes are central to development.
  1. Jean Piaget's Cognitive-Stage Theory
     Clinical method: Technique combining observation with flexible questioning.
        - **Organization:** The tendency to create increasingly complex cognitive structures (schemes).
        - **Schemes**: Organized patterns of behavior that a person uses to think about and act in a situation.
        - **Adaptation:** How children handle new information in light of what they already know.

- **Assimilation**: Part of adaptation, taking in new information and incorporating into existing cognitive structures.
- **Accommodation**: Part of adaptation, changing one's cognitive structures to include new information.
- **Equilibration**: The constant striving for a stable balance in the shift from assimilation to accommodation.

2. **Information-processing approach**: Approach to the study of cognitive development by observing and analyzing the mental processes involved in perceiving and handling information.
   a. Computer-Based Models: Flowcharts that analyze the specific steps people go through in gathering, storing, retrieving, and using information.
   b. Neo-Piagetian Theories
3. The Cognitive Neuroscience Approach
   - **Cognitive neuroscience approach**: Approach to the study of cognitive development that links brain processes with cognitive ones.
   - **Social cognitive neuroscience**: An emerging interdisciplinary field that draws on cognitive neuroscience, information processing, and social psychology.

D. Perspective 4: Evolutionary/Sociobiological
   - *Survival of the fittest:* Darwinian process in which the animal most capable of survival (the one with the most adaptable traits) survives to pass on its genes in offspring.
   - *Natural selection:* Darwinian process in which the weak and those with maladaptive traits are removed from the gene pool, leaving only the healthiest and strongest to survive and continue the species.
   - **Ethology**: Study of distinctive adaptive behaviors of species of animals that have evolved to increase survival of the species.
   - **Sociobiological perspective**: View of development that focuses on biological bases of social behavior.
   - **Evolutionary psychology**: Application of Darwinian principles of natural selection and survival of the fittest to individual behavior.

E. Perspective 5: Contextual

Contextual perspective: View of development that sees the individual as inseparable from the social context.
   1. Urie Bronfenbrenner's **Bioecological Theory**: Approach to understanding processes and contexts of development:
      - **Microsystem**: A setting in which a child interacts with others on an everyday, face-to-face basis.
      - **Mesosystem**: Linkages between two or more microsystems.
      - **Exosystem**: Linkages between two or more settings, one of which does not contain the child.
      - **Macrosystem**: A society's overall cultural patterns.
      - **Chronosystem**: Effects of time on other developmental systems.
   2. Lev Vygotsky's Sociocultural Theory
      - **Sociocultural theory**: Vygotsky's theory of how contextual factors affect children's development.
      - **Zone of proximal development (ZPD)**: Vygotsky's term for the difference between what a child can do alone and with help.

- **Scaffolding**: Temporary support to help a child master a task.

F. How Theory and Research Work Together

II. RESEARCH METHODS
- **Quantitative research**: Research that focuses on "hard" data and numerical or statistical measures.
- **Qualitative research**: Research that focuses on "soft" data, such as subjective experiences, feelings, or beliefs.
- **Scientific method**: System of established principles and processes of scientific inquiry. The usual steps in the method are:
    1. *Identify a problem* to be studied.
    2. *Formulate hypotheses* to be tested by research.
    3. *Collect data.*
    4. *Analyze the data* to determine whether they support the hypothesis.
    5. *Disseminate findings* so that other observers can check, learn from, analyze, repeat, and build on the results.

A. Sampling
- *Population:* A group to whom the findings in research may apply.
- **Sample**: Group of participants chosen to represent the entire population under study.
- *Generalized:* Application of results from a sample study to the population as a whole.
- *Random selection:* Method of selecting participants in a study so that each person in a population has an equal and independent chance of being chosen.

B. Forms of Data Collection
1. Self-Reports: Diaries, Interviews, Questionnaires
    - *Diary:* A log or record of activities.
    - *Parental self-reports:* A log or record of activities kept by the parents of young children, concerning the children's activities.
    - *Interview:* Method in which researchers, either face-to-face or on the telephone, ask questions about attitudes, opinions, or behavior.
        - ➤ *Structured interview:* Interview in which each participant is asked the same set of questions.
        - ➤ *Open-ended interview:* Interview in which the interviewer can vary the topics and order of questions and can ask follow-up questions based on the responses.
    - *Questionnaire:* Printed questions that participants fill out and return.
2. Behavioral and Performance Measures
    - *Valid:* A test that measures the abilities it claims to measure is said to be valid.
    - *Reliable:* A test that provides consistent results from one testing to another is reliable.
    - *Standardized:* A test that is given and scored by the same methods and criteria for all test-takers is said to be standardized.
    - **Operational definitions**: Definitions stated solely in terms of the operations or procedures used to produce or measure a phenomenon.
3. Naturalistic and Laboratory Observation
    - **Naturalistic observation**: Research method in which behavior is studied in natural settings without intervention or manipulation.

- **Laboratory observation**: Research method in which all participants are observed under the same controlled conditions.
- *Observer bias:* The researcher's tendency to interpret data to fit expectations or to emphasize some aspects and minimize others.

C. Basic Research Designs
1. Case Studies
   Case study: Study of an individual.
2. Ethnographic Studies
   - **Ethnographic study**: In-depth study of a culture, which uses a combination of methods including participant observation.
   - **Participant observation**: Research method in which the observer lives with the people or participates in the activity being observed.
3. Correlational Studies
   - **Correlational study**: Research design intended to discover whether a statistical relationship between variables exists.
   - *Correlation:* A statistical relationship between two or more variables.
   - *Variables:* Phenomena that change or vary among people or can be varied for purposes of research.
   - *Positive correlation:* Variables that are related increase or decrease together.
   - *Negative correlation:* Variables have an inverse relationship; as one increases, the other decreases.
4. Experiments
   - **Experiment**: Rigorously controlled, replicable procedure in which the researcher manipulates variables to assess the effect of one on the other.
   - *Replicate:* Repeating an experiment in exactly the same way with different participants to verify the results and conclusions.
   a. Groups and Variables
      - **Experimental group**: In an experiment, the group receiving the treatment under study.
      - **Control group**: In an experiment, a group of people, similar to those in the experimental group, who do not receive the treatment whose effects are to be measured.
      - *Treatment:* The phenomenon the researcher wants to study.
      - *Treatment groups:* In an experiment, groups that each receive one of the treatments under study.
      - *Dialogic reading:* A method of reading picture books to very young children.
      - **Independent variable**: In an experiment, the condition over which the experimenter has direct control.
      - **Dependent variable**: In an experiment, the condition that may or may not change as a result of changes in the independent variable.
   b. Random Assignment
      - *Random assignment:* Assigning the participants in an experiment to groups in such a way that each person has an equal chance of being placed in any group.
      - *Confound:* Contamination of an experiment by unintended differences between the groups.

c. Laboratory, Field, and Natural Experiments
   - *Laboratory experiments:* Experiment in which the participants are brought to a special place where they experience conditions manipulated by the experimenter.
   - *Field experiment:* A controlled study conducted in an everyday setting, such as home or school.
   - *Natural experiment:* Study comparing people who have been accidentally "assigned" to separate groups by circumstances of life (a correlational study).
D. Developmental Research Designs
   1. Longitudinal, Cross-Sectional, and Sequential Designs
      - **Longitudinal study**: Study designed to assess changes in a sample over time.
      - **Cross-sectional study**: Study design in which people of different ages are assessed on one occasion.
      - **Sequential study**: Study design that combines cross-sectional and longitudinal techniques.
   2. **Microgenetic Studies**: Study designs that allows researchers to directly observe change by repeated testing over a short time.
E. Ethics of Research
   1. Right to Informed Consent
   2. Avoidance of Deception
   3. Right to Privacy and Confidentiality

True/False Self-Test

Place a T or an F in the space provided. These questions are taken from the chapter content, tables, key terms, Guideposts for Study, and Checkpoints.

1. ___ A theory is used to explain data and to generate hypotheses that can be tested by research.

2. ___ The psychoanalytic perspective sees development as motivated by unconscious emotional conflicts.

3. ___ Freud described two stages of psychosocial development.

4. ___ The learning perspective is concerned with hidden, mental behavior.

5. ___ Social cognitive neuroscience uses brain imaging and the study of people with brain injuries to determine how the brain controls and influences behavior.

6. ___ The information-processing approach analyzes the mental processes underlying sexual behavior.

7. ___ Piaget's theory includes four stages of increasingly complex cognition.

8. ___ Bandura's social learning theory stresses observational learning and imitation of models.

9. ___ Bronfenbrenner identified three interlocking levels of cognitive influence.

10. ___ Vygotsky's sociocultural theory focuses on interaction between the individual and social context.

11. ___ The ethological perspective is represented by Piaget and Vygotsky.

12. ___ Random selection of a research sample can ensure generalizability.

13. ___ To arrive at sound conclusions, researchers use the scientific method.

14. ___ Only experiments can firmly establish causal relationships.

15. ___ Laboratory experiments are difficult to control and replicate.

16. ___ The learning perspective views people as fostering their own development through choice, creativity, and self-realization.

17. ___ Dominant beliefs and ideologies are part of Bronfenbrenner's microsystem.

18. ___ The ethological perspective focuses on biological and evolutionary bases of behavior.

19. ___ Two kinds of associative learning are classical conditioning and operant conditioning.

20. ___ Behaviorism is a mechanistic theory.

21. ___ Erikson's crisis of infancy has been disproved.

22. ___ The learning perspective is concerned with finding out the objective laws that govern observable behavior.

23. ___ The superego, according to Freud, develops at about age 10.

24. ___ Adaptation involves two steps: assimilation and accommodation.

25. ___ Although researchers take the principles of beneficence, respect, and justice into consideration, ultimately their decisions will be made on the basis of how useful they believe their findings will be.

Multiple-Choice Self-Test

Circle the letter of the best answer. These questions are based on many aspects of the chapter content, in no particular order.

1. Margaret Mead's major contribution to the field of human development is
a. operant conditioning.
b. the value of a cross cultural perspective.
c. observational learning.
d. social learning theory.

2. A set of logically related concepts or statements, which seeks to describe and explain human development, is
a. reliability.
b. validity.
c. theory.
d. hypothesis.

3. The model of human development that sees people as active, growing organisms that set their own development in motion is the
a. mechanistic model.
b. psychosocial model.
c. behaviorist model.
d. organismic model.

4. Research concerning the influences of heredity and environment on almost all characteristics has found that there is
a. a strong genetic influence.
b. an interaction between the two forces.
c. a strong environmental influence.
d. None of the above.

5. Mechanistic theorists
a. see development as continuous.
b. focus on quantitative change.
c. see development as always governed by the same processes.
d. All of the above.

6. The theoretical perspective that is concerned with observable behavior is
a. psychoanalytic.
b. ethological.
c. contextual.
d. learning.

7. According to Freud, newborns are governed by
a. the id.
b. the superego.
c. the ego.
d. None of the above.

8. Erik Erikson developed a theory that included
a. eight stages across the life span.
b. psychosocial development.
c. lifelong ego development.
d. All of the above.

9. Learning theorists see development as
a. occurring in stages.
b. qualitatively changing.
c. continuous.
d. impossible to define.

10. Behaviorism is
a. focused on associative learning.
b. an organismic theory.
c. experimental at this time.
d. an information-processing tool.

11. Ivan Pavlov developed
a. a hierarchy of human needs.
b. the principles of classical conditioning.
c. social learning theory.
d. bioecological theory.

12. According to social cognitive theory, children gradually develop a sense of
a. self-actualization.
b. guilt.
c. self-efficacy.
d. transcendence.

13. Piaget's cognitive stage theory, the neo-Piagetian theories, and the information-processing approach are all part of
a. the ethological perspective.
b. the contextual perspective.
c. the psychoanalytic view.
d. the cognitive perspective.

14. Piaget's term for the way a child handles new information that seems to conflict with what the child already knows is
a. adaptation.
b. organization.
c. schemes.
d. demarcation.

15. The information-processing approach
a. is a single theory.
b. is invalid today.
c. compares the brain to a computer.
d. focuses on the unconscious.

16. The adaptive values of immaturity include
a. protection from overstimulation.
b. facilitation of early language development.
c. extended period of play.
d. All of the above.

17. Bioecological theory was developed by
a. Albert Bandura.
b. Sigmund Freud.
c. Urie Bronfenbrenner.
d. Erik Erikson.

18. According to bioecological theory, a system that includes personal, face-to-face relationships and bidirectional influences that flow back and forth is a
a. mesosystem.
b. microsystem.
c. exosystem.
d. chronosystem.

19. Vygotsky describes the gap between what children are able to do and what they are not quite ready to accomplish by themselves as
a. assimilation.
b. actualization.
c. adaptation.
d. the zone of proximal development.

20. The simplest form of self-report is
a. a questionnaire.
b. a diary or log.
c. an interview.
d. the Denver Developmental Screening Test.

21. The researcher's tendency to interpret data to fit expectations, or to emphasize some facts and minimize others, is known as
a. quantification.
b. correlation.
c. observer bias.
d. naturalistic observation.

22. An in-depth study of a culture or subculture is known as
a. an ethnographic study.
b. a case study.
c. a bioecological study.
d. an experiment.

23. Laboratory experiments are
a. generalized.
b. easiest to control and replicate.
c. microgenetic studies.
d. ways to resolve ethical issues.

24. A microgenetic study
a. allows direct observation of a change over a short period of time.
b. is intended to overcome the weakness of the longitudinal study.
c. resolves ethical issues.
d. compares age groups.

25. Observation may take the form of
a. naturalistic observation.
b. laboratory observation.
c. experimenter observation.
d. Both a and b.

Organize It!

Making lists helps organize information into easily recalled form. The following lists are based on the chapter content, Guideposts for Study, and Checkpoints.

1. List and briefly describe three basic theoretical issues on which developmental scientists differ.

    1.
    2.
    3.

2. List and describe four forms of data collection.

    1.

    2.

    3.

    4.

3. List and describe four research designs used to study child development.

    1.

    2.

    3.

    4.

4. List and briefly describe the eight stages of Erikson's theory.

    1.

    2.

    3.

    4.

    5.

    6.

    7.

    8.

5. List and summarize the five steps in the scientific method.

    1.

    2.

    3.

    4.

    5.

Short Essay Questions

These short essay questions are based in part on the Checkpoints in the chapter. Answer each question as completely and succinctly as possible.

1. Discuss the three practical applications of the information-processing approach to human development.

2. Describe the five interlocking contextual systems proposed by Bronfenbrenner.

3. Discuss Vygotsky's zone of proximal development, using examples.

4. Describe two types of observation and discuss the advantages and disadvantages of each.

5. What ethical problems may arise in research?

Critical Thinking Questions

These questions may be used in small group discussions or as extra-credit reports.

1. After reading the article, can you identify the researcher's main hypothesis?

2. What do you think of the methods the researchers used to investigate their research questions?

3. If you were going to repeat this study, what would you change?

Answer Keys

True/False Self-Test

1. T	p. 27	GP 1		14. T	p. 50	GP 4
2. F	p. 29	GP 3		15. F	p. 51	GP 4
3. F	p. 30	GP 3		16. F	p. 33	GP 3
4. F	p. 33	GP 3		17. F	p. 39	GP 3
5. T	p. 38	GP 3		18. T	p. 38	GP 3
6. F	p. 37	GP 3		19. T	p. 33	GP 3
7. T	p. 36	GP 3		20. T	p. 33	GP 3
8. F	p. 35	GP 3		21. F	p. 33	GP 3
9. F	p. 39	GP 3		22. T	p. 33	GP 3
10. T	p. 42	GP 3		23. F	p. 31	GP 3
11. F	p. 38	GP 3		24. T	p. 36	GP 3
12. T	p. 44	GP 4		25. F	p. 55	GP 5
13. T	p. 44	GP 4				

Multiple-Choice Self-Test

1. b	p. 26	—		14. a	p. 36	GP 3
2. c	p. 27	GP 1		15. c	p. 37	GP 3
3. d	p. 28	GP 2		16. d	p. 40	GP 3
4. b	p. 28	GP 2		17. c	p. 39	GP 3
5. b	p. 28	GP 2		18. b	p. 39	GP 3
6. d	p. 33	GP 3		19. d	p. 42	GP 3
7. a	p. 31	GP 3		20. b	p. 45	GP 4
8. d	p. 33	GP 3		21. c	p. 46	GP 4
9. c	p. 33	GP 3		22. a	p. 48	GP 4
10. a	p. 33	GP 3		23. b	p. 51	GP 4
11. b	p. 33	GP 3		24. a	p. 54	GP 4
12. c	p. 35	GP 3		25. d	p. 46	GP 4
13. d	p. 35	GP 3				

Organize It!

1.	pp. 27-29	GP 2
2.	pp. 45-47	GP 4
3.	pp. 52-55	GP 4
4.	p. 32	GP 3
5	p. 44	GP 4

Short Essay Questions

1.	p. 37	GP 3
2.	pp. 39-41	GP 3
3.	pp. 42-43	GP 3
4.	p. 46	GP 4
5.	pp. 55-56	GP 5

PART 2: BEGINNINGS

CHAPTER 3: FORMING A NEW LIFE

This chapter focuses on the mechanisms of heredity, the influences of heredity and environment, and on prenatal development. The issues of fetal alcohol syndrome, cloning and genetic testing and genetic engineering are addressed in the three focus boxes.

Guideposts for Study

1. How does conception normally occur?

2. What causes multiple births?

3. How does heredity operate in determining sex and transmitting normal and abnormal traits?

4. How do scientists study the relative influences of heredity and environment, and how do heredity and environment work together?

5. What roles do heredity and environment play in physical health, intelligence, and personality?

6. What are the three stages of prenatal development, and what happens during each stage?

7. What can fetuses do?

8. What environmental influences can affect prenatal development?

9. What techniques can assess a fetus's health and well-being, and what is the importance of prenatal care?

Detailed Chapter Outline with Key Terms

I. CONCEIVING NEW LIFE
- *Animalculists:* Early school of biological thought that claimed that fully formed "little people" were contained in the heads of sperm, ready to grow in the nurturing womb.
- *Ovists:* Early school of biological thought that claimed that a female's ovaries contained tiny, already formed humans whose growth was activated by the male's sperm.
- **Clone:** (*verb*) To make a genetic copy of an individual; (noun) a genetic copy of an individual.
- A. How Fertilization Takes Place
  - **Fertilization:** Union of sperm and ovum fuse to produce a zygote; also called *conception.*
  - *Gametes:* The sex cells, ovum and sperm.
  - **Zygote:** One-celled organism resulting from fertilization.
  - *Follicle:* Small sac in the ovary containing the immature ova.
  - *Ovulation:* The rupture of a mature follicle and expulsion of the ovum.
  - *Cilia:* Tiny hair cells in the fallopian tubes that sweep the ovum along.
  - *Cervix:* The opening of the uterus.

B. What Causes Multiple Births?
- **Dizygotic (two-egg) twins**: Twins conceived by the union of two different ova (or a single ovum that has split) with two different sperm cells; also called *fraternal twins*.
- **Monozygotic (one-egg) twins**: Twins resulting from the division of a single zygote after fertilization; also called *identical twins*.
- **Temperament**: Characteristic disposition or style of approaching and reacting to situations.

II. MECHANISMS OF HEREDITY

Heredity: The inborn factors, inherited from the biological parents, that affect development.

A. The Genetic Code
- **Deoxyribonucleic acid (DNA)**: Chemical that carries inherited instructions for the formation and function of body cells.
- *Bases:* Chemical units that make up DNA; adenine, thymine, cytosine, and guanine.
- **Genetic code**: Sequence of base pairs within DNA, which determine inherited characteristics.
- **Chromosomes**: Coils of DNA that carry the genes.
- **Genes**: Small segments of DNA located in definite positions on particular chromosomes.
- **Human genome**: Complete sequence or mapping of genes in the human body and their location.
- *Meiosis:* Type of cell division in which each sex cell (gamete) ends up with only 23 chromosomes.
- *Mitosis:* Type of cell division in which each cell divides in half repeatedly, resulting in new cells with 46 chromosomes.

B. What Determines Sex?
- **Autosomes**: The 22 pairs of chromosomes not related to sexual expression.
- **Sex chromosomes**: Pair of chromosomes that determines sex: XX in the normal female, XY in the normal male.
- *X chromosomes:* Chromosomes containing the genes for femaleness.
- *Y chromosomes:* Chromosomes containing the genes for maleness.
- *Wnt-4:* A signaling molecule that appears to control the development of female characteristics.

C. Patterns of Genetic Transmission
1. Dominant and Recessive Inheritance
   - **Alleles**: Paired genes (alike or different) that affect a trait.
   - **Homozygous**: Possessing two identical alleles for a trait.
   - **Heterozygous**: Possessing differing alleles for a trait.
   - **Dominant inheritance**: Pattern of inheritance in which, when a child receives contradictory alleles, only the dominant one is expressed.
   - **Recessive inheritance**: Pattern of inheritance in which a child receives identical recessive alleles, resulting in expression of a nondominant trait.
   - *Codominance:* Situation occurring when neither of two alleles is dominant, and the resulting trait reflects the influence of both.
   - **Polygenic inheritance**: Pattern of inheritance in which multiple genes affect a complex trait.

- *Molecular genetics:* Area of study in which researchers have identified specific genes that contribute to particular behavioral traits.
- *Quantitative trait loci (QTL):* In molecular genetics, the locations and relative effect sizes of contributing genes.
- **Multifactorial transmission**: Combination of genetic and environmental factors to produce certain complex traits.
    2. Genotypes and Phenotypes: Multifactorial Transmission
    - **Phenotype**: Observable characteristics of a person.
    - **Genotype**: Genetic makeup of a person, containing both expressed and unexpressed characteristics.
D. Genetic and Chromosomal Abnormalities
Mutations: Permanent alterations in genes or chromosomes that may produce harmful characteristics.
    1. Defects Transmitted by Dominant or Recessive Inheritance
    Incomplete dominance: Partial expression of a trait.
    2. Defects Transmitted by Sex-Linked Inheritance
    - **Sex-linked inheritance**: Pattern of inheritance in which certain characteristics carried on the X chromosome inherited from the mother are transmitted differently to her male and female offspring.
    - *Carrier:* Person who does not have an expressed genetic trait but can pass on the gene for it to offspring.
    3. **Genome (Genetic) Imprinting**: The phenomenon in which some genes seem to be temporarily imprinted, or chemically altered, in either the mother or the father. When transmitted to offspring, these genes have different effects than do counterpart genes from the other parent.
    4. Chromosomal Abnormalities
    - **Down syndrome**: Chromosomal disorder characterized by moderate-to-severe mental retardation and by such physical signs as a downward-sloping skin fold at the inner corners of the eyes.
    - *Trisomy-21:* Down syndrome in which there is an extra 21st chromosome or a translocation of part of the 21st chromosome onto another chromosome.
E. Genetic Counseling and Testing
    - **Genetic counseling**: Clinical service that advises couples of their probable risk of having children with hereditary defects.
    - *Karyotype:* Arranged enlarged photographic chart of the chromosomes in a cell.

III. NATURE AND NURTURE: INFLUENCES OF HEREDITY AND ENVIRONMENT
A. Studying Heredity and Environment
Behavioral genetics: Quantitative study of relative hereditary and environmental influences.
    1. Measuring Heritability
    - **Heritability**: Statistical estimate of contribution of heredity to individual differences in a specific trait within a given population.
    - *Family studies:* Study in which researchers measure the degree to which biological relatives share certain traits and whether the closeness of the familial relationship is associated with the degree of similarity.

- *Adoption studies:* Study in which researchers look at similarities between adopted children and their adoptive families, and also between adopted children and their biological families.
- *Studies of twins:* Study in which researchers compare pairs of monozygotic and same-sex dizygotic twins.
- **Concordant**: Term describing twins who share the same trait or disorder.

2. Effects of the Prenatal Environment
- *Co-twin control study:* Study in which the prenatal (or postnatal) development and experiences of one monozygotic twin are compared with the other, who serves as a one-person "control group."
- *Chorion control study:* Study in which two types of monozygotic twins—monochorionic and dichorionic—are compared.
- *Monochorionic twins:* Twins who developed within the same fluid-filled sac.
- *Dichorionic twins:* Twins who developed within two separate sacs.

B. How Heredity and Environment Work Together
Developmental system: The combination of constitutional factors (related to biological and psychological makeup), social, economic, and cultural factors that help shape development.
1. Reaction Range and Canalization
- **Reaction range**: Potential variability, depending on environmental conditions, in the expression of a hereditary trait.
- *Norm of reaction:* Term used in the developmental system model in place of reaction range; the idea that the limits set by heredity are unknowable and their effects unpredictable because of the complexity of development.
- **Canalization**: Limitation on variance of expression of certain inherited characteristics.

2. **Genotype-Environment Interaction**: The portion of phenotypic variation that results from the reactions of genetically different individuals to similar environmental conditions.

3. **Genotype-Environment Correlation** *(genotype-environment covariance)*: Tendency of certain genetic and environmental influences to reinforce each other; may be passive, reactive (evocative), or active.
- *Passive correlations:* The parents, who provide the genes that predispose a child toward a trait, also tend to provide an environment that encourages development of that trait.
- *Reactive, or evocative, correlations:* Children with differing genetic makeups evoke different responses from adults.
- *Active correlations:* Older children actively choose or create experiences consistent with their genetic tendencies.
- **Niche-picking**: Tendency of a person, especially after early childhood, to seek out environm

4. What Makes Siblings Different? The Nonshared Environment
Nonshared environmental effects: The unique environment in which each child grows up, consisting of distinctive influences or influences that affect one child differently than another.

C. Some Characteristics Influenced by Heredity and Environment
  1. Physical and Physiological Traits
     Obesity: Extreme overweight. Research suggests that as much as 80 percent of the risk of obesity is genetic.
  2. Intelligence and School Achievement
  3. Personality
  4. Psychopathology
     - **Schizophrenia**: Mental disorder marked by a loss of contact with reality; symptoms include hallucinations and delusions.
     - **Autism**: Pervasive developmental disorder of the brain, characterized by lack of normal social interaction, impaired communication and imagination, and repetitive, obsessive behaviors.
     - *Autistic spectrum disorders (ASD):* Mild to severe disorders of the autistic type.
     - *Pervasive developmental disorder (PDD):* A disorder related to classic autism.
     - *Asperger's disorder:* The most common PDD; children with this disorder usually have normal or even high verbal intelligence, are curious, and do well in school, but they have limited, fixed interests, repetitive speech and behavior, and difficulty understanding social and emotional cues.
     - *HOXA1:* Gene involved in the development of the brain stem that may predispose an infant to autism in one variant.

IV. PRENATAL DEVELOPMENT
  - *Gestation:* The approximately nine-month period of development between conception and birth.
  - *Gestational age:* Age of the organism from conception.
  - *Zygote:* A fertilized ovum.
  - *Morphogens:* Molecules produced by certain genes. These molecules are switched on after fertilization and direct the differentiation of the various body parts.
  A. Stages of Prenatal Development
     - **Cephalocaudal principle**: Principle that development proceeds in a head-to-tail direction; that is, the upper parts of the body develop before lower parts.
     - **Proximodistal principle**: Principle that development proceeds from within to without; that is, that parts of the body near the center develop before the extremities.
     1. Germinal Stage (Fertilization to 2 Weeks)
        - **Germinal stage**: First 2 weeks of prenatal development, characterized by rapid cell division, increasing complexity and differentiation, and implantation in the wall of the uterus.
        - *Mitosis:* Period of rapid cell division and duplication.
        - *Blastocyst:* A fluid-filled sphere of cells that will float into the uterus and implant in the lining.
        - *Embryonic disk:* A thickened cell mass located on the blastocyst, from which the embryo begins to develop.
        - *Ectoderm:* The upper layer of the embryonic disk that will form into the outer layer of skin, the nails, hair, teeth, sensory organs, and the nervous system.
        - *Endoderm:* The lower layer of the embryonic disk that will form into the digestive system, liver, pancreas, salivary glands, and respiratory system.

- *Mesoderm:* The inner layer of the embryonic disk that will form into the inner layer of skin, muscles, skeleton, and excretory and circulatory systems.
- *Placenta:* Organ that provides oxygen and nourishment to the developing baby and removes its body wastes.
- *Umbilical cord:* Cord that connects the placenta to the baby and vice versa.
- *Amniotic sac:* Fluid-filled membrane that encases the developing baby, protecting it and giving it room to move.
- *Chorion:* Outermost layer of the amniotic sac.
- *Trophoblast:* The outer cell layer of the blastocyst.
- *HOXA10:* A gene that appears to control whether an embryo will be successfully implanted in the uterine wall.

2. Embryonic Stage (2 to 8 Weeks)
   - **Embryonic stage**: Second stage of gestation (2 to 8 weeks), characterized by rapid growth and development of major body systems and organs.
   - *Trimester:* A three-month period of pregnancy.
   - **Spontaneous abortion**: Natural expulsion from the uterus of a conceptus that cannot survive outside the womb; also called *miscarriage.*
   - *Stillborn:* Term for a baby that is dead at its birth.

3. Fetal Stage (8 Weeks to Birth)
   - **Fetal stage**: Final stage of gestation (from 8 weeks to birth), characterized by increased detail of body parts and greatly enlarged body size.
   - **Ultrasound**: Prenatal medical procedure using high-frequency sound waves to detect the outline of a fetus and its movements, to determine whether a pregnancy is progressing normally.

B. Environmental Influences: Maternal Factors
   - **Teratogenic**: Capable of causing birth defects.
   - *Transforming growth factor alpha:* A variant of a growth gene, this factor causes a fetus to have six times more risk than other fetuses of developing a cleft palate if the mother smokes while pregnant.

   1. Nutrition
   2. Physical Activity
   3. Drug Intake
      a. Medical Drugs
      b. Alcohol
         - **Fetal alcohol syndrome (FAS)**: Combination of mental, motor, and developmental abnormalities affecting the offspring of some women who drink heavily during pregnancy.
         - *Corpus callosum:* Brain tissue that connects and coordinates signals between the right and left hemispheres of the brain.
         - *Fetal alcohol effects:* A less severe condition that can include mental retardation, retardation of intrauterine growth, and minor congenital abnormalities.
      c. Nicotine
      d. Caffeine
      e. Marijuana, Opiates, and Cocaine
   4. Sexually Transmitted Diseases
      Acquired immune deficiency syndrome (AIDS): Viral disease that undermines effective functioning of the immune system.

5. Other Maternal Illnesses
   Toxoplasmosis: An infection caused by a parasite harbored in the bodies of cattle, sheep, pigs, and in the intestinal tract of cats.
6. Maternal Age
7. Outside Environmental Hazards
C. Environmental Influences: Paternal Factors
D. Monitoring Prenatal Development
   1. Ultrasound and Amniocentesis
      * *Sonogram:* A picture of the uterus, fetus, and placenta created by ultrasound directed into the mother's abdomen.
      * *Sonoembriology:* Technique in which high-frequency transvaginal probes and digital image processing are used to detect unusual defects during the embryonic stage.
      * *Amniocentesis:* Technique in which a sample of the amniotic fluid, which contains fetal cells, is withdrawn and analyzed to detect genetic or multifactorial defects and chromosomal disorders.
   2. Other Assessment Methods
      * *Chorionic villus sampling (CVS):* A technique in which tissue from the ends of the hairlike projections (villi) of the chorion are tested for the presence of birth defects and disorders.
      * *Embryoscopy:* The insertion of a tiny viewing scope into a pregnant woman's abdomen.
      * *Preimplantation genetic diagnosis:* Technique in which embryos of four to eight cells, conceived by in vitro fertilization, are examined for defects before implantation.
      * *Umbilical cord sampling or fetal blood sampling:* Technique in which a needle is inserted into tiny blood vessels of the umbilical cord under the guidance of ultrasound.
      * *Maternal blood test:* Examination of a blood sample, taken from the mother between the 16th and 18th weeks of pregnancy, for the presence of alpha fetoprotein (AFP), an indicator of neural tube defects.
E. Prenatal Care

True/False Self-Test

Place a T or an F in the appropriate space. These questions are taken from the chapter content, tables, key terms, Guideposts for Study, and Checkpoints.

1. _____ Fertilization results in a one-celled zygote.

2. _____ Dizygotic twins have the same genetic makeup.

3. _____ Monozygotic twins are always of the same sex.

4. _____ Differences in pre- and postnatal experiences may cause differences in the personalities of identical twins.

5. _____ The basic unit of heredity is the neuron.

6. ____ Each gene is located by function in a definite position on the chromosome.

7. ____ At conception, each human being receives 46 chromosomes from each parent.

8. ____ A child who receives an X chromosome from each parent will be female.

9. ____ The male parent's chromosome determines the sex of the child.

10. ___ The phenotype is a person's observable characteristics.

11. ___ Most human characteristics are the result of a single gene.

12. ___ Birth defects are transmitted through simple dominant, recessive, or sex-linked genes.

13. ___ Down syndrome is a rare chromosomal abnormality.

14. ___ Through genetic counseling, prospective parents can receive information about the mathematical odds of having children with certain birth defects.

15. ___ Through genetic testing, certain birth defects like Tay-Sachs disease are on the decline.

16. ___ Monozygotic twins tend to be less concordant for genetically influenced traits than do dizygotic twins.

17. ___ Siblings tend to be more different than alike in intelligence and personality.

18. ___ Obesity is an example of a characteristic influenced by heredity and environment.

19. ___ Prenatal development occurs in six stages.

20. ___ Growth and development both before and after birth is erratic and unpredictable.

21. ___ More males are spontaneously aborted than females.

22. ___ Fetal activity can be observed via ultrasound.

23. ___ Fetuses seem to be able to hear, exercise sensory discrimination, learn, and remember.

24. ___ Nutrition, physical activity, smoking, and drinking are all important prenatal influences involving the mother.

25. ___ External influences in the environment may affect the father's sperm.

Multiple-Choice Self-Test

Circle the letter of the best answer. These questions are based on many aspects of the chapter content, in no particular order.

1. The process by which male and female gametes combine to form a single-celled zygote is known as
   a. cloning.
   b. fertilization.
   c. meiosis.
   d. mitosis.

2. The rupture of a mature follicle and the expulsion of the ovum is known as
   a. ovulation.
   b. intercourse.
   c. fertilization.
   d. menopause.

3. Sperm are produced by the
   a. cilia.
   b. fallopian tubes.
   c. cervix.
   d. testes.

4. Fertilization takes place in
   a. the ovaries.
   b. the fallopian tube.
   c. the cervix.
   d. the uterus.

5. Normal human females are born with
   _____ ova.
   a. 100
   b. 400,000
   c. 1,000,000
   d. 28

6. Fertilization is most likely if intercourse occurs
   a. during the menstrual period.
   b. on the day after the menstrual period.
   c. on the day of ovulation or five days preceding ovulation.
   d. None of the above.

7. Dizygotic twins occur when
   a. one fertilized egg splits in two.
   b. two eggs are released and fertilized at the same time.
   c. one egg is fertilized by two sperm.
   d. None of the above.

8. Monozygotic twins are
   a. identical in genetic makeup.
   b. likely to be mirror images of each other in some physical characteristics.
   c. not always identical in temperament.
   d. All of the above.

9. The incidence of multiple births in the United States is
   a. declining rapidly.
   b. rising rapidly.
   c. unchanged in the last 50 years.
   d. declining slightly.

10. Dizygotic twins are least common among
    a. Asians.
    b. white northern Europeans.
    c. African Americans.
    d. East Indians.

11. Multiple births are
    a. more likely to lead to disability and death in infancy.
    b. rising in the United States, partly as a result of delayed childbearing.
    c. partly related to the increased use of fertility drugs.
    d. All of the above.

12. Each genome in the human body contains approximately _____ genes.
a. 46
b. 100
c. 30,000 to 40,000
d. 23 to 46

13. Each gene is located by function in a definite position on the
a. cell wall.
b. mitochondria.
c. chromosome.
d. cell.

14. The process by which body cells divide in half repeatedly is
a. meiosis.
b. metamorphosis.
c. mitosis.
d. crossover.

15. Each sperm and each egg contains _____ chromosomes
a. 23
b. 46
c. 92
d. 69

16. The cell division of sperm and egg is a process known as
a. mitosis.
b. morphogenesis.
c. meiosis.
d. polygenesis.

17. The sex of the human baby is determined by the genetic contribution of the
a. father.
b. mother.
c. paternal grandmother.
d. maternal grandmother.

18. Male embryos begin producing testosterone at
a. 16 weeks after conception.
b. 6 to 8 weeks after conception.
c. 20 weeks before birth.
d. None of the above.

19. Genes that produce alternative expressions of a characteristic are
a. clones.
b. homozygous.
c. alleles.
d. chromatophores.

20. The array of observable characteristics that expresses one's genetic makeup is known as
a. genotype.
b. homozygous.
c. heterozygous.
d. phenotype.

21. Permanent alterations in genes or chromosomes that often produce harmful characteristics are
a. dominant.
b. mutations.
c. clones.
d. multifactors.

22. Defects such as Tay-Sachs disease are transmitted by
a. dominant inheritance.
b. gene splicing.
c. recessive inheritance.
d. IVF.

23. Red-green color blindness and hemophilia are examples of genetic disorders that
a. almost always appear in male children.
b. show up differently in male and female children.
c. are carried on the X chromosomes of an unaffected mother.
d. All of the above.

24. The condition caused by an extra copy of chromosome 21 or by the translocation of a part of chromosome 21 onto another chromosome is
a. Down syndrome.
b. Marfan syndrome.
c. Turner syndrome.
d. Klinefelter syndrome.

25. Prenatal development occurs in
a. six stages.
b. four stages.
c. three stages.
d. 40 stages.

Organize It!

Making a list is an easy way to remember clusters of related concepts, facts, and ideas. Below is a group of lists to make, based on Checkpoints in the chapter. Have fun!

1. List the three stages of prenatal development. Include one important feature of each.

    1.

    2.

    3.

2. List and describe three methods of prenatal assessment and intervention.

    1.

    2.

    3.

3. List three maternal illnesses that have adverse effects on the embryo or fetus.

    1.

    2.

    3.

4. List three ethnically related genetic diseases and the ethnic group most at risk for each.

    1.

    2.

    3.

5. List four genetically influenced psychopathological conditions.

   1.

   2.

   3.

   4.

6. List three kinds of influences that contribute to nonshared environmental effects.

   1.

   2.

   3.

Short Essay Questions

These short essay questions are based on the Checkpoints in the chapter. Answer each question as completely and succinctly as possible.

1. Briefly describe the process of normal conception. When is the best time for intercourse if a couple wishes to have a child?

2. Multiple births have increased significantly in the last decade in the United States. Discuss several possible reasons for this statistic. Base your answer on the chapter material.

3. Discuss the role of heredity and environment in determining physical health, intelligence, and personality.

4. Describe the ways in which environmental hazards may affect prenatal development.

Critical Thinking Questions

These questions can be used in small group discussions or for extra-credit reports.

1. Now that the human genome has been completed, how far do you think scientists and medical professionals should go in altering the genetic makeup of human beings? Consider these areas: eradication/correction of genetic diseases, gender selection, alteration of existing conditions such as vision defects or growth deficiencies, and physical trait selection such as hair, eye, and skin color.

2. Building on question 1, what are some potential benefits and problems with altering the genetic makeup of humans?

3. In what ways are you more like your mother, and in what ways are you more like your father? How are you similar or dissimilar to your siblings? How might these similarities and differences be influenced by heredity or environment?

4. How far should government go in protecting the unborn fetus from the pregnant mother's use of drugs and/or alcohol?

Answer Keys

True/False Self-Test

1. T   p. 63   GP 1
2. F   p. 64   GP 2
3. T   p. 64   GP 2
4. T   p. 64   GP 2
5. F   p. 65   GP 3
6. T   p. 65   GP 3
7. F   p. 65   GP 3
8. T   p. 66   GP 3
9. T   p. 66   GP 3
10. T   p. 69   GP 3
11. F   p. 68   GP 3
12. T   p. 71   GP 3
13. F   p. 73   GP 3
14. T   p. 74   GP 3
15. T   p. 75   GP 3
16. F   p. 76   GP 4
17. T   p. 81   GP 4
18. T   p. 82   GP 5
19. F   p. 86   GP 6
20. F   p. 87   GP 6
21. T   p. 91   GP 6
22. T   p. 91   GP 7
23. T   p. 91   GP 7
24. T   p. 92   GP 8
25. T   p. 99   GP 8

Multiple-Choice Self-Test

1. b   p. 63   GP 1
2. a   p. 64   GP 1
3. d   p. 64   GP 1
4. b   p. 64   GP 1
5. b   p. 64   GP 1
6. c   p. 64   GP 1
7. b   p. 64   GP 2
8. b   p. 64   GP 2
9. b   p. 65   GP 2
10. a   p. 65   GP 2
11. d   p. 65   GP 2
12. c   p. 65   GP 3
13. c   p. 65   GP 3
14. c   p. 66   GP 3
15. a   p. 65   GP 3
16. c   p. 65   GP 3
17. a   p. 66   GP 3
18. b   p. 67   GP 3
19. c   p. 68   GP 3
20. d   p. 69   GP 3
21. b   p. 71   GP 3
22. c   p. 71   GP 3
23. d   p. 72   GP 3
24. a   p. 73   GP 3
25. c   p. 86   GP 6

Organize It!

1.   p. 86   GP 6
2.   pp. 100-101   GP 9
3.   p. 98   GP 8
4.   p. 72   GP 3
5.   p. 84   GP 5
6.   pp. 81-82   GP 4

Short Essay Questions

1.   pp. 63-64   GP 1
2.   pp. 64-65   GP 2
3.   pp. 82-84   GP 5
4.   pp. 92-100   GP 8

CHAPTER 4: PHYSICAL DEVELOPMENT DURING THE FIRST THREE YEARS

This chapter introduces the birth process and the physical development of the child from infancy to the beginning of early childhood. The principles of early physical development are explored in depth in this informative chapter. The first part of the chapter focuses on birth and the newborn. The second part of the chapter explores early physical development, including brain development, reflex behaviors, and motor development.

Guideposts for Study

1. What happens during each of the four stages of childbirth?

2. What alternative settings and methods of delivery are available today?

3. How do newborn infants adjust to life outside the womb?

4. How can we tell whether a new baby is healthy and is developing normally?

5. What complications of childbirth can endanger newborn babies' adjustment or even their lives?

6. How can we enhance babies' chances of survival and health?

7. What influences the growth of body and brain?

8. When do the senses develop?

9. What are some early milestones in motor development, and what are some influences on it?

Detailed Chapter Outline with Key Terms

I. THE BIRTH PROCESS
  - *Labor:* Contractions of the uterus during childbirth.
  - **Parturition**: Process of uterine, cervical, and other changes, usually lasting about two weeks, preceding childbirth.
  - *Corticotropin-releasing hormone (CRH):* A protein produced by the placenta that seems to determine the timing of parturition. Also promotes maturation of fetal lungs.
  A. Stages of Childbirth
    - *First stage:* Usually the longest stage, may last 12 hours or more, in which regular and increasingly frequent uterine contractions widen the cervix.
    - *Second stage:* Lasting about 1-1/2 hours or less, this stage begins when the baby's head moves through the cervix and into the vaginal canal, and ends when the baby emerges from the mother's body.
    - *Third stage:* Lasting only about 5 to 30 minutes, this stage is the expulsion of the placenta and remaining tissues from the uterus.
    - *Fourth stage:* The first couple of hours after delivery, when the mother rests in bed while her recovery is monitored.

- **Electronic fetal monitoring**: Mechanical monitoring of fetal heartbeat during labor and delivery.
  B. Settings, Attendants, and Methods of Delivery
  1. Vaginal versus Cesarean Delivery
     Cesarean delivery: Delivery of a baby by surgical removal from the uterus.
  2. Medicated versus Unmedicated Delivery
     - **Natural childbirth**: Method of childbirth that seeks to prevent pain by eliminating the mother's fear through education about the physiology of reproduction and training in breathing and relaxation during delivery.
     - **Prepared childbirth**: Method of childbirth that uses instruction, breathing exercises, and social support to induce a controlled physical response to uterine contractions and reduce fear and pain.

II. THE NEWBORN BABY

Neonatal period: First 4 weeks of life, a time of transition from intrauterine dependency to independent existence.
  A. Size and Appearance
   - **Neonate**: Newborn baby, up to 4 weeks old.
   - *Fontanels:* Places on a baby's head where the bones have not yet grown together.
   - *Lanugo:* The birth hair, a fuzzy prenatal hair that will eventually drop off.
   - *Vernix caseosa:* An oily protective covering against infection, which dries within the first few days and sloughs off.
  B. Body Systems
   - **Anoxia**: Lack of oxygen, which may cause brain damage.
   - **Meconium**: Fetal waste matter, excreted during the first few days after birth.
   - **Neonatal jaundice**: Condition, in many newborn babies, caused by immaturity of liver and evidenced by yellowish appearance; can cause brain damage if not treated promptly.
  C. **State of Arousal**: An infant's physiological and behavioral status at a given moment in the periodic daily cycle of wakefulness, sleep, and activity.

III. SURVIVAL AND HEALTH

  A. Medical and Behavioral Assessment
  1. **Apgar scale**: Standard measurement of a newborn's condition; it assesses appearance, pulse, grimace, activity, and respiration.
  2. Assessing Neurological Status: The Brazelton Scale
     Brazelton Neonatal Behavioral Assessment Scale (NBAS): Neurological and behavioral test to measure neonate's responses to the environment. It assesses:
     - Motor organization (such as activity level or motor coordination)
     - Reflexes
     - State changes (such as irritability or the ability to calm down after an upset)
     - Attention and interactive capacities (such as general alertness and responsiveness)
     - Central nervous system instability (such as tremors and skin color changes)
  3. Neonatal Screening for Medical Conditions
  B. Complications of Childbirth
     Birth trauma: Injury sustained at the time of birth.

1. Postmaturity
   Postmature: Referring to a fetus not yet born as of 2 weeks after the due date or 42 weeks after the mother's last menstrual period.
2. Prematurity and Low Birthweight
   - **Low birthweight**: Weight of less than 5-1/2 pounds (2,500 grams) at birth because of prematurity or being small for date.
   - **Preterm (premature) infants**: Infants born before completing the 37th week of gestation.
   - **Small-for-date (small-for-gestational age)**: Infants whose birthweight is less than that of 90 percent of babies of the same gestational age, as a result of slow fetal growth.
   a. Who Is More Likely to Have a Low-Birthweight Baby?
      - *Demographic and socioeconomic factors:* Factors such as atypical age of the mother, poverty, unmarried status, or low educational level of the mother.
      - *Medical factors predating the pregnancy:* Factors such as a mother having either no children or more than four, being thin or short, having had previous low-birthweight babies or miscarriages, having been a low-birthweight baby herself, or having genital or urinary abnormalities or chronic hypertension.
      - *Prenatal behavioral and environmental factors:* Factors such as poor nutrition, poor prenatal care, smoking, use of alcohol or other drugs, or exposure to stress, high altitude, or toxic substances.
      - *Medical conditions associated with the pregnancy:* Factors such as vaginal bleeding, infections, high or low blood pressure, anemia, too little weight gain, and having given birth either less than six months before or more than ten years before.
   b. Immediate Treatment and Outcomes
      Hyaline membrane disease: Respiratory distress syndrome.
   c. Long-Term Outcomes
      - *Very-low-birthweight babies:* Babies weighing less than 1,500 grams.
      - *Extremely low-birthweight babies:* Babies weighing between 501 and 1,000 grams, or about 1 to 2 pounds.
C. Can a Supportive Environment Overcome Effects of Birth Complications?
   1. The Infant Health and Development Studies
   2. The Kauai Study
   Protective factors: Influences that reduce the impact of early stress and tend to predict positive outcomes.
D. Death during Infancy
   1. Improving Infant Survival
   Infant mortality rate: Proportion of babies born alive who die within the first year.
   2. **Sudden Infant Death Syndrome (SIDS)**: Sudden and unexplained death of an apparently healthy infant.
E. Immunization for Better Health

IV. EARLY PHYSICAL DEVELOPMENT
A. Principles of Development
   - *Cephalocaudal principle:* Principle stating that growth (including sensory and motor development) occurs from the top down.

- *Proximodistal principle:* Principle stating that growth and motor development proceed from the center of the body outward.
B. Physical Growth
   1. Influences on Growth
C. Nutrition
   1. Early Feeding: Past and Present
   2. Breast or Bottle?
   3. Obesity and Cholesterol
      - *Cholesterol:* A waxy substance found in human and animal tissue, associated with heart disease.
      - *Atherosclerosis:* A condition in which high levels of LDL, or "bad" cholesterol, can dangerously narrow blood vessels, leading to heart disease.
D. The Brain and Reflex Behavior
   - **Central nervous system**: Brain and spinal cord.
   - *Spinal cord:* A bundle of nerves running through the backbone.
   1. Building the Brain
   2. Major Parts of the Brain
      - *Brain stem:* The part of the brain responsible for such basic bodily functions as breathing heart rate, body temperature, and the sleep-wake cycle.
      - *Cerebellum:* The part of the brain that maintains balance and motor coordination.
      - *Cerebrum:* The largest part of the brain, divided into left and right hemispheres.
      - **Lateralization**: Tendency of each of the brain's hemispheres to have specialized functions.
      - *Corpus callosum:* A tough band of tissue joining the right and left hemispheres.
      - *Occipital lobe:* Section of the cerebral hemisphere that processes visual information.
      - *Parietal lobe:* Section of the cerebral hemisphere that processes touch and spatial information.
      - *Temporal lobe:* Section of the cerebral hemisphere that processes hearing and language.
      - *Frontal lobe:* Section of the cerebral hemisphere that permits high-level functioning such as speech and reasoning.
      - *Cerebral cortex:* The outer surface of the cerebrum.
   3. Brain Cells
      - **Neurons**: Nerve cells.
      - *Glial cells:* Cells that support and protect the neurons.
      - *Axons:* Branching extension from the neuron that sends signals to other neurons.
      - *Dendrites:* Branching extensions from the neuron that receive incoming messages from other cells.
      - *Synapses:* Tiny gaps between neurons.
      - *Neurotransmitters:* Chemicals that bridge the synapse between neurons.
      - **Integration**: Process by which neurons coordinate the activities of muscle groups.
      - **Differentiation**: Process by which neurons acquire specialized structure and function.
      - **Cell death**: Elimination of excess brain cells to achieve more efficient functioning.

4. Myelination
   - *Myelin:* Fatty substance that coats the neural pathways.
   - **Myelination**: Process of coating neurons with a fatty substance (myelin) that enables faster communication between cells.
   - *Hippocampus:* A structure deep in the temporal lobe that plays a key role in memory.
5. Early Reflexes
   - **Reflex behavior**: Automatic, involuntary, innate response to stimulation.
   - *Primitive reflexes:* Reflexes related to instinctive needs for survival and protection.
   - *Postural reflexes:* Reactions to changes in position or balance.
   - *Locomotor reflexes:* Reflexes that resemble voluntary movements that do not appear until months after the reflexes have disappeared, such as walking and swimming.
6. Molding the Brain: The Role of Experience
   Plasticity: Modifiability, or "molding," of the brain through experience.

E. Early Sensory Capacities
   1. Touch and Pain
   2. Smell and Taste
   3. Hearing
   4. Sight
   Binocular vision: The use of both eyes to focus, allowing perception of depth and distance.

F. Motor Development
   1. Milestones of Motor Development
      - **Systems of action**: Increasingly complex combinations of skills, which permit a wider or more precise range of movement and more control of the environment.
      - *Pincer grasp:* Grasp in which thumb and index finger meet at the tips to form a circle.
      - **Denver Developmental Screening Test**: Screening test given to children one month to six years old to determine whether they are developing normally.
      - **Gross motor skills**: Physical skills that involve the large muscles.
      - **Fine motor skills**: Physical skills that involve the small muscles and eye-hand coordination.
      a. Head Control
      b. Hand Control
      c. Locomotion
         Self-locomotion: The ability of babies to get around under their own power by means of creeping or crawling.
   2. How Motor Development Occurs: Maturation in Context
      Walking reflex: Stepping movements a neonate makes when held upright with the feet touching a surface.
   3. Motor Development and Perception
      - **Visual guidance**: The use of the eyes to guide the movement of the hands (or other parts of the body).
      - **Visual cliff**: Apparatus designed to give an illusion of depth and used to assess depth perception in infants.
      - **Depth perception**: Ability to perceive objects and surfaces three-dimensionally.

- **Haptic perception**: Ability to acquire information about properties of objects, such as size, weight, and texture, by handling them.
4. Eleanor and James Gibson's Ecological Theory
   - **Affordances**: In the Gibsons' ecological theory of perception, the fit between a person's physical attributes and capabilities and characteristics of the environment.
   - **Ecological theory of perception**: Theory developed by Eleanor and James Gibson, which describes developing motor and perceptual abilities as interdependent parts of a functional system that guides behavior in varying contexts.
5. Cultural Influences on Motor Development

True/False Self-Test

Place a T or an F in the appropriate space. These questions are taken from the chapter content, tables, key terms, Guideposts for Study, and Checkpoints.

1. ___ Today, nearly two-thirds of new mothers in the United States breast-feed.

2. ___ Breast-feeding may reduce the risks of SIDS.

3. ___ As of the year 2000, almost 25 percent of births in the United States were by cesarean section delivery.

4. ___ At one year of age, an infant's brain is 25 percent of its adult weight.

5. ___ Periods of rapid brain growth coincide with feeding changes.

6. ___ The cerebellum grows slowly in the first year of life.

7. ___ The brain is composed of two types of cells: neurons and glial cells.

8. ___ At birth, most of the 100 billion neurons are formed but not yet fully developed.

9. ___ The neurons coat the glial cells with myelin.

10. ___ Reflex behaviors play an important part in stimulating early development of the central nervous system and muscles.

11. ___ Sucking and the Moro reflex are primitive reflexes.

12. ___ Most of the early reflexes disappear during the first 6 months to 1 year.

13. ___ Touch is the most mature sensory system in the first several months of life.

14. ___ Newborns prefer sour or bitter tastes over sweetness.

15. ___ Hearing is only functional after birth.

16. ___ Vision is the least developed sense at birth.

17. ___ The Denver Developmental Screening Test measures cognitive awareness.

18. ___ Normal development need not follow the same timetable to reach the same destination.

19. ___ By the age of one year, most babies can balance on one foot and begin to hop.

20. ___ Although motor development follows a virtually universal sequence, its pace does seem to respond to certain contextual factors.

21. ___ African babies tend to be more advanced than American and European babies in sitting, walking, and running.

22. ___ Some cultures discourage early motor development.

23. ___ Babies develop depth perception after one year of age.

24. ___ Walkers are considered dangerous by the American Academy of Pediatrics.

25. ___ The Brazelton Neonatal Behavioral Assessment Scale is used to assess responses to the environment and to predict future development.

Multiple-Choice Self-Test

Circle the letter of the best answer. These questions are based on many aspects of the chapter content, in no particular order.

1. The uterine contractions that expel the fetus typically begin how many days after conception?
   a. 65
   b. 266
   c. 170
   d. 435

2. The changes that bring on labor typically begin about two weeks before delivery, as a result of
   a. size of the baby.
   b. increased anxiety of the mother.
   c. the shifting balance between estrogen and progesterone.
   d. size of the placenta.

3. Normal vaginal childbirth is accomplished in
   a. six periods.
   b. four stages.
   c. seven stages.
   d. forty stages.

4. The second stage of childbirth begins when
   a. the cervix begins to dilate.
   b. the placenta is delivered.
   c. the baby's head begins to move through the cervix.
   d. contractions become regular.

5. Cesarean delivery is a procedure that
a. is used to surgically deliver the baby.
b. is no longer used.
c. requires an episiotomy.
d. is never required in the United States.

6. Advocates of natural childbirth argue that medicated birth
a. poses risks for the baby.
b. deprives mothers of the empowering experience of childbirth.
c. Both a and b.
d. Neither a or c.

7. Settings and attendants for birth
a. should be hospitals and doctors.
b. reflect the overall cultural system.
c. should be homes and midwives.
d. should be government regulated.

8. The neonatal period is generally regarded as
a. the first 2 days of life.
b. the first 3 months of life.
c. the first 24 hours of life.
d. the first 4 weeks of life.

9. The layers of fat that develop during the last two months of gestation function to help newborns
a. roll over easil.
b. appeal to their mothers.
c. regulate body temperature.
d. float in the bath.

10. A baby who is sleeping with eyes closed, with no eye movement, and cannot be aroused by mild stimuli is in the state of
a. drowsiness.
b. alert inactivity.
c. irregular sleep.
d. regular sleep.

11. The Apgar Scale is used primarily for
a. immediate assessment of the newborn.
b. fetal heart rate measurement.
c. behavioral assessment at one year.
d. weighing the newborn.

12. Babies who inherit the enzyme disorder phenylketonuria (PKU) will
a. adjust within one month.
b. become jaundiced.
c. become mentally retarded unless placed on a special diet.
d. cry frequently at night.

13. Birth trauma may be caused by
a. anoxia.
b. infection.
c. disease.
d. All of the above.

14. Low-birthweight babies are those babies who weigh less than
a. 2,500 grams.
b. 5,000 grams.
c. 7 pounds but more than 6 pounds.
d. None of the above.

15. Postmature babies are typically
a. long and thin.
b. at risk for death.
c. at risk for brain damage.
d. All of the above.

16. In the United States, the leading cause of infant death is
a. SIDS.
b. Respiratory Distress Syndrome (RDS).
c. birth defects.
d. low birthweight.

17. Sudden infant death syndrome (SIDS)
a. is caused by choking.
b. occurs most often between 1 month and 4 months of age.
c. strikes only poor babies.
d. affects only African American babies.

18. Growth and development before and after birth follows these two principles:
a. cephalocaudal and proximodistal
b. body and brain
c. Apgar and Brazelton
d. All of the above.

19. The best food for infants up to one year of age is
a. cow's milk.
b. breast milk.
c. goat's milk.
d. iron-enriched formula.

20. Babies who are fed plain cow's milk in the early months may suffer from
a. low carbohydrate intake.
b. iron-deficiency anemia.
c. Vitamin C deficiency.
d. Vitamin A deficiency.

Organize It!

Making a list is an efficient and fun way to remember many types of information, including conceptual information. Once you have made your list, use it! Memorize it by singing it, saying it rhythmically, or dancing it into your memory. All of these methods put the information into your brain in easily recalled ways.

1. List the four stages of labor and one characteristic of each.

    1.

    2.

    3.

    4.

2. List three distinctive features of a newborn baby.

    1.
    2.
    3.

3. List three protective factors identified by the Kauai Study.

    1.
    2.
    3.

4. List the five infant states of arousal and the characteristics of each (see Table 4-1).

    1.

    2.

    3.

    4.

    5.

5. List the five subtests of the Apgar Scale.

    1.
    2.
    3.
    4.
    5.

6. List four factors that increase the likelihood that a woman will have an underweight or low-birthweight baby.

    1.

    2.

    3.

    4.

7. List in descending order, the four leading causes of infant deaths in the United States.

    1.

    2.

    3.

    4.

Short Essay Questions

These short essay questions are based on the Checkpoints in the chapter. Answer each question as completely and succinctly as possible.

1. Summarize trends in infant mortality, and explain why African American infants are less likely to survive than white infants. Discuss risk factors, causes, and prevention of sudden infant death syndrome.

2. Explain why full immunization of all preschool children is important.

3. Summarize pediatric recommendations regarding infant nutrition. Include in your essay breastfeeding versus formula; when to introduce cow's milk, solid foods, and fruit juices; and the most common nutritional deficiencies.

4. Describe the changes in sleep patterns after the first few months of life. Discuss the role of culture in influencing sleep patterns and arrangements.

5. Summarize the development of the senses during infancy.

6. What are the milestones of motor development during the first three years? Describe several important influences on motor development in your essay, and give examples.

Critical Thinking Questions

These questions may be used for small group discussions or research papers.

1. Should pregnant women who smoke, drink, take drugs, or take other actions that will hurt an unborn baby be held accountable in a court of law?

2. How far should parents go in trying to advance their infant's motor skills or cognitive skills?

Answer Keys

True/False Self-Test

1.	T	p. 127	GP 7		14.	F	p. 137	GP 8
2.	T	p. 128	GP 7		15.	F	p. 137	GP 8
3.	T	p. 112	GP 2		16.	T	p. 137	GP 8
4.	F	p. 129	GP 7		17.	F	p. 138	GP 9
5.	F	p. 129	GP 7		18.	T	p. 143	GP 9
6.	F	p. 129	GP 7		19.	F	p. 139	GP 9
7.	T	p. 130	GP 7		20.	T	p. 141	GP 9
8.	T	p. 130	GP 7		21.	T	p. 143	GP 9
9.	F	p. 132	GP 7		22.	T	p. 143	GP 9
10.	T	p. 134	GP 7		23.	F	p. 142	GP 9
11.	T	p. 134	GP 7		24.	T	p. 141	GP 9
12.	T	p. 134	GP 7		25.	T	p. 117	GP 4
13.	T	p. 136	GP 8					

Multiple-Choice Self-Test

1.	b	p. 109	GP 1		11.	a	p. 116	GP 4
2.	c	p. 109	GP 1		12.	c	p. 117	GP 4
3.	b	p. 109	GP 1		13.	d	p. 118	GP 5
4.	c	p. 109	GP 1		14.	a	p. 118	GP 5
5.	a	p. 111	GP 2		15.	d	p. 118	GP 5
6.	c	p. 112	GP 2		16.	c	p. 123	GP 6
7.	b	p. 110	GP 2		17.	b	p. 124	GP 6
8.	d	p. 113	GP 3		18.	a	p. 125	GP 7
9.	c	p. 114	GP 3		19.	b	p. 127	GP 7
10.	d	p. 115	GP 3		20.	b	p. 127	GP 7

Organize It!

1.	pp. 109-110	GP 1
2.	pp. 113-114	GP 3
3.	p. 122	GP 6
4.	pp. 114-115	GP 3
5.	p. 117	GP 4
6.	p. 119	GP 5
7.	p. 123	GP 6

Short Essay Questions

1.	pp. 123-124	GP 6
2.	p. 125	GP 6
3.	pp. 127-129	GP 7
4.	pp. 115-116	GP 3
5.	pp. 136-137	GP 8
6.	pp. 137-143	GP 9

CHAPTER 5: COGNITIVE DEVELOPMENT DURING THE FIRST THREE YEARS

This chapter introduces the classic and the newer approaches to the study of cognitive development in early childhood. Language development is presented in depth in the second part of the chapter.

Guideposts for Study

1. How do infants learn, and how long can they remember?

2. Can infants' and toddlers' intelligence be measured, and how can it be improved?

3. How did Piaget describe infants' and toddlers' cognitive development, and how have his claims stood up?

4. How can we measure infants' ability to process information, and how does this ability relate to future intelligence?

5. When do babies begin to think about characteristics of the physical world?

6. What can brain research reveal about the development of cognitive skills?

7. How does social interaction with adults advance cognitive competence?

8. How do babies develop language?

9. What influences contribute to linguistic progress?

Detailed Chapter Outline with Key Terms

I. STUDYING COGNITIVE DEVELOPMENT: CLASSIC APPROACHES
   - *Cognitive development:* The study of learning, thinking, problem solving, memory, and intelligence.
   - **Behaviorist approach**: Approach to the study of cognitive development that is concerned with basic mechanics of learning.
   - **Psychometric approach**: Approach to the study of cognitive development that seeks to measure the quantity of intelligence a person possesses.
   - **Piagetian approach**: Approach to the study of cognitive development that describes qualitative stages in cognitive functioning.
   A. Behaviorist Approach: Basic Mechanics of Learning
      1. Classical and Operant Conditioning
         - **Classical conditioning**: Learning based on associating a stimulus that does not ordinarily elicit a response with another stimulus that does elicit the response.
         - *Extinct:* The fading of classically conditioned learning that occurs when that learning is not reinforced.
         - **Operant conditioning**: Learning based on reinforcement or punishment.
      2. Infant Memory
         Infantile amnesia: The inability to remember events before the age of 3 years.

B. Psychometric Approach: Developmental and Intelligence Testing
- **Intelligent behavior**: Behavior that is goal-oriented and adaptive to circumstances and conditions of life.
- **IQ (intelligence quotient) tests**: Psychometric tests that seek to measure intelligence by comparing a test-taker's performance with standardized norms.
1. Testing Infants and Toddlers
   - **Bayley Scales of Infant Development**: Standardized test of infants' mental and motor development.
   - *Mental scale:* Measures such abilities as perception, memory, learning, and vocalization.
   - *Motor scale:* Measures gross (large-muscle) and fine (manipulative) motor skills, including sensorimotor coordination.
   - *Behavior rating scale:* Completed by the examiner based in part on information from the child's caregiver.
   - *Developmental quotients (DQs):* Separate scores based on deviation from the mean established by comparison with a normal sample.
2. Assessing the Impact of the Home Environment
   Home Observation for Measurement of the Environment (HOME): Checklist to measure home environment's influence on children's cognitive growth.
3. Socioeconomic Status, Parenting Practices, and IQ
4. Early Intervention
   - **Early intervention**: Systematic process of providing services to help families meet young children's developmental needs.
   - **Developmental priming mechanisms**: Aspects of the home environment that seem necessary for normal cognitive and psychosocial development.
C. Piagetian Approach: The Sensorimotor Stage
   Sensorimotor stage: In Piaget's theory, the first stage in cognitive development, during which infants learn through senses and motor activity.
1. Substages of the Sensorimotor Stage
   - **Schemes**: Piaget's term for organized patterns of behavior used in particular situations.
   - **Circular reactions**: Piaget's term for processes by which an infant learns to reproduce desired occurrences originally discovered by chance.
     - ➢ *First substage (birth to about 1 month):* Neonates begin to exercise some control over inborn reflexes, modifying and extending their schemes.
     - ➢ *Second substage (about 1 to 4 months):* Babies learn to repeat a pleasant bodily sensation first achieved by chance (called a *primary circular reaction*).
     - ➢ *Third substage (about 4 to 8 months):* Babies are interested in manipulating objects and engage in *secondary circular reactions*—intentional actions repeated not merely for their own sake but to get results beyond the infant's own body.
     - ➢ *Fourth substage, coordination of secondary schemes (about 8 to 12 months):* Infants have learned to generalize from the past to solve new problems and exhibit complex, goal-directed behavior.
     - ➢ *Fifth substage (about 12 to 18 months):* Infants experiment with new behavior to see what will happen. They engage in *tertiary circular reactions*—the varying of an action to get a similar result instead of mere repetition. Trial and error is used for problem solving.

> *Sixth substage, mental combinations (about 18 months to two years):* A transition into the preoperational stage of early childhood.
- **Representational ability**: Piaget's term for the capacity to mentally represent objects and experiences, largely through symbols.
- **Deferred imitation**: Piaget's term for reproduction of an observed behavior after the passage of time by calling up a stored symbol of it.

2. Development of Knowledge about Objects and Space
Object concept: The idea that objects have their own independent existence, characteristics, and location in space.
  a. Object Permanence
- **Object permanence**: Piaget's term for the understanding that a person or object still exists when out of sight.
- **A, not-B error**: Tendency for 8- to 12-month-old infants to search for a hidden object in a place where they previously found it, rather than in the place where they most recently saw it being hidden.
- **Egocentric**: Piaget's term for the self-centered view of spatial relations in the infant and young child.

  b. Objects in Space
Allocentric: Objective; referring to the more objective view of the world held by babies at the end of the sensorimotor period.

3. Which Abilities May Develop Earlier Than Piaget Thought?
  a. Object Permanence
  b. Categorization
- *Perceptual:* Categorization based on how things look.
- *Conceptual:* Categorization based on what things are.

  c. Invisible and Deferred Imitation
- **Invisible imitation**: Imitation with parts of one's body that one cannot see.
- **Visible imitation**: Imitation with parts of one's body that one can see.

II. STUDYING COGNITIVE DEVELOPMENT: NEWER APPROACHES
- **Information-processing approach**: Approach to the study of cognitive development by analyzing processes involved in perceiving and handling information.
- **Cognitive neuroscience approach**: Approach to the study of cognitive development that links brain processes with cognitive ones.
- **Social-contextual approach**: Approach to the study of cognitive development by focusing on environmental influences, particularly parents and other caregivers.

A. Information-Processing Approach: Perceptions and Representations
  1. Habituation
- **Habituation**: Simple type of learning in which familiarity with a stimulus reduces, slows, or stops a response.
- **Dishabituation**: Increase in responsiveness after presentation of a new stimulus.

  2. Early Perceptual and Processing Abilities
- **Visual preference**: Tendency of infants to spend more time looking at one sight than another.
- *Novelty preference:* Tendency of infants to pay more attention to new stimuli than to familiar ones.

- **Visual-recognition memory**: Ability to distinguish a familiar visual stimulus from an unfamiliar one when shown both at the same time.
- **Cross-modal transfer**: Ability to use information gained by one sense to guide another.

3. Information Processing as a Predictor of Intelligence
   - *Visual reaction time:* The measure of how quickly an infant's gaze will shift to a picture that has just appeared.
   - *Visual anticipation:* The measure of how quickly an infant's gaze will shift to the place where the infant expects the next picture to appear.
   - *Visual expectation paradigm:* Method of showing a series of computer-generated pictures briefly to an infant, some on the left and some on the right side of the infant's peripheral visual field.

4. Violation of Expectations and the Development of Thought
   - **Violation-of-expectations**: Research method in which dishabituation to a stimulus that conflicts with experience is taken as evidence that an infant recognizes the new stimulus as surprising.
   - *Innate learning mechanisms:* Reasoning abilities that may be present at an infant's birth.
     - ➤ Object Permanence
     - ➤ Number
     - ➤ **Causality:** The principle that one event causes another.
     - ➤ Evaluating Violation-of-Expectations Research

B. Cognitive Neuroscience Approach: The Brain's Cognitive Structures
   - **Explicit memory**: Intentional and conscious memory, generally of facts, names, and events.
   - **Implicit memory**: Unconscious recall, generally of habits and skills; sometimes called *procedural memory*.
   - **Working memory:** Short-term storage of information being actively processing.
   - *Striatum:* Part of the brain involved in some forms of procedural memory.
   - *Cerebellum:* Part of the brain at the back and base, involved in memory of conditioning.
   - *Brain stem:* Lower parts of the brain, linked to the cerebellum.
   - *Hippocampus:* Part of the brain located in the center, may be responsible for much of explicit memory.
   - *Medial temporal lobe:* Part of the brain in which the hippocampus is located.
   - *Semantic memory:* General knowledge.
   - *Episodic memory:* Memory of specific experiences.
   - *Prefrontal cortex:* The large portion of the frontal lobe directly behind the forehead, believed to control many aspects of cognition.

C. Social-Contextual Approach: Learning from Interactions with Caregivers
   Guided participation: Participation of an adult in a child's activity in a manner that helps structure the activity and bring the child's understanding of it closer to an adult's.

III. LANGUAGE DEVELOPMENT
- **Language**: Communication system based on words and grammar.
- **Literacy**: Ability to read and write.

A. Sequence of Early Language Development
    Prelinguistic speech: Forerunner of linguistic speech; utterance of sounds that are not words. Includes crying, cooing, babbling, and accidental and deliberate imitations of sounds without understanding their meaning.
    1. Early Vocalization
        *   *Crying:* Newborn's means of communication; can signal hunger, sleepiness, or anger.
        *   *Cooing:* Squealing, gurgling, and making vowel sounds like "ahhh."
        *   *Babbling:* Repeating consonant-vowel strings, such as "ma-ma-ma-ma."
    2. Recognizing Language Sounds
    3. Gestures
        *   *Conventional social gestures:* Gestures such as waving goodbye or nodding the head to signify "yes," taught to a child by an adult or older child.
        *   *Representational gestures:* Gestures that represent the desired action directly, such as holding an empty cup to one's mouth to signify wanting a drink.
        *   *Symbolic gestures:* Gestures that function much like words and are symbolic of the desired concept, such as blowing to mean hot or sniffing to mean flower.
    4. First Words
        *   **Linguistic speech**: Verbal expression designed to convey meaning.
        *   **Holophrase**: Single word that conveys a complete thought.
        *   *Expressive:* Referring to spoken vocabulary.
    5. First Sentences
        *   **Telegraphic speech**: Early form of sentence consisting of only a few essential words.
        *   **Syntax**: Rules for forming sentences in a particular language.
B. Characteristics of Early Speech
    *   *Simplify:* Children use telegraphic speech to say just enough to get their meaning across.
    *   *Understand grammatical relationships they cannot yet express:* Although unable to string together enough words to express a complete action, children can understand action.
    *   *Underextend word meanings:* Certain words may be used by children to mean only a single object, but not other, similar objects.
    *   *Overextend word meanings:* Children will overgeneralize a word to objects that are only similar to the original referent.
    *   *Overregularize rules:* Children will apply rules rigidly, without recognizing exceptions, such as "mouses" instead of "mice."
C. Classic Theories of Language Acquisition: The Nature-Nurture Debate
    *   **Nativism**: Theory that human beings have an inborn capacity for language acquisition.
    *   **Language acquisitions device (LAD)**: In Chomsky's terminology, an inborn mechanism that enables children to infer linguistic rules from the language they hear.
    *   *Planum temporale:* A brain structure that is larger on one side than on the other and may contain the inborn mechanism for language.
    *   *Hand-babbling:* The gestures of deaf babies that are repeated over and over.
D. Influences on Early Language Development
    1. Maturation of the Brain

2. Social Interaction: The Role of Parents and Caregivers
   a. Prelinguistic Period
   b. Vocabulary Development
      - **Code mixing**: Use of elements of two languages, sometimes in the same utterance, by young children in households where both languages are spoken.
      - **Code switching**: Changing one's speech to match the situation, as in people who are bilingual.
   c. **Child-directed speech (CDS)**: Form of speech often used in talking to babies or toddlers; includes slow, simplified speech, a high-pitched tone, exaggerated vowel sounds, short words and sentences, and much repetition. Also called *parentese*.

E. Preparing for Literacy: The Benefits of Reading Aloud
   - *Describer style:* Adult style of reading to a child in which the adult focuses on describing what is going on in the pictures and invites the child to do so.
   - *Comprehender style:* Adult style of reading to a child in which the adult encourages the child to look more deeply at the meaning of a story and to make inferences and predictions.
   - *Performance-oriented style:* Adult style of reading to a child in which the reader reads the story straight through, introducing the main themes beforehand and asking questions afterward.
   - *Dialogic reading:* Shared reading in which the parent asks challenging questions and the child is encouraged to become the storyteller.
   - *Prereading skills:* The competencies helpful in learning to read, such as learning how letters look and sound.

True/False Self-Test

Place a T or an F in the appropriate space. These questions are taken from the chapter content, tables, key terms, Guideposts for Study, and Checkpoints.

1. _____ The behaviorist approach to the study of intelligent behavior is concerned with measuring quantitative factors that make up intelligence.

2. _____ The Bayley Scales of Infant Development is a widely used test that is an accurate predictor of later intelligence.

3. _____ Research using operant conditioning has found that infants' memory processes are much like those of older children and adults.

4. _____ Two simple types of learning that behaviorists study are classical conditioning and operant conditioning.

5. _____ Infants' memory of an action is closely linked to contextual clues.

6. _____ In normal infants, psychometric tests can indicate current functioning but are generally poor predictors of later intelligence.

7. ____ Parental responsiveness and the ability to create a stimulating home environment have been shown to be associated with cognitive development.

8. ____ The Piagetian approach is concerned with quantitative stages of cognitive development.

9. ____ According to Piaget, self-locomotion has no influence on the object concept.

10. ___ Research suggests that several abilities develop earlier than Piaget described.

11. ___ Deferred imitation that Piaget placed in the last half of the fifth year has been reported as early as 2 weeks.

12. ___ The information-processing approach is concerned with literacy skills.

13. ___ Indicators of the efficiency of infants' information processing include speed of habituation and dishabituation, visual preference, and cross-modal transfer.

14. ___ Violation-of-expectations research suggests that infants as young as 3-1/2 to 5 months may have a rudimentary grasp of object permanence.

15. ___ Cognitive neuroscience researchers have found that some forms of implicit memory develop in the first few months of life.

16. ___ Explicit memory and working memory do not merge before 3 years of age.

17. ___ Neurological developments cannot explain the emergence of Piagetian skills and information-processing abilities.

18. ___ Through guided participation in play and other shared everyday activities, parents or caregivers help children learn the skills, knowledge, and values important in their culture.

19. ___ Babies use gestures such as pointing only after they have spoken their first word.

20. ___ A "naming explosion" typically occurs some time between 16 and 24 months of age.

21. ___ Children in households where two languages are spoken generally choose one language and stick to it.

22. ___ Telegraphic speech generally occurs between 18 and 24 months of age.

23. ___ Simplification, underextending and overextending word meanings, and overregularizing rules characterize early speech.

24. ___ Chomsky's nativistic theory maintains that children are born with a language acquisition device (LAD).

25. ___ Reading aloud to a child from an early age helps pave the way for literacy.

Multiple-Choice Self-Test

Circle the letter of the best answer. These questions are based on many aspects of the chapter content, in no particular order.

1. The behaviorist approach to the study of cognitive development is concerned with
   a. the mechanics of learning.
   b. the quantitative factors that make up intelligence.
   c. predicting later intelligence from tests.
   d. qualitative stages of cognitive development.

2. According to the Home Observation for Measurement of Environment (HOME), two important factors in cognitive development are
   a. television and art supplies.
   b. extended family status and socioeconomic status.
   c. education of the parents and type of community.
   d. parental responsiveness and the ability to create a stimulating home environment.

3. The sensorimotor stage, according to Piaget, lasts from
   a. 3 to 5 years.
   b. 5 to 7 years.
   c. birth to 2 years.
   d. 10 to 12 years.

4. According to Piaget, self-locomotion promotes development of
   a. the A, not-B error.
   b. the object concept.
   c. imitation.
   d. problem solving.

5. According to Piaget, children in the sensorimotor stage progress in cognitive and behavioral schemes in the following order:
   a. deferred imitation, problem solving, tertiary circular reaction
   b. tertiary circular reactions, secondary circular reactions, deferred imitation
   c. primary circular reactions, deferred imitation, secondary circular reactions
   d. primary, secondary, tertiary circular reactions, mental combinations

6. One indicator of the efficiency of infants' information processing includes
   a. cross-modal transfer.
   b. object permanence.
   c. imitation.
   d. None of the above.

7. Explicit memory and working memory emerge between what ages?
   a. 13 and 22 months
   b. 6 and 12 months
   c. 22 and 36 months
   d. 2 and 4 months

8. Children in households where two languages are spoken tend to do
   a. better in one language than the other.
   b. poorly in school.
   c. code mixing and code switching.
   d. holophrasic speech until the age of 3.

9. A "naming explosion" typically occurs at what age?
   a. 10 to 14 months
   b. 22 to 36 months
   c. 16 to 24 months
   d. 3 to 6 months

10. Syntax and communicative abilities are fairly well developed in most children by the age of
a. 2 years.
b. 1 year.
c. 18 months.
d. 3 years.

11. Early speech is characterized by
a. underextending word meanings.
b. overextending word meanings.
c. simplification.
d. overregularizing rules.
e. All of the above.

12. The language acquisition device (LAD) is a key component of whose theory of language development?
a. Piaget
b. Chomsky
c. Vygotsky
d. Skinner

13. Child-directed speech (CDS)
a. crosses language barriers.
b. is not limited to spoken language.
c. helps children respond to emotional cues.
d. All of the above.

14. Repetitive babbling may emerge with the maturation of parts of the
a. cerebellum.
b. brain stem.
c. motor cortex.
d. medulla oblongata.

15. Young John says "I thinked!" instead of "I thought." His speech is an example of
a. overextending word meanings.
b. overregularization of rules.
c. underextending word meanings.
d. holophrasic speech.

16. Betsy's mother hands her a glass of milk, which Betsy does not want. She says, "No drink milk!" Betsy's speech is an example of
a. telegraphic speech.
b. underextension of meanings.
c. theory of mind.
d. code mixing.

17. Children show increasing competence in syntax at the age of
a. 20 to 30 months.
b. 12 to 14 months.
c. 5 to 7 months.
d. 12 to 15 months.

18. Waving bye-bye, nodding the head to mean yes and no, and shaking the head to signify no are examples of
a. nativist theory.
b. behaviorist theory.
c. conventional social gestures.
d. habituation.

19. Learning gestures before speech
a. confers a linguistic advantage.
b. deters children from learning to speak.
c. should be discouraged.
d. is not natural.

20. The expressive (spoken) vocabulary
a. develops faster than the ability to understand words.
b. relies more on gestures.
c. develops before the understanding of words.
d. develops more slowly than the understanding of words.

21. The single-word stage lasts until
a. 18 months.
b. 36 months
c. 24 months.
d. 10 months.

22. Child-directed speech (CDS) teaches children how to
a. carry on a conversation.
b. introduce a topic.
c. respond to emotional cues.
d. All of the above.

23. A form of learning in which a person tends to repeat a behavior that has been reinforced or to cease a behavior that has been punished is called
a. social learning.
b. operant conditioning.
c. classical conditioning.
d. imitation.

24. The understanding, in Piaget's terminology, that a person or object still exists when it is out of sight is called
a. visible imitation.
b. information processing.
c. deferred imitation.
d. object permanence.

Organize It!

Making a list is an easy way to categorize information into a unit that is readily recalled. Here are a few lists to make. You may want to add others of your own.

1. List the six substages of Piaget's sensorimotor stage.

    1.
    2.
    3.
    4.
    5.
    6.

2. List six developmental priming mechanisms that help make children ready for formal learning.

    1.
    2.
    3.
    4.
    5.
    6.

3. List the brain structures responsible for implicit, preexplicit, explicit, and working memory.

    1.
    2.
    3.
    4.

4. List five milestones of language development during the first three years.

1.
2.
3.
4.
5.

5. List five ways in which early speech differs from adult speech.

1.
2.
3.
4.
5.

6. List three examples of how parents or caregivers help babies learn to talk.

1.
2.
3.

Short Essay Questions

These short essay questions are based in part on the Checkpoints in the chapter. Answer each question as completely and succinctly as possible.

1. Summarize how learning theory and nativism seek to explain language acquisition, and point out strengths and weaknesses of each.

2. Summarize the evidence for plasticity in the brain's linguistic areas.

3. Compare two cultural patterns of guided participation in toddlers' learning.

4. Discuss three areas in which violation-of-expectations research seems to contradict Piaget's account of cognitive development.

5. Explain why Piaget may have underestimated some of infants' cognitive abilities, and discuss the implications of research on imitation in infants and toddlers.

6. Summarize what studies of operant conditioning have shown about infant memory.

Critical Thinking Questions

1. What might be some drawbacks of early educational intervention programs?

2. Much of Piaget's theory was developed from his observations of his own children as they grew from infancy to childhood. What are some disadvantages of this kind of observation?

3. Using Piaget's research findings as a guide, what kind of toy would you buy for a child in each of his or her four stages of cognitive development?

4. Based on the findings concerning child-directed speech, is "baby talk" good or bad for babies? Why or why not?

Answer Keys

True/False Self-Test

1. F p. 149 GP 1
2. F p. 153 GP 2
3. T p. 151 GP 1
4. T p. 149 GP 1
5. T p. 152 GP 1
6. T p. 153 GP 2
7. T p. 153 GP 2
8. F p. 156 GP 3
9. F p. 161 GP 3
10. T p. 161 GP 3
11. F p. 164 GP 3
12. F p. 164 GP 4
13. T p. 165 GP 4
14. T p. 168 GP 5
15. T p. 171 GP 6
16. F p. 171 GP 6
17. F p. 171 GP 6
18. T p. 172 GP 7
19. F p. 174 GP 8
20. T p. 175 GP 8
21. F p. 181 GP 9
22. T p. 176 GP 8
23. T p. 176 GP 8
24. T p. 178 GP 8
25. T p. 182 GP 9

Multiple-Choice Self-Test

1. a p. 149 GP 1
2. d p. 153 GP 2
3. c p. 156 GP 3
4. b p. 161 GP 3
5. d p. 157 GP 3
6. a p. 166 GP 4
7. b p. 171 GP 6
8. c p. 181 GP 9
9. c p. 175 GP 8
10. d p. 176 GP 8
11. e p. 176 GP 8
12. b p. 178 GP 8
13. d p. 181 GP 9
14. c p. 179 GP 9
15. b p. 177 GP 8
16. a p. 176 GP 8
17. a p. 176 GP 8
18. c p. 174 GP 8
19. a p. 175 GP 8
20. d p. 175 GP 8
21. a p. 175 GP 8
22. d p. 181 GP 9
23. b p. 150 GP 1
24. d p. 159 GP 3

Organize It!

1. p. 157 GP 3
2. p. 155 GP 2
3. p. 171 GP 6
4. p. 173 GP 8
5. p. 176 GP 8
6. pp. 180-181 GP 9

Short Essay Questions

1. p. 177-179 GP 8
2. pp. 179-180 GP 9
3. pp. 172 GP 7
4. pp. 167-170 GP 5
5. pp. 161-164 GP 3
6. pp. 151-152 GP 1

CHAPTER 6: PSYCHOSOCIAL DEVELOPMENT DURING THE FIRST THREE YEARS

This chapter explores the development of trust, attachment, and the emerging sense of self in the first three years. Relationships with siblings, parents, and other children are presented in the second part of the chapter. The issues of early child care and parental employment are also discussed.

Guideposts for Study

1. What are emotions, when do they develop, and how do babies show them?

2. How do infants show temperamental differences, and how enduring are those differences?

3. What roles do mothers and fathers play in early personality development?

4. How do infants gain trust in their world and form attachments?

5. How do infants and caregivers "read" each other's nonverbal signals, and what happens when communication breaks down?

6. When and how do the self and self-concept arise?

7. How do toddlers develop autonomy and standards for socially acceptable behavior?

8. How do infants and toddlers interact with siblings and other children?

9. How do parental employment and early child care affect infants' and toddlers' development?

Detailed Chapter Outline With Key Terms

I. FOUNDATIONS OF PSYCHOSOCIAL DEVELOPMENT
   A. Emotions
   - **Emotions**: Subjective reactions to experience that are associated with physiological and behavioral changes.
   - *Stranger anxiety:* Wariness shown by babies by about 8 months of age.
   - *Nonorganic failure to thrive:* Failure of an infant to grow and gain weight despite adequate nutrition.
   1. First Signs of Emotion
      a. Crying
      - *Hunger cry:* A rhythmic cry, not always associated with hunger.
      - *Angry cry:* A variation of the rhythmic cry in which excess air is forced through the vocal cords.
      - *Pain cry:* A sudden onset of loud crying without preliminary moaning, sometimes followed with holding the breath.
      - *Frustration cry:* Two or three drawn-out cries, with no prolonged breath-holding.
      b. Smiling and Laughing
      Waking smiles: Voluntary smiles.

2. When Do Emotions Appear?
   a. Basic Emotions
   b. Emotions Involving the Self
      - **Self-conscious emotions**: Emotions such as embarrassment, empathy, and envy that require a degree of self-awareness.
      - **Self-awareness**: Realization that one's existence and functioning are separate from those of other people and things.
      - **Self-evaluative emotions**: Emotions such as pride, guilt, and shame that involve evaluation of one's own thoughts and behavior against socially appropriate thoughts and behavior.
   c. Empathy: Feeling What Others Feel
      - **Empathy**: The ability to put oneself in another person's place and feel what that person feels, or would be expected to feel, in a particular situation.
      - *Sympathy:* Sorrow or concern for another person's plight.
      - *Prosocial behavior:* Behavior that is intended to help without expectation of personal gain.
      - *Social cognition:* The cognitive ability to understand that others have mental states.
3. Brain Growth and Emotional Development
   - *Cerebral cortex:* Outer covering of the brain where higher mental functions occur.
   - *Frontal lobes:* Front section of the cerebral cortex (one on each side of the brain), responsible in part for emotional responses.
   - *Hippocampus:* Structure in the limbic system of the brain.
   - *Hypothalamus:* Structure of the brain involved in the limbic system and emotion.

B. **Temperament**: Characteristic disposition or style of approaching and reacting to situations.
   1. Studying Temperamental Patterns
      - **"Easy" children**: Children with a generally happy temperament, regular biological rhythms, and readiness to accept new experiences.
      - **"Difficult" children**: Children with irritable temperament, irregular biological rhythms, and intense emotional responses.
      - **"Slow-to-warm-up" children**: Children whose temperament is generally mild but who are hesitant about accepting new experiences.
      - **Goodness of fit**: Appropriateness of environmental demands and constraints to a child's temperament.
      - *Extraversion:* Characteristics of impulsiveness, intense pleasure, high activity level, boldness, risk taking, and comfort in new social situations.
      - *Negative affect:* Characteristics of sadness, discomfort, anger, frustration, fear, and high reactivity.
      - *Effortful control:* Characteristics of inhibitory control, low-intensity pleasure, ability to focus attention, and perceptual sensitivity.
   2. How Stable is Temperament?
   3. Biological Bases of Temperament
      Inhibition to the unfamiliar: Shyness, or how sociable a child is with strange children and how boldly or cautiously the child approaches unfamiliar objects and situations.
   4. Cross-Cultural Differences

C. Earliest Social Experiences: The Infant in the Family
   1. The Mother's Role
   2. The Father's Role
   3. How Parents Shape Gender Differences
      - **Gender**: Significance of being male or female.
      - **Gender-typing**: Socialization process by which children, at an early age, learn appropriate gender roles.

II. DEVELOPMENTAL ISSUES IN INFANCY
   A. Developing Trust
      - **Basic trust versus basic mistrust**: Erikson's first stage in psychosocial development, in which infants develop a sense of the reliability of people and objects.
      - *Hope:* The belief of infants that they can fulfill their needs and obtain their desires.
   B. Developing Attachments
      Attachment: Reciprocal, enduring tie between infant and caregiver, each of whom contributes to the quality of the relationship.
      1. Studying Patterns of Attachment
         - **Strange Situation**: Laboratory technique used to study attachment.
         - **Secure attachment**: Pattern in which an infant cries or protests when the primary caregiver leaves and actively seeks out the caregiver upon his or her return.
         - **Secure base**: Infant's use of a parent or other familiar caregiver as a departure point for exploration and a safe place to return periodically for emotional support.
         - **Avoidant attachment**: Pattern in which an infant rarely cries when separated from the primary caregiver and avoids contact upon his or her return.
         - **Ambivalent (resistant) attachment**: Pattern in which an infant becomes anxious before the primary caregiver leaves, is extremely upset during his or her absence, and both seeks and resists contact on his or her return.
         - **Disorganized-disoriented attachment**: Pattern in which an infant, after separation from the primary caregiver, shows contradictory behaviors upon his or her return.
      2. How Attachment Is Established
      3. Influences on Attachment
      4. The Role of Temperament
      5. Intergenerational Transmission of Attachment Patterns
         Adult Attachment Interview (AAI): A semistructured interview that asks adults to recall and interpret feelings and experiences related to their childhood attachments.
      6. Long-Term Effects of Attachment
   C. Emotional Communication with Caregivers: Mutual Regulation
      - **Mutual regulation**: Process by which infant and caregiver communicate emotional states to each other and respond appropriately.
      - **"Still-face" paradigm**: Research method used to measure mutual regulation in infants 2 to 9 months old.
      - *Still-face:* In the "still-face" paradigm, referring to the mother suddenly becoming stony-faced, silent, and unresponsive.
      - *Reunion:* In the "still-face" paradigm, referring to the mother's resumption of normal interaction after the "still-face" episode.

D. Stranger Anxiety and Separation Anxiety
- **Stranger anxiety**: Wariness of strange people and places, shown by some infants during the second half of the first year.
- **Separation anxiety**: Distress shown by an infant when a familiar caregiver leaves.

E. **Social Referencing**: Understanding an ambiguous situation by seeking out another person's perception of it.

III. DEVELOPMENTAL ISSUES IN TODDLERHOOD

- *Sense of self:* The development of the toddler's knowledge of being a separate person from those around him or her.
- *Autonomy:* Self-determination.
- *Internalization of behavioral standards:* The toddler's tendency to make the behavioral standards of others, such as parents, a part of the toddler's mental structures and memories.

A. The Emerging Sense of Self
- **I-self**: James's term for the subjective entity that seeks to know about itself.
- **Me-self**: James's term for what a person objectively knows about himself or herself. Also called *self-concept*.
- **Self-concept**: Sense of self; descriptive and evaluative mental picture of one's abilities and traits.
  1. Emergence of the I-Self (birth to 15 months)
     - *Agency:* A feature of the I-self in which the baby realizes that one can control external events.
     - **Self-efficacy**: Sense of capability to master challenges and achieve goals.
     - *Self-coherence:* The sense of being a physical whole with boundaries, within which agency resides.
  2. Emergence of the Me-Self (15 to 30 months)
     Self-awareness: Conscious knowledge of the self as a distinct, identifiable being.

B. Development of Autonomy
- **Autonomy versus shame and doubt**: Erikson's second stage in psychosocial development, in which children achieve a balance between self-determination and control by others.
- *Negativism:* The tendency of a toddler to shout "No!" just for the sake of resisting authority.

C. Socialization and Internalization: Developing a Conscience
- **Socialization**: Development of habits, skills, values, and motives shared by responsible, productive members of a society.
- **Internalization**: Process by which children accept societal standards of conduct as their own; fundamental to socialization.
- **Conscience**: Internal standards of behavior, which usually control one's conduct and produce emotional discomfort when violated.
- *Superego:* Freud's term for the conscience.
- **Self-regulation**: Child's independent control of behavior to conform to understood social expectations.
- *Attentional processes:* The ability to pay attention to stimuli.
  1. Developing Self-Regulation

2. Committed Compliance
   - **Inhibitory control**: Conscious, or effortful, holding back of impulses.
   - **Committed compliance**: Kochanska's term for wholehearted obedience of a parent's orders without reminders or lapses.
   - **Situational compliance**: Kochanska's term for obedience of a parent's orders only in the presence of signs of ongoing parental control.

IV. CONTACT WITH OTHER CHILDREN
   A. Siblings
   B. Sociability With Nonsiblings

V. CHILDREN OF WORKING PARENTS
   A. Effects of Parental Employment
   B. The Impact of Early Child Care

True/False Self-Test

Place a T or an F in the appropriate space. These questions are taken from the chapter content, tables, key terms, Guideposts for Study, and Checkpoints.

1. _____ Crying, smiling, and laughing are reflexes, not emotions.

2. _____ Complex emotions seem to develop from earlier, simpler ones.

3. _____ The repertoire of basic emotions seems to be universal, but there are cultural variations in their expression.

4. _____ Children all fall into one category of temperament.

5. _____ Temperamental patterns appear largely to be inborn and are generally stable, but can be modified by experience.

6. _____ There are very few differences in child-raising practices worldwide.

7. _____ In most cultures, mothers, even when employed outside the home, provide more infant care than fathers.

8. _____ Mothers and fathers in some cultures have different styles of play with babies.

9. _____ Significant gender differences appear before infancy.

10. ___ Parents begin gender-typing boys and girls almost from birth.

11. ___ Erikson's first crisis of personality is autonomy versus shame and doubt.

12.____ Attachment to fathers occurs much later than attachment to mothers.

13. ___ Separation anxiety and stranger anxiety do not appear until the age of 3 years.

14. ___ Researchers gauge mutual regulation by the still-face paradigm.

15. ___ Separation anxiety and stranger anxiety are no longer considered to be components of attachment.

16. ___ The Adult Attachment Interview can predict the security of attachment on the basis of a parent's memories of her or his own childhood attachment.

17. ___ The belief that babies, after about the age of 6 months, show social referencing has been established.

18. ___ The self-concept begins to emerge at the age of 3 years.

19. ___ The self-concept includes both cognition and emotion.

20. ___ Negativism is a normal manifestation of the shift from external control to self-control.

21. ___ Mothers' workforce participation during a child's first three years seems to have little or no impact on the child's development.

22. ___ High-quality day care may offset insensitive mothering.

23. ___ Self-awareness is demonstrated when recognizing oneself in the mirror.

24. ___ Children with a generally happy temperament, regular biological rhythms, and a readiness to accept new experiences are known as "easy children."

25. ___ Self-conscious and evaluative emotions arise before the development of self-awareness.

Multiple-Choice Self-Test

Circle the letter of the best answer. These questions are based on many aspects of the chapter content, in no particular order.

1. Infants are intensely preoccupied with their principal caregiver, may become afraid of strangers, and act subdued in new situations at the age of
   a. birth to 3 months.
   b. 6 to 9 months.
   c. 9 to 12 months.
   d. 18 to 36 months.

2. Infants begin to play "social games" and try to get responses from people at the age of
   a. 6 to 9 months.
   b. 9 to 12 months.
   c. 12 to 18 months.
   d. 3 to 6 months.

3. The first and most powerful way that infants communicate their needs is through
   a. laughing.
   b. smiling.
   c. crying.
   d. eye contact.

4. A cry characterized by two or three drawn-out cries, with no prolonged breath-holding, is a
   a. hunger cry.
   b. pain cry.
   c. angry cry.
   d. frustration cry.

5. A cry characterized by sudden onset with no preliminary moaning, sometimes followed by holding the breath, is a
   a. basic hunger cry.
   b. pain cry.
   c. frustration cry.
   d. angry cry.

6. Babies indicate their emotions by
   a. facial expression.
   b. motor activity.
   c. body language.
   d. All of the above.

7. Emotions such as embarrassment, empathy, and envy arise
   a. before the development of self-awareness.
   b. in early infancy.
   c. after the development of self-awareness.
   d. between 3 and 6 months of age.

8. The fourth cognitive shift in brain organization comes at
   a. birth.
   b. age 1.
   c. age 2.
   d. age 3.

9. Self-awareness and self-conscious emotions develop during the
   a. first year.
   b. second year.
   c. fifth year.
   d. eighth year.

10. The New York Longitudinal Study is considered
    a. invalid today.
    b. the pioneering study on temperament.
    c. a foundation study of motor skill.
    d. a conclusive study of day care.

11. A child who has mildly intense reactions, both positive and negative, responds slowly to novelty and change, and gradually develops liking for new stimuli after repeated, unpressured exposures is a
    a. easy child.
    b. difficult child.
    c. slow-to-warm-up child.
    d. None of the above.

12. Research evidence points to the idea that temperament is
    a. unpredictable.
    b. stable, inborn, and largely hereditary.
    c. totally influenced by environment.
    d. unstable in early childhood.

13. In China, children who exhibit shyness and inhibition are
    a. considered immature.
    b. considered incompetent.
    c. rejected by their mothers.
    d. socially approved.

14. In Canada, children who exhibit shyness and inhibition are
    a. considered immature.
    b. socially approved.
    c. considered well-behaved.
    d. None of the above.

15. Harlow's research with monkeys showed that
a. feeding is not the most important thing babies get from their mothers.
b. mothering includes the comfort of close body contact.
c. Both of the above.
d. Neither of the above.

16. Trust versus mistrust
a. has a definite critical period.
b. is similar to imprinting.
c. forms immediately after birth.
d. continues until about 18 months of age.

17. Measurable differences between baby boys and girls are
a. few.
b. many and varied.
c. well established.
d. None of the above.

18. Overall, fathers are
a. more talkative than mothers.
b. less talkative, negative, and supportive in their speech than mothers.
c. more involved with toddlers than mothers.
d. less likely to promote gender-typing.

19. According to Erikson, the critical element in developing trust is
a. consistent feeding.
b. the sex of the baby.
c. the age of the mother.
d. sensitive, responsive, consistent caregiving.

20. A baby who cries when the mother leaves and greets her happily when she returns is displaying
a. ambivalent attachment.
b. secure attachment.
c. avoidant attachment.
d. None of the above.

21. A baby who does not cry when the mother leaves and avoids her when she returns is displaying
a. avoidant attachment.
b. secure attachment.
c. ambivalent attachment.
d. disorganized-disoriented behavior.

22. Researchers measure attachment by
a. what happens when the mother leaves.
b. what happens when the mother returns.
c. how long the baby cries.
d. None of the above.

23. Securely attached toddlers are
a. more sociable with peers.
b. more sociable with unfamiliar adults.
c. Both of the above.
d. Neither of the above.

24. The "still-face" paradigm is a research method used to study
a. attachment.
b. smiling.
c. mutual regulation.
d. cognitive ability.

25. Both as infants and preschoolers, children with severely or chronically depressed mothers tend to be
a. securely attached.
b. insecurely attached.
c. ambivalent-avoidant.
d. None of the above.

Organize It!

Making lists is a fun and useful way to categorize information in your mind. After making each list, think of ways to memorize it so that you have immediate recall. Singing a list, dancing while you recite it, or simply saying it in a rhythmic pattern as you are walking, driving, or jogging allows your brain to store the information in easily retrievable form. Try it!

1. List and briefly describe the three categories of children's temperament.

    1.

    2.

    3.

2. List five criteria for good child care.

    1.
    2.
    3.
    4.
    5

3. List and describe nine aspects of temperament identified by the New York Longitudinal Study.

    1.

    2.

    3.

    4.

    5.

    6.

    7.

    8.

    9.

Short Essay Questions

These short essay questions are based on the Checkpoints in the chapter. Answer each question as completely and succinctly as possible.

1. Discuss the role of temperament and goodness of fit in the success of socialization.

2. In view of Kochanska's research on the roots of conscience, what questions would you ask about the early socialization of antisocial adolescents and adults, whose conscience appears to be severely underdeveloped?

3. Compare the roles of fathers and mothers, and compare parenting practices in at least two cultures. Include a comparison of the cultural differences in the ways fathers play with their babies.

4. Describe long-term behavioral differences influenced by attachment patterns.

Critical Thinking Questions

These questions may be used for small group discussions or research papers.

1. Based on the information about temperament in the text, do you think that it is best for parents of a shy child to accept the child's shyness or to try to change it?

2. Fathers are becoming more and more active in their role as parents today. Despite this, many people feel that a mother will always be more important to babies and young children than a father. Do you agree or disagree? Why or why not?

3. What ethical problems might exist in the Strange Situation paradigm?

4. Should parents place infants under one year of age in day care? Why or why not?

Answer Keys

True/False Self-Test

1.	F	p. 191	GP 1	14.	T	p. 208	GP 5
2.	T	p. 193	GP 1	15.	T	p. 210	GP 5
3.	T	p. 193	GP 1	16.	T	p. 206	GP 4
4.	F	p. 195	GP 2	17.	F	p. 211	GP 5
5.	T	p. 197	GP 2	18.	F	p. 212	GP 6
6.	F	p. 198	GP 3	19.	T	p. 212	GP 6
7.	T	p. 199	GP 3	20.	T	p. 214	GP 7
8.	T	p. 198	GP 3	21.	T	p. 218	GP 9
9.	F	p. 201	GP 3	22.	T	p. 220	GP 9
10.	T	p. 201	GP 3	23.	T	p. 212	GP 6
11.	F	p. 202	GP 4	24.	T	p. 195	GP 2
12.	F	p. 205	GP 4	25.	F	p. 193	GP 1
13.	F	p. 210	GP 5				

Multiple-Choice Self-Test

1.	c	p. 190	GP 1	14.	a	p. 198	GP 2
2.	a	p. 190	GP 1	15.	c	p. 199	GP 3
3.	c	p. 191	GP 1	16.	d	p. 202	GP 4
4.	d	p. 191	GP 1	17.	a	p. 201	GP 3
5.	b	p. 191	GP 1	18.	b	p. 201	GP 3
6.	d	p. 192	GP 1	19.	d	p. 202	GP 4
7.	c	p. 193	GP 1	20.	b	p. 203	GP 4
8.	d	p. 194	GP 1	21.	a	p. 203	GP 4
9.	b	p. 194	GP 1	22.	b	p. 203	GP 4
10.	b	p. 195	GP 2	23.	c	p. 207	GP 4
11.	c	p. 196	GP 2	24.	c	p. 208	GP 5
12.	b	p. 197	GP 2	25.	b	p. 211	GP 5
13.	d	p. 198	GP 2				

Organize It!

1.	p. 196	GP 2
2.	p. 219	GP 9
3.	p. 195	GP 2

Short Essay Questions

1.	p. 196	GP 2
2.	p. 214	GP 7
3.	pp. 198-200	GP 3
4.	pp. 206-207	GP 4

PART 3: EARLY CHILDHOOD

CHAPTER 7: PHYSICAL AND COGNITIVE DEVELOPMENT IN EARLY CHILDHOOD

This chapter introduces the student to normal physical and cognitive development from 3 to 6 years. Body growth and change, sleep patterns, and motor skills are discussed in the first part of the chapter. The preoperational child and cognitive development are explored in the second part of the chapter.

Guideposts for Study

1. How do children's bodies change between ages 3 and 6, and what are their nutritional needs?

2. What sleep patterns and problems tend to develop during early childhood?

3. What are the main motor achievements of early childhood?

4. What are the major health and safety risks for young children?

5. What are typical cognitive advances and immature aspects of young children's thinking?

6. How does language improve, and what happens when its development is delayed?

7. What memory abilities expand in early childhood?

8. How is preschoolers' intelligence measured, and what are some influences on it?

9. What purposes does early childhood education serve, and how do children make the transition to kindergarten?

Detailed Chapter Outline with Key Terms

PHYSICAL DEVELOPMENT
I. ASPECTS OF PHYSICAL DEVELOPMENT
   A. Bodily Growth and Change
   B. Nutrition and Oral Health
   - **Obesity**: Extreme overweight in relation to age, sex, height, and body type; sometimes defined as having a body mass index (weight-for-height) at or above the 85th or 95th percentile of growth curves for children of the same age and sex.
   - *Body mass index (BMI)*: Comparison of weight to height.
   C. Sleep Patterns and Problems
      1. Sleep Disturbances and Disorders
      - *Bedtime struggles:* The tendency of children, usually in the first four years of life, to resist going to sleep for more than an hour and to wake the parents frequently at night.
      - *Nightmare:* A frightening dream, usually occurring in the morning and vividly recalled.

- *Sleep terror:* The abrupt awakening of a child or adult from deep sleep in a state of panic, usually about one hour after falling asleep. The person typically remembers nothing about the episode in the morning.
  2. Bed-Wetting
Enuresis: Repeated urination in clothing or in bed.
  D. Motor Skills
- **Gross motor skills**: Physical skills that involve the large muscles.
- **Fine motor skills**: Physical skills that involve the small muscles and eye-hand coordination.
- **Systems of action**: Increasingly complex combinations of skills, which permit a wider or more precise range of movement and more control of the environment.
  1. Artistic Development
     - *Scribble:* In the first stage of children's artistic development, the vertical and zigzag lines drawn in patterns by young children.
     - *Shapes:* Circles, squares, triangles, and other figures drawn by young children in the second stage of artistic development.
     - *Pictorial:* The stage of artistic development in which children draw actual depictions of objects, such as houses and trees.
  2. **Handedness**: Preference for using a particular hand.

II. HEALTH AND SAFETY
  A. Minor Illnesses
  B. Accidental Injuries and Deaths
  C. Health in Context: Environmental Influences
     1. Exposure to Smoking
     2. SES and Poverty
     3. Exposure to Lead
     4. Homelessness

COGNITIVE DEVELOPMENT
III. PIAGETIAN APPROACH: THE PREOPERATIONAL CHILD
Preoperational stage: In Piaget's theory, the second major stage of cognitive development, in which children become more sophisticated in their use of symbolic thought but are not yet able to use logic.
  A. Advances of Preoperational Thought
     1. **Symbolic function**: Piaget's term for ability to use mental representations (words, numbers, or images) to which a child has attached meaning.
        - *Deferred imitation:* Imitation of an action at a later time, based on a mental representation of the observed action.
        - *Pretend play:* Play involving imaginary people or situations.
        - *Language:* The use of a system of symbols (words) to communicate.
     2. Symbolic Development and Spatial Thinking
        Dual representation hypothesis: Proposal that children younger than age 3 have difficulty grasping spatial relationships because of the need to keep more than one mental representation in mind at the same time.

3. Causality

Transduction: In Piaget's terminology, a preoperational child's tendency to mentally link particular experiences, whether or not a logical causal relationship exists.

4. Understanding of Identities and Categorization
   - *Identities:* The concept that people and many things are basically the same even if they change in form, size, or appearance.
   - **Animism**: Tendency to attribute life to objects that are not alive.

5. Number
   - Five Principles of Counting:
     1. The *1-1 principle:* Say only one number-name for each item being counted.
     2. The *stable-order principle:* Say number-names in a set order.
     3. The *order-irrelevance principle:* Start counting with any item, and the total count will be the same.
     4. The *cardinality principle:* The last number-name used is the total number of items being counted.
     5. The *abstraction principle:* The principles above apply to any kind of object.
   - *Ordinality:* The concept of *more* or *less*, *bigger* or *smaller*.

B. Immature Aspects of Preoperational Thought
   - **Centration**: In Piaget's theory, tendency of preoperational children to focus on one aspect of a situation and ignore others.
   - **Decenter**: In Piaget's terminology, to think simultaneously about several aspects of a situation.

1. **Conservation**: Piaget's term for awareness that two objects that are equal according to a certain measure remain equal in the face of perceptual alteration so long as nothing has been added to or taken away from either object.
   - **Irreversibility**: Piaget's term for a preoperational child's failure to understand that an operation can go in two or more directions.
   - *Focus on successive states:* In Piaget's theory, the tendency for preoperational children to focus on the end states rather than the transformations from one state to another.

2. Egocentrism
   - **Egocentrism**: Piaget's term for inability to consider another person's point of view.
   - *Three-mountain task:* Piagetian assessment in which a child sits facing a table that holds three large mounds, with a doll in the opposite chair. The child is asked how the "mountains" would look to the doll.

C. Do Young Children Have Theories of Mind?

Theory of mind: Awareness and understanding of mental processes.

1. Knowledge about Thinking and Mental States

Social cognition: Ability to understand that others have mental states and to judge their feelings and intentions.

2. False Beliefs and Deception
3. Distinguishing between Appearance and Reality
4. Distinguishing between Fantasy and Reality
5. Influences on Theory-of-Mind Development

IV. LANGUAGE AND OTHER COGNITIVE ABILITIES

A. Language Development
  1. Vocabulary

     Fast mapping: Process by which a child absorbs the meaning of a new word after hearing it once or twice in conversation.
  2. Grammar and Syntax
  3. Pragmatics and Social Speech
     - **Pragmatics**: Practical knowledge needed to use language for communication.
     - **Social speech**: Speech intended to be understood by a listener.
  4. Private Speech
     - **Private speech**: Talking aloud to oneself with no intent to communicate.
     - *Egocentric:* Piaget's term for the young child's inability to recognize the viewpoints of others.
  5. Delayed Language Development

     Dialogic reading: A method of reading picture books to very young children.
  6. Social Interaction and Preparation for Literacy
     - **Emergent literacy**: Preschooolers' development of skills, knowledge, and attitudes that underlie reading and writing.
     - *Phonemic awareness:* The realization that words are composed of distinct sounds.
     - *Phonemes:* The basic units of sound that compose words.
     - *Phoneme-grapheme correspondence:* The ability to link sounds with the corresponding letters or combinations of letters.

B. Information-Processing Approach: Memory Development
   - **Encoding**: Process by which information is prepared for long-term storage and later retrieval.
   - **Storage**: Retention of memories for future use.
   - **Retrieval**: Process by which information is accessed or recalled from memory storage.
  1. Recognition and Recall
     - **Recognition**: Ability to identify a previously encountered stimulus.
     - **Recall**: Ability to reproduce material from memory.
     - *Strategies:* Techniques that help the memory process, such as rehearsal.
     - **Prospective memory**: Remembering to perform future actions.
  2. Forming Childhood Memories
     - **Generic memory**: Memory that produces scripts of familiar routines to guide behavior.
     - **Script**: General remembered outline of a familiar, repeated event, used to guide behavior.
     - **Episodic memory**: Long-term memory of specific experiences or events, linked to time and place.
     - **Autobiographical memory**: Memory of specific events in one's own life.
  3. Influences on Autobiographical Memory
     - *Repetitive conversational style:* When adults tend to repeat their own previous statements or questions to help a child who is "stuck."
     - *Elaborative conversational style:* When adults tend to move on to a new aspect of the event or add more information to help a child who is "stuck."

C. Intelligence: Psychometric and Vygotskian Approaches
   1. Traditional Psychometric Measures
      - **Stanford-Binet Intelligence Scale**: Individual intelligence test used to measure memory, spatial orientation, and practical judgment.
      - **Wechsler Preschool and Primary Scale of Intelligence, Revised (WPPSI-R)**: Individual intelligence test for children ages 3 to 7, which yields verbal and performance scores as well as a combined score.
   2. Influences on Measured Intelligence
   3. Testing and Teaching Based on Vygotsky's Theory
      - **Dynamic testing**: A test based on Vygotsky's theory that measures potential abilities by giving a child leading questions, examples, and demonstrations that may help the child master a task.
      - *Scaffolding:* Temporary support to help a child master a task.

V. EARLY CHILDHOOD EDUCATION
   A. Goals and Types of Preschools: A Cross-Cultural View
      - *Society-centered:* A preschool that emphasizes skills and attitudes that promote group harmony.
      - *Child-centered:* A preschool that encourages self-expression and creativity, and in which children freely choose exercises.
      - *Role-centered:* A preschool that concentrates on preparing children for roles in society.
      - *Child-initiated:* A preschool in which the child actively directs his or her own learning experience.
      - *Academically directed:* A preschool in which the focus is on the subject matter and teachers direct learning.
      - *Middle-of-the-road:* A blend of the child-initiated and academically directed types of preschools.
   B. Compensatory Preschool Programs
   C. The Transition to Kindergarten

True/False Self-Test

Place a T or an F in the appropriate space. These questions are taken from the chapter content, tables, key terms, Guideposts for Study, and Checkpoints.

1. _____ Physical growth decreases from years 3 to 6.

2. _____ Girls are larger than boys throughout childhood.

3. _____ Preschool children eat less than in infancy and toddlerhood for their weight, but the prevalence of obesity has increased.

4. _____ Sleep patterns are affected by cultural expectations.

5. _____ Sleep terrors tend to occur within an hour after falling asleep.

6. ____ Enuresis (bed-wetting) is common and is usually outgrown without special help.

7. ____ Handedness reflects dominance by one hemisphere of the brain.

8. ____ Stages of art production appear to reflect personality rather than brain development.

9. ____ Accidents are the leading cause of death in childhood in the United States.

10. ____ Preventable disease is no longer a problem in the developing world.

11. ____ Most fatal nonvehicular accidents occur at home.

12. ____ Minor illnesses help build immunity to disease.

13. ____ Environmental factors, such as exposure to stress, have no effect on the risk of illness or injury.

14. ____ Children in the preoperational stage of cognitive development always show maturity of thought.

15. ____ The symbolic function enables children to reflect on people, objects, and events only when they are present.

16. ____ Preoperational children can understand the concept of identity.

17. ____ Centration, or the inability to decenter, prevents preoperational children from understanding principles of conservation.

18. ____ The theory of mind occurs after age 12.

19. ____ Preoperational children are capable of empathy.

20. ____ Preoperational children often focus on states rather than transformations.

21. ____ Children become less competent in pragmatics as they engage in social speech.

22. ____ Interaction with adults can promote emergent literacy.

23. ____ At all ages, recall is better than recognition.

24. ____ Autobiographical memory is linked with the development of language.

25. ____ Children are less likely to remember unusual activities that they actually participate in.

Multiple-Choice Self-Test

Circle the letter of the best answer. These questions are based on many aspects of the chapter content, in no particular order.

1. Homeless families are typically headed by
   a. senior citizens.
   b. single mothers.
   c. single fathers.
   d. adolescents.

2. Many poor children do not receive the medical care they need because
   a. parents are not responsible.
   b. they are too healthy.
   c. they are uninsured.
   d. they have behavior problems.

3. Homeless preschoolers
   a. are three times more likely to lack immunizations than other children.
   b. suffer more health problems than children who have homes.
   c. experience high rates of diarrhea, tooth decay, and hunger.
   d. All of the above.

4. Advances of preoperational thought include
   a. a growing understanding of identities.
   b. an ability to spell.
   c. an ability to do geometric and algebraic math problems.
   d. focusing on one aspect of a situation.

5. Marie lists which of her classmates are "nice" and which are "mean." She says, "The nice ones are all my friends." Marie is demonstrating
   a. empathy.
   b. understanding of cause and effect.
   c. ability to classify.
   d. theory of mind.

6. Jeffrey cries when his father gives him a cookie that is broken in half. Because each half is smaller than the whole cookie, Jeffrey thinks he is getting less. Jeffrey is demonstrating
   a. egocentrism.
   b. centration.
   c. animism.
   d. transductive reasoning.

7. Marie thinks clouds are alive because they move. She is demonstrating
   a. theory of mind.
   b. centration.
   c. egocentrism.
   d. animism.

8. The absence of sensory or motor cues, such as Wang Yani's paintings from memory, is known as
   a. the symbolic function.
   b. fine motor skills.
   c. irreversibility.
   d. centration.

9. The awareness of having experienced a particular incident that occurred at a specific time and place is known as
   a. generic memory.
   b. episodic memory.
   c. script.
   d. None of the above.

10. Autobiographical memory and the decline of childhood amnesia may be linked to
    a. generic memory.
    b. age of the parents.
    c. development of language.
    d. vividness of an event.

11. The fourth edition of the Stanford-Binet IQ Test provides
a. a single, overall measure of intelligence.
b. assessment of patterns and levels of cognitive development.
c. separate verbal and performance scores.
d. None of the above.

12. Handedness is usually evident by age
a. 3.
b. 6.
c. 8.
d. 10.

13. Preventable disease
a. includes common colds.
b. is no longer a problem worldwide.
c. is rare today because of worldwide immunization.
d. remains a major problem in the developing world.

14. The environmental influences that increase a child's risk of illness and injury include
a. homelessness.
b. smoking.
c. poverty.
d. All of the above.

15. The symbolic function is shown in
a. egocentrism.
b. pretend play.
c. centration.
d. animism.

16. Which of the following can preoperational children generally NOT do?
a. understand classification
b. understand principles of counting
c. distinguish reality from fantasy
d. make fairly accurate judgments about spatial relationships

17. The existence of imaginary companions in the lives of children aged 3 to 10 is
a. disturbing and should be investigated.
b. normal.
c. a desperate bid for attention.
d. a sign of intense stress.

18. Who is most likely to have an imaginary companion?
a. girls
b. boys
c. both
d. later-born children

19. A boy's imaginary companion is most often
a. an animal.
b. a human.
c. a fantasy creature.
d. None of the above.

20. Children who have imaginary companions are
a. more cooperative with other children.
b. likely to watch less television.
c. more fluent with language.
d. All of the above.

21. Children use imaginary companions to
a. provide support in difficult situations.
b. provide wish fulfillment mechanisms.
c. be scapegoats.
d. All of the above.

22. The process of "fast mapping" allows young children to
a. find their way home from school.
b. increase their vocabulary rapidly.
c. enhance spatial abilities.
d. All of the above.

23. Private speech is
a. a sign of autism.
b. a sign of nervousness.
c. normal and common in childhood.
d. a speech problem.

24. The development of skills, knowledge, and attitudes that underlie reading and writing is known as
a. phonics.
b. morphemes.
c. emergent literacy.
d. theory of mind.

25. _____ memory begins at about age 2 and produces a script.
a. Generic
b. Episodic
c. Semantic
d. Procedural

Organize It!

Making lists is a fun and useful way to categorize information in your mind. After making each list, think of ways to memorize it so that you have immediate recall. Singing a list, dancing while you recite it, or simply saying it in a rhythmic pattern as you are walking, driving, or jogging allows your brain to store the information in easily retrievable form. Try it!

1. List and briefly describe the three types of childhood memory.

1.

2.

3.

2. List and describe three ways that preschoolers increase their vocabulary.

1.

2.

3.

3. List and briefly describe the seven limitations of preoperational thought, according to Piaget (see Table 7-4).

1.

2.

3.

4.

5.

6.

4. List and briefly describe the seven cognitive advances during early childhood (see Table 7-3).

1.

2.

3.

4.

5.

6.

7.

Short Essay Questions

These short essay questions are based on the Checkpoints in the chapter. Answer each question as completely and succinctly as possible.

1. Who should be responsible for children's well-being when parents cannot provide adequate food, clothing, shelter, and health care: government, religious and community institutions, the private sector, or a combination of these?

2. What do you think accounts for the rising prevalence of obesity in preschoolers? What suggestions can you make for preventing it?

3. What are the main motor achievements of early childhood?

4. Give examples of research that challenges Piaget's views on young children's cognitive limitations.

5. Explain why preoperational children have trouble with conservation tasks involving two glasses of different shapes with the same amount of water in each.

6. Compare and discuss Piaget's "three mountains task" and Hughes' "doll and police officer task" in terms of theory and results.

Critical Thinking Questions

These questions may be used in small group discussions or as extra-credit reports.

1. What are some of the ways that television promotes poor nutrition for children?

2. How far should the government go in protecting children from their own parents?

3. Should teachers be permitted to know a child's IQ score? Should parents be told the score? Should the child be told the score? What are some implications of telling each of these individuals?

4. Do we place children in educational settings too early? Why or why not?

Answer Keys

True/False Self-Test

1. F p. 229 GP 1
2. F p. 229 GP 1
3. T p. 230 GP 1
4. T p. 231 GP 1
5. T p. 232 GP 2
6. T p. 232 GP 2
7. T p. 234 GP 3
8. F p. 233 GP 3
9. T p. 235 GP 4
10. F p. 234 GP 4
11. T p. 235 GP 4
12. T p. 235 GP 4
13. F p. 236 GP 4
14. F p. 238 GP 5
15. F p. 240 GP 5
16. T p. 241 GP 5
17. T p. 243 GP 5
18. F p. 245 GP 5
19. T p. 246 GP 5
20. T p. 244 GP 5
21. F p. 251 GP 6
22. T p. 253 GP 6
23. F p. 254 GP 7
24. T p. 256 GP 7
25. F p. 257 GP 7

Multiple-Choice Self-Test

1. b p. 237 GP 4
2. c p. 237 GP 4
3. d p. 238 GP 4
4. a p. 241 GP 5
5. c p. 241 GP 5
6. b p. 243 GP 5
7. d p. 241 GP 5
8. a p. 238 GP 5
9. b p. 255 GP 7
10. c p. 256 GP 7
11. b p. 258 GP 8
12. a p. 234 GP 3
13. d p. 234 GP 4
14. d p. 236 GP 4
15. b p. 240 GP 5
16. c p. 247 GP 5
17. b p. 248 GP 5
18. a p. 248 GP 5
19. a p. 248 GP 5
20. d p. 248 GP 5
21. d p. 248 GP 5
22. b p. 250 GP 6
23. c p. 251 GP 6
24. c p. 253 GP 6
25. a p. 255 GP 7

Organize It!

1. pp. 255-256 GP 7
2. pp. 249-250 GP 6
3. p. 239 GP 5
4. p. 239 GP 5

Short Essay Questions

1. pp. 236-238 GP 4
2. pp. 230-231 GP 1
3. pp. 232-234 GP 3
4. pp. 245-248 GP 5
5. pp. 243-244 GP 5
6. pp. 244-245 GP 5

CHAPTER 8: PSYCHOSOCIAL DEVELOPMENT IN EARLY CHILDHOOD

This chapter introduces the various aspects of psychosocial development: the developing self, gender differences, play, parenting, and relationships with other children.

Guideposts for Study

1. How does the self-concept develop during early childhood, and how do children advance in understanding their emotions?

2. How do young children develop initiative and self-esteem?

3. How do boys and girls become aware of the meaning of gender, and what explains differences in behavior between the sexes?

4. How do preschoolers play, and how does play contribute to and reflect development?

5. What forms of discipline do parents use, and how do parenting styles and practices influence development?

6. Why do young children help or hurt others, and why do they develop fears?

7. What causes child abuse and neglect, and what are the effects of maltreatment?

8. How do young children get along with—or without—siblings?

9. How do young children choose playmates and friends, and why are some children more popular than others?

Detailed Chapter Outline with Key Terms

I. THE DEVELOPING SELF
   A. The Self-Concept and Cognitive Development
   - **Self-concept**: Sense of self; descriptive and evaluative mental picture of one's abilities and traits.
   - *Cognitive construction:* A system of descriptive and evaluative representations about the self.
   - **Self-definition**: Cluster of characteristics used to describe oneself.
   - **Single representations**: In neo-Piagetian terminology, first stage in development of self-definition, in which children describe themselves in terms of individual, unconnected characteristics and in all-or-nothing terms.
   - **Real self**: The self one actually is.
   - **Ideal self**: The self one would like to be.
   - **Representational mappings**: In neo-Piagetian terminology, second stage in development of self-definition, in which a child makes logical connections between aspects of the self but still sees these characteristics in all-or-nothing terms.

- *Representational systems:* In neo-Piagetian terminology, third stage in development of self-definition, in which a child begins to integrate specific features of the self into a general, multidimensional concept and to articulate a sense of self-worth.
B. Understanding Emotions
  1. Emotions Directed Toward the Self
  2. Simultaneous Emotions
C. Erikson: Initiative versus Guilt
  - **Initiative versus guilt**: Erikson's third crisis in psychosocial development, in which children balance the urge to pursue goals with moral reservations that may prevent carrying them out.
  - *Purpose:* In Erikson's third crisis, the courage to envision and pursue goals without being unduly inhibited by guilt or fear of punishment.
D. **Self-esteem**: The judgment a person makes about his or her self-worth.
  1. Developmental Changes in Self-Esteem
  2. Contingent Self-Esteem: The "Helpless" Pattern

II. GENDER
  Gender identity: Awareness, developed in early childhood, that one is male or female.
  A. *Gender Differences*: Psychological or behavioral differences between males and females.
  B. Perspectives on Gender Development: Nature and Nurture
    - **Gender roles**: Behaviors, interests, attitudes, skills, and traits that a culture considers appropriate for males or females.
    - **Gender-typing**: Socialization process whereby children, at an early age, learn appropriate gender roles.
    - **Gender stereotypes**: Preconceived generalizations about male or female behavior.
    1. *Biological Approach*: Perspective on gender development that looks at the biological bases of gender.
      - *Corpus callosum:* The band of tissue joining the right and left cortical hemispheres.
      - *Androgens:* Male sex hormones.
      - *Estrogens:* Female sex hormones.
    2. *Psychoanalytic Approach*: Perspective on gender development that looks at gender from a Freudian viewpoint.
      Identification: In Freudian theory, the process by which a young child adopts the characteristics, beliefs, attitudes, values, and behaviors of the same-sex parent.
    3. *Cognitive Approach*: Perspective on gender development that focuses on thought processes and active construction of gender concepts.
      - **Gender constancy**: Awareness that one will always be male or female. Also called *sex-category constancy*.
      - **Gender-schema theory**: Theory, proposed by Bem, that children socialize themselves in their gender roles by developing a mentally organized network of information about what it means to be male or female in a particular culture.
      - *Schema:* A mentally organized network of information that influences a particular category of behavior.

4. *Socialization-Based Approach*: Perspective on gender development that emphasizes the influence of socialization and observational learning on forming gender concepts.
   - **Social cognitive theory**: Albert Bandura's expansion of social learning theory; holds that children learn gender roles through socialization.
   - *Socialization:* The process by which children acquire socially accepted standards of behavior in their culture.
   a. Family Influences
   b. Peer Influences
   c. Cultural Influences

III. PLAY: THE BUSINESS OF EARLY CHILDHOOD
   - *Content:* What children do when they play.
   - *Social dimension:* Whether children play alone or with others.
   A. Types of Play
   As defined by Piaget and Smilansky:
   - **Functional play**: The lowest cognitive level of play, involving repetitive muscular movements.
   - **Constructive play**: The second cognitive level of play, involving use of objects or materials to make something.
   - **Pretend play**: The third cognitive level of play, involving imaginary people or situations; also called *fantasy play*, *dramatic play*, or *imaginative play*.
   - *Formal games with rules:* The fourth cognitive level of play, involving organized games with known procedures and penalties, such as hopscotch and marbles.
   B. The Social Dimension of Play
   Parallel constructive play: A type of nonsocial play in which a child plays separately from, but in the presence of, another child.
   C. How Gender Influences Play
   D. How Culture Influences Play

IV. PARENTING
   A. Forms of Discipline
   Discipline: Methods of molding children's character and of teaching them to exercise self-control and engage in acceptable behavior.
   1. Behaviorist Techniques: Reinforcement and Punishment
      - *External reinforcements:* Rewards for behavior that come from outside the child, such as candy or praise.
      - *Internal reward:* A sense of pleasure or accomplishment.
      - **Corporal punishment**: Use of physical force with the intention of causing pain, but not injury, to correct or control behavior.
   2. Power Assertion, Induction, and Withdrawal of Love
      - **Power assertion**: Disciplinary strategy designed to discourage undesirable behavior through physical or verbal enforcement of parental control.
      - **Inductive techniques**: Disciplinary techniques designed to induce desirable behavior by appealing to a child's sense of reason and fairness.
      - **Withdrawal of love**: Disciplinary strategy that may involve ignoring, isolating, or showing dislike for a child.

B. Parenting Styles
  1. Baumrind's Model
     - **Authoritarian**: Parenting style emphasizing control and obedience.
     - **Permissive**: Parenting style emphasizing self-expression and self-regulation.
     - **Authoritative**: Parenting style blending respect for a child's individuality with an effort to instill social values.
     - *Neglectful, or uninvolved:* Parenting style in which parents focus on their own needs rather than those of the child, sometimes because of stress or depression.
  2. Cultural Factors
C. Promoting Altruism and Dealing with Aggression and Fearfulness
  1. Prosocial Behavior
     - **Altruism**: Behavior intended to help others out of inner concern and without expectation of external reward; may involve self-denial or self-sacrifice.
     - **Prosocial behavior**: Any voluntary behavior intended to help others.
  2. Aggression
     - **Instrumental aggression**: Aggressive behavior used to achieve a goal.
     - **Overt aggression**: Aggression that is openly directed at its target.
     - **Relational aggression**: Aggression aimed at damaging or interfering with another person's relationships, reputation, or psychological well-being; also called *covert, indirect,* or *psychological aggression.*
     a. Sources of Aggression
     b. Triggers of Aggression
     c. Influence of Culture
  3. Fearfulness
     Systematic desensitization: Therapeutic technique involving gradual exposure to a feared object or situation.

V. FAMILIES IN TROUBLE: CHILD ABUSE AND NEGLECT
  - *Maltreatment:* Deliberate or avoidable endangerment of a child.
  - *Abuse:* Action that inflicts harm.
  - **Physical abuse**: Action taken to endanger a child involving potential bodily injury.
  - **Neglect**: Failure to meet a child's basic needs.
  - **Sexual abuse**: Sexual activity involving a child and an older person.
  - **Emotional maltreatment**: Action or inaction that may cause behavioral, cognitive, emotional, or mental disorders.
  A. Maltreatment: Facts and Figures
  B. Contributing Factors: An Ecological View
     1. Characteristics of Abusive Families
     2. Characteristics of Neglectful Families
     3. Neighborhood and Social Support
  C. Effects of Maltreatment
     1. Helping Families in Trouble or at Risk

VI. RELATIONSHIPS WITH OTHER CHILDREN

Self-efficacy: A child's growing sense of capability to master challenges and acieve goals.

A. Siblings—or Their Absence
 1. Brothers and Sisters
 2. The Only Child
B. Playmates and Friends
 1. Choosing Playmates and Friends
 2. Characteristics and Benefits of Friendships
 3. Parenting and Popularity

True/False Self-Test

Place a T or an F in the appropriate space. These questions are taken from the chapter content, tables, key terms, Guideposts for Study, and Checkpoints.

1. ____ Children incorporate into their self-image their growing understanding of how others see them.

2. ____ Emotions such as shame and pride develop in middle childhood, not early childhood.

3. ____ Harter's research includes 12 levels of development.

4. ____ Children who have developed representational systems can integrate their sets of positive and negative emotions.

5. ____ Older children can describe conflicting feelings toward the same target, whereas younger children cannot.

6. ____ Self-esteem in early childhood tends to be global and unrealistic, reflecting adult approval.

7. ____ The main gender difference in early childhood is girls' greater aggressiveness.

8. ____ Gender stereotypes peak during the preschool years.

9. ____ Gender differences are exclusively behaviorally based.

10. ____ According to Parten, play becomes less social during early childhood.

11. ____ Nonsocial play is not necessarily immature; it depends on what children do when they play.

12. ____ Discipline can be a powerful tool for socialization.

13. ____ Authoritative parents tend to raise less competent children.

14. ___ Power assertion, inductive techniques, and withdrawal of love can be effective in certain situations.

15. ___ Most children become more aggressive after age 6 or 7.

16. ___ Family conflict can be used to help children learn rules and standards of behavior and negotiating skills.

17. ___ Boys tend to practice relational aggression and girls engage in overt aggression.

18. ___ Preschool children show temporary fears of real and imagined objects.

19. ___ The incidence of reported maltreatment and abuse of children has decreased since 1970.

20. ___ Sibling and peer relationships contribute to self-efficacy.

21. ___ Most sibling interactions are negative.

22. ___ Siblings tend to resolve disputes on the basis of moral principles, although not always the same ones parents use.

23. ___ Same-sex siblings, especially girls, tend to get along best.

24. ___ Friends have more positive and negative interactions than do other playmates.

25. ___ Parenting does not affect children's social competence with peers.

Multiple-Choice Self-Test

Circle the letter of the best answer. These questions are based on many aspects of the chapter content, in no particular order.

1. The self-concept undergoes major change in
a. early childhood.
b. middle childhood.
c. late childhood.
d. fourth grade.

2. According to neo-Piagetians, self-definition
a. never changes.
b. changes unpredictably.
c. shifts from single representations to representational mappings.
d. changes according to gender only.

3. Self-esteem in early childhood tends to be
a. unpredictable.
b. dependent on school popularity.
c. global and unrealistic.
d. conservative and realistic.

4. According to Erikson, the chief developmental crisis of early childhood is
a. hopelessness vs. despair.
b. integrity vs. popularity.
c. initiative vs. guilt.
d. freedom vs. control.

5. The main gender difference in early childhood is
a. girls' greater aggressiveness.
b. boys' greater aggressiveness.
c. girls' greater cognitive ability.
d. boys' greater athletic ability.

6. Gender stereotypes
a. decline in the preschool years.
b. are unchanged until adolescence.
c. decline until adolescence.
d. peak during the preschool years.

7. The idea that gender differences are biologically based is suggested by
a. Freud.
b. Vygotsky.
c. Erikson.
d. differences in brain size and hormonal activity.

8. According to social cognitive theory, children learn gender roles through
a. parental instruction.
b. church.
c. socialization.
d. None of the above.

9. According to Piaget and Smilansky, the order of cognitive progression in children's play is:
a. pretend, cognitive, functional, formal games with rules
b. cognitive, pretend, functional, formal games with rules
c. formal, functional, pretend, cognitive, constructive
d. functional, constructive, pretend, formal games with rules

10. In early childhood, children prefer to play
a. with others of the opposite sex.
b. with others of the same sex.
c. with others of both sexes.
d. alone.

11. The most effective method of discipline is
a. power assertion.
b. withdrawal of love.
c. inductive techniques.
d. spanking.

12. Baumrind identified
a. three parenting styles.
b. five levels of emotional development.
c. four methods of discipline.
d. four stages of moral leadership.

13. The most common type of aggression in early childhood is
a. overt aggression.
b. relational aggression.
c. hostile aggression.
d. instrumental aggression.

14. Maltreatment includes
a. physical abuse.
b. neglect.
c. sexual abuse.
d. All of the above.

15. Sibling and peer relationships contribute to
a. self-efficacy.
b. aggression.
c. the helpless syndrome.
d. shyness.

16. Most sibling interactions are
a. negative.
b. altruistic.
c. positive.
d. undefined.

17. Only children seem to develop
a. less well socially than children with siblings.
b. as well as children with siblings.
c. with unusual grace.
d. behind children with siblings, academically speaking.

18. Preschoolers choose playmates and friends who are
a. unlike them.
b. like them.
c. leaders.
d. None of the above.

19. Aggressive children of preschool age are
a. more popular than prosocial children.
b. less popular than prosocial children.
c. a disappointment to their parents.
d. None of the above.

20. The cluster of characteristics used to describe oneself is known as
a. self-concept.
b. self-definition.
c. real self.
d. ideal self.

21. When a child adopts the characteristics, beliefs, attitudes, values, and behavior of the same-sex parent, it is known as
a. gender constancy.
b. gender stereotype.
c. identification.
d. gender schema.

22. Play involving use of objects or materials to make something is classified as
a. pretend play.
b. functional play.
c. dramatic play.
d. constructive play.

23. A discipline strategy designed to discourage undesirable behavior through physical or verbal enforcement of parental control is known as
a. permissive.
b. power assertion.
c. altruism.
d. instrumental aggression.

24. After age 6 or 7, children become
a. less aggressive.
b. more aggressive.
c. more inclined to pout.
d. more likely to have temper tantrums.

25. According to Kohlberg, gender constancy leads to
a. frustration.
b. acquisition of gender roles.
c. preadolescence.
d. cognitive competence.

Organize It!

Here are several helpful lists to make. Practice memorizing the lists and you will find that the chapter information is organized in a meaningful whole in your mind!

1. List and briefly describe the four perspectives of gender development (see Table 8-1).

    1.

    2.

    3.

    4.

2. List and describe the four parenting styles described by Baumrind, Maccoby and Martin.

    1.

    2.

    3.

    4.

3. List and describe the common fears of childhood, including the ages when they most commonly appear (see Table 8-3).

    1.

    2.

    3.

    4.

    5.

    6.

    7.

    8.

    9.

    10.

4. List and describe four cognitive levels of play, according to Piaget and others.

    1.

    2.

    3.

    4.

5. List Parten's six categories of social and nonsocial play.

1.

2.

3.

4.

5.

6.

Short Essay Questions

These short essay questions are based on the Checkpoints in the chapter. Answer each question as completely and succinctly as possible.

1. Describe the emergence of altruism and the ways it is influenced in early childhood.

2. Discuss the benefits of the sibling relationship and the ways sibling interactions help children to develop.

3. Explain why Baumrind's parenting styles may not be appropriate for all cultures.

4. Discuss the ways in which children become aware of gender in early childhood.

Critical Thinking Questions

These questions may be used in small group discussions or as extra-credit reports.

1. What are some ways in which your parents or other adults helped you develop self-esteem?

2. Should parents encourage their children to play with toys that are typically for the other gender, such as boys playing with dolls and girls playing with trucks? How might parents discourage sex-role stereotypes?

3. Have computers and calculators been good for children's cognitive development? Why or why not?

4. In what situations is spanking a child acceptable?

5. What kind of parent do you think you are or will be, according to Baumrind's categories? What kind of parenting style did your own parents use?

6. Are there situations in which a child should be encouraged to be aggressive?

7. What kind of problems do you foresee if the United States adopted a "one child" policy as in China?

Answer Keys

True/False Self-Test

1.	T	p. 269	GP 1		14.	T	p. 285	GP 5
2.	F	p. 271	GP 1		15.	F	p. 291	GP 6
3.	F	p. 271	GP 1		16.	T	p. 289	GP 5
4.	T	p. 270	GP 1		17.	F	p. 291	GP 6
5.	T	p. 271	GP 1		18.	T	p. 293	GP 6
6.	T	p. 272	GP 2		19.	F	p. 294	GP 7
7.	F	p. 274	GP 3		20.	T	p. 298	GP 8
8.	T	p. 275	GP 3		21.	F	p. 298	GP 8
9.	F	p. 275	GP 3		22.	T	p. 298	GP 8
10.	F	p. 282	GP 4		23.	T	p. 299	GP 8
11.	T	p. 283	GP 4		24.	T	p. 301	GP 9
12.	T	p. 284	GP 5		25.	F	p. 301	GP 9
13.	F	p. 288	GP 5					

Multiple-Choice Self-Test

1.	a	p. 269	GP 1		14.	d	p. 294	GP 7
2.	c	p. 270	GP 1		15.	a	p. 298	GP 8
3.	c	p. 272	GP 2		16.	c	p. 298	GP 8
4.	c	p. 271	GP 2		17.	b	p. 299	GP 8
5.	b	p. 274	GP 3		18.	b	p. 299	GP 9
6.	d	p. 275	GP 3		19.	b	p. 300	GP 9
7.	d	p. 275	GP 3		20.	b	p. 269	GP 1
8.	c	p. 279	GP 3		21.	c	p. 277	GP 3
9.	d	p. 281	GP 4		22.	d	p. 281	GP 4
10.	b	p. 283	GP 4		23.	b	p. 285	GP 5
11.	c	p. 285	GP 5		24.	a	p. 291	GP 6
12.	a	p. 288	GP 5		25.	b	p. 277	GP 3
13.	d	p. 290	GP 6					

Organize It!

1.	p. 276	GP 3
2.	p. 288	GP 5
3.	p. 293	GP 6
4.	p. 281	GP 4
5.	p. 282	GP 4

Short Essay Questions

1.	p. 290	GP 6
2.	pp. 298-299	GP 8
3.	p. 289	GP 5
4.	p. 275	GP 3

PART 4: MIDDLE CHILDHOOD

CHAPTER 9: PHYSICAL AND COGNITIVE DEVELOPMENT IN MIDDLE CHILDHOOD

Chapters 9 and 10 make up Part 4 of the text, which explores middle childhood. The middle years from 6 to 11 are often termed the *school years*. School is a focal point of physical, cognitive, and psychosocial development. Children grow taller, heavier, and stronger, and they acquire the motor skills needed to participate in organized games and sports. This chapter focuses on physical and cognitive skills.

Guideposts for Study

1. What gains in growth and motor development occur during middle childhood, and what nutritional hazards do children face?

2. What are the principal health and safety concerns about school-age children?

3. How is school-age children's thinking and moral reasoning different from that of younger children?

4. What advances in memory and other information-processing skills occur during middle childhood?

5. How accurately can schoolchildren's' intelligence be measured?

6. How do communicative abilities and literacy expand during middle childhood?

7. What influences school achievement?

8. How do schools meet the needs of foreign-speaking children and those with learning problems?

9. How is giftedness assessed and nurtured?

Detailed Chapter Outline with Key Terms

PHYSICAL DEVELOPMENT
I. ASPECTS OF PHYSICAL DEVELOPMENT
    A. Growth
    B. Nutrition and Oral Health
        1. Malnutrition
        2. Obesity and Body Image
            *   *Inherited tendency:* A characteristic, such as obesity, that is at least partially under the control of the genes.
            *   *Leptin:* Protein found in the brain that is associated with obesity.
            *   *Environment:* One of the factors influencing obesity, includes types of foods available and eating habits of influential people such as parents.

- *Inactivity:* One of the factors influencing obesity, refers to a lack of physical activity.
- **Body image**: Descriptive and evaluative beliefs about one's appearance.
- C. Motor Development
  1. **Rough-and-Tumble Play**: Vigorous play involving wrestling, hitting, and chasing, often accompanied by laughing and screaming.
  2. Physical Fitness

II. HEALTH AND SAFETY
A. Medical Problems
- **Acute medical conditions**: Illnesses that last a short time.
- **Chronic medical conditions**: Illnesses or impairments that persist for at least 3 months.
1. Vision and Hearing Problems
2. **Asthma**: A chronic respiratory disease characterized by sudden attacks of coughing, wheezing, and difficulty in breathing.
3. HIV and AIDS
B. Accidental Injuries

COGNITIVE DEVELOPMENT
III. PIAGETIAN APPROACH: THE CONCRETE OPERATIONAL CHILD
Concrete operations: Third stage of Piagetian cognitive development (approximately from ages 7 to 12), during which children develop logical but not abstract thinking.
A. Cognitive Advances
1. Space and Causality
2. Categorization
- **Seriation**: Ability to order items along a dimension.
- **Transitive inference**: Understanding of the relationship between two objects by knowing the relationship of each to a third object.
- **Class inclusion**: Understanding the relationship between a whole and its parts.
3. Inductive and Deductive Reasoning
- **Inductive reasoning**: Type of logical reasoning that moves from particular observations about members of a class to a general conclusion about that class.
- **Deductive reasoning**: Type of logical reasoning that moves from a general premise about a class to a conclusion about a particular member(s) of the class.
4. Conservation
- *Identity:* Knowledge that a substance retains its nature even when it looks different.
- *Reversibility:* Knowledge that reversing an action will cause the substance to revert to its former appearance.
- *Decenter:* Ability to focus on more than one feature of a stimulus at a time.
- **Horizontal décalage**: Piaget's term for the inability to transfer learning about one type of conservation to other types, which causes a child to master different types of conservation tasks at different ages.
B. Moral Reasoning
Equity: The belief that one person may be treated differently than another because of special circumstances that are taken into account.

IV. INFORMATION PROCESSING AND INTELLIGENCE

A. Memory and Other Processing Skills
  1. Basic Processes and Capacities
     - **Sensory memory**: Initial, brief, temporary storage of sensory information.
     - **Working memory**: Short-term storage of information being actively processed.
     - *Prefrontal cortex:* The large portion of the frontal lobe directly behind the forehead.
     - **Central executive**: In Baddeley's model, the element of working memory that controls the processing of information.
     - **Long-term memory**: Storage of virtually unlimited capacity, which holds information for very long periods.
  2. Metamemory: Understanding Memory
  Metamemory: Understanding of processes of memory.
  3. Mnemonics: Strategies for Remembering
     - **External memory aids**: Mnemonic strategies using something outside the person.
     - **Rehearsal**: Mnemonic strategy to keep an item in working memory through conscious repetition.
     - **Organization**: Mnemonic strategy of categorizing material to be remembered.
     - **Elaboration**: Mnemonic strategy of making mental associations involving items to be remembered.
  4. Selective Attention
  5. Information Processing and Piagetian Tasks
     - *Operational:* Referring to mental structures in Piagetian theory such as concrete and formal operations.
     - *Conceptual:* Referring to the theory of Case, in which mental structures exist within specific domains such as number, story understanding, and spatial relations.

B. Psychometric Approach: Testing Intelligence
Achievement tests: Standardized tests that assess how much children have learned in various subject areas.
  1. Traditional Group and Individual Tests
     - **Otis-Lennon School Ability Test**: Group intelligence test for kindergarten through 12th grade.
     - **Wechsler Intelligence Scale for Children (WISC-III)**: Individual intelligence test for schoolchildren, which yields verbal and performance scores as well as a combined score.
  2. The IQ Controversy
     a. Influence of Schooling
     b. Influences of Ethnicity and Culture
        - **Cultural bias**: Tendency of intelligence tests to include items calling for knowledge or skills that are more familiar or meaningful to some cultural groups than to others.
        - **Culture-free**: Describing an intelligence test that, if it were possible to design, would have no culturally linked content.
        - **Culture-fair**: Describing an intelligence test that deals with experiences common to various cultures, in an attempt to avoid cultural bias.

3. Is There More Than One Intelligence?
   a. Gardner's **Theory of Multiple Intelligences**: Each person has several distinct forms of intelligence.
   b. Sternberg's **Triarchic Theory of Intelligence**: Three types of intelligence: componential (analytic ability), experiential (insight and originality), and contextual (practical thinking).
      - *Intelligence:* According to Sternberg, a group of mental abilities necessary for children or adults to adapt to any environmental context and to select and shape the contexts in which they live and act.
      - **Componential element**: The analytic aspect of intelligence. *Analytic:* The ability to process information efficiently, as in problem-solving.
      - **Experiential element**: The insightful aspect of intelligence. *Insightful:* In Sternberg's theory, the ability to think originally and creatively.
      - **Contextual element**: The practical aspect of intelligence. *Practical:* The ability to size up a situation and decide what to do: adapt to it, change it, or get out of it.
      - *The Sternberg Triarchic Abilities Test (STAT):* Test that seeks to measure each of the three components of intelligence through multiple-choice and essay questions in three domains: verbal, quantitative, and figural (or spatial).
4. Other New Directions in Intelligence Testing
   - **Kaufman Assessment Battery for Children (K-ABC)**: Nontraditional individual intelligence test designed to provide fair assessments of minority children and children with disabilities.
   - *Dynamic testing:* Testing of intelligence based on Vygotsky's theory of cognitive development and the zone of proximal development.

V. LANGUAGE AND LITERACY
A. Vocabulary, Grammar, and Syntax
   - *Simile* and *metaphor:* Figures of speech in which a word or phrase that usually designates one thing is compared or applied to another.
   - *Syntax:* How words are organized into phrases and sentences.
B. Pragmatics: Knowledge about Communications
   Pragmatics: Set of linguistic rules that govern the use of language for communication.
C. Literacy
   1. Identifying Words: Decoding Versus Visually Based Retrieval
      - *Decoding:* Process by which a child sounds out a word, translating it from print to speech before retrieving it from long-term memory.
      - *Visually based retrieval:* Process by which a child simply looks at a word and then retrieves it.
      - **Phonetic, or code emphasis approach**: Approach to teaching reading that emphasizes decoding of unfamiliar words.
      - **Whole-language approach**: Approach to teaching reading that emphasizes visual retrieval and use of contextual cues.
   2. Comprehension
      Metacognition: Awareness of a person's own mental processes.
   3. Writing

VI. THE CHILD IN SCHOOL
A. Entering First Grade
B. Influences on School Achievement
 1. The Child: Self-Efficacy Beliefs and Academic Motivation
 Self-efficacy: Belief that one's actions will bring about a particular result, either favorable or unfavorable.
 2. Parenting Practices
 - *Extrinsic:* Refers to things that are external to oneself, such as money or rewards.
 - *Intrinsic:* Refers to things that are internal, such as pride of accomplishment.
 - *Authoritative:* Parenting style blending respect for a child's individuality with an effort to instill social values.
 - *Authoritarian:* Parenting style emphasizing control and obedience.
 - *Permissive:* Parenting style emphasizing self-expression and self-regulation.
 3. Socioeconomic Status
 Social capital: Family and community resources on which a child can draw.
 4. Teacher Expectations
 Self-fulfilling prophecy: False expectation or prediction of behavior that tends to come true because it leads people to act as if it were already true.
 5. The Educational System
 Social promotion: Policy of automatically promoting children even if they do not meet academic standards.
 6. The Culture
 Jukus: Private remedial and enrichment schools in Japan.
C. Second-Language Education
 - **English immersion**: Approach to teaching English as a second language in which instruction is presented only in English.
 - **Bilingual education**: System of teaching non-English-speaking children in their native language while they learn English, and later switching to all-English instruction.
 - **Bilingual**: Fluent in two languages.
 - **Two-way (dual-language) learning**: Approach to second-language education in which English speakers and non-English speakers learn together in their own and each other's languages.
 - *Biliteracy:* Proficiency in reading and writing two languages.
D. Children with Learning Problems
 1. **Mental Retardation**: Significantly subnormal cognitive functioning.
 2. Learning Disabilities
 - **Dyslexia**: Developmental disorder in which reading achievement is substantially lower than predicted by IQ or age.
 - **Learning disabilities (LDs)**: Disorders that interfere with specific aspects of learning and school achievement.
 3. Hyperactivity and Attention Deficits
 - **Attention-deficit/hyperactivity disorder (ADHD)**: Syndrome characterized by persistent inattention and distractibility, impulsivity, low tolerance for frustration, and inappropriate overactivity.
 - *Atomoxetine:* A newer drug for treating ADHD.
 4. Educating Children with Disabilities

E. Gifted Children

Giftedness: Term applied to children who meet some criteria, such as high scores (130 or above) on tests of intelligence.

1. Identifying Gifted Children
2. The Lives of Gifted Children
3. Defining and Measuring Creativity
   - **Creativity**: Ability to see situations in a new way, to produce innovations, or to discern previously unidentified problems and find novel solutions.
   - **Convergent thinking**: Thinking aimed at finding the "one" right answer to a problem.
   - **Divergent thinking**: Thinking that produces a variety of fresh, diverse possibilities.
4. Educating Gifted Children
   - **Enrichment**: Approach to educating the gifted, which broadens and deepens knowledge and skills through extra activities, projects, field trips, or mentoring.
   - **Acceleration**: Approach to educating the gifted, which moves them through the curriculum at an unusually rapid pace.

True/False Self-Test

Place a T or an F in the appropriate space. These questions are taken from the chapter content, tables, key terms, Guideposts for Study, and Checkpoints.

1. ____ Physical development is more rapid in middle childhood than in early childhood.

2. ____ On the average, children need 5, 000 calories per day to maintain growth and development.

3. ____ In the United States, one child in five does not get enough to eat.

4. ____ Concern with body image increases in middle childhood.

5. ____ Malnutrition can affect cognitive and psychosocial development.

6. ____ Obesity is increasingly rare among U.S. children.

7. ____ Lack of exercise affects mental health.

8. ____ About 89 percent of schoolchildren's free play is rough-and-tumble play.

9. ____ Rough-and-tumble play is more common in boys than girls.

10. ___ Vision becomes keener in middle childhood.

11. ___ Chronic infections, such as asthma, are more common among upper-class children.

12. ___ Children's understanding of health and illness is related to their cognitive level.

13. ___ Accidents are the leading cause of death in middle childhood.

14. ___ Children are less proficient at tasks involving conservation, spatial thinking, transitive inference, and inductive reasoning in middle childhood.

15. ___ Cultural experience seems to contribute to the rate of development of conservation and other Piagetian skills.

16. ___ According to Piaget, the first stage of moral reasoning in middle childhood is the morality of obedience.

17. ___ Information-processing theory looks at eight stages of memory.

18. ___ The capacity of working memory increases greatly during middle childhood.

19. ___ Metamemory disappears in middle childhood.

20. ___ Rehearsal, organization, and elaboration are all mnemonic strategies.

21. ___ The WISC-III and the Stanford-Binet IQ tests are both group tests.

22. ___ Conventional IQ tests may miss important aspects of intelligent behavior.

23. ___ According to Robert Sternberg's triarchic theory of intelligence, IQ tests measure mainly the componential element of intelligence, not the experiential or contextual elements.

24. ___ Schooling seems to increase measured intelligence.

25. ___ Studies on bilingualism have shown that being bilingual lowers a child's cognitive achievement.

Multiple-Choice Self-Test

Circle the letter of the best answer. These questions are based on many aspects of the chapter content, in no particular order.

1. Mental retardation
a. appears after age 18.
b. is indicated by an IQ of about 70 or less.
c. occurs in 20 percent of the U.S. population.
d. is the same as dyslexia.

2. Creativity and IQ are
a. closely linked.
b. likely to go together.
c. not closely linked.
d. the same thing.

3. In Terman's study, most of the children were
a. millionaires in adulthood.
b. well-adjusted and successful.
c. below average in IQ.
d. mildly retarded.

4. Tests of creativity attempt to measure
a. divergent thinking.
b. convergent thinking.
c. sensory memory.
d. working memory.

5. Programs for gifted children are often based on
a. enrichment.
b. acceleration.
c. Both a and b.
d. None of the above.

6. A common standard for identifying gifted children for special programs is an IQ of
a. 130 or higher.
b. 200 or higher.
c. 65 or higher.
d. 44 or higher.

7. An understanding of the relationship between two objects by knowing the relationship of each to a third object is
a. class inclusion.
b. seriation.
c. transitive inference.
d. inductive reasoning.

8. The ability to order items along a dimension is
a. inductive reasoning.
b. seriation.
c. class inclusion.
d. cross-modal transfer.

9. In Piaget's terminology, a child's inability to transfer learning about one type of conservation to other types, because of which the child masters different types of conservation at different ages, is called
a. encoding.
b. morality of constraint.
c. morality of cooperation.
d. horizontal décalage.

10. In Baddeley's model, the element of working memory that controls the processing of information is the
a. cerebellum.
b. islets of Langerhans.
c. central executive.
d. retrieval.

11. Understanding the processes of memory is
a. central executive.
b. storage.
c. metamemory.
d. encoding.

12. A type of logical reasoning that moves from a general premise about a class to a conclusion about a particular member or members of the class is
a. deductive reasoning.
b. inductive reasoning.
c. metacognition.
d. horizontal décalage.

13. A developmental disorder in which reading achievement is substantially lower than predicted by IQ or age is
a. ADD.
b. ODD.
c. dyslexia.
d. autism.

14. A set of linguistic rules that govern the use of language for communication is
a. metacognition.
b. pragmatics.
c. child-directed speech.
d. bilingualism.

15. Thinking that is aimed at finding the "one right answer" to a problem is
a. divergent thinking.
b. convergent thinking.
c. enrichment.
d. acceleration of ideas.

16. The most commonly diagnosed learning disability is
a. ADHD.
b. dyslexia.
c. mental retardation.
d. autism.

17. The superior achievement of children of East Asian extraction seems to stem from
a. cultural factors.
b. homework assigned.
c. parental discipline.
d. higher IQ.

18. The major area of linguistic growth in middle childhood is in
a. vocabulary.
b. grammar.
c. syntax.
d. pragmatics.

19. According to Piaget, moral development
a. is linked with cognitive maturation.
b. occurs in two stages.
c. Both a and b.
d. Neither a nor b.

20. In order to reduce injuries and fatalities in middle childhood, parents should
a. keep their children inside as much as possible.
b. encourage the use of bicycle helmets.
c. encourage children to stay in and watch television.
d. avoid riding bicycles.

21. Children in the stage of concrete operations are
a. largely limited in their reasoning to the here and now.
b. less egocentric than before.
c. more proficient at tasks requiring logical reasoning.
d. All of the above.

22. Rough-and-tumble play
a. is more common among boys than girls.
b. is more common among girls than boys.
c. consumes 90 percent of the free play of middle school children.
d. increases dramatically after age 11.

23. On the average, children need how many calories per day to maintain growth and development?
a. 3,600
b. 2,400
c. 4,500
d. 6,500

24. African American children grow
a. faster than white children.
b. slower than white children.
c. at the same rate as white children.
d. less muscle and less bone mass than white children.

25. Obesity is
a. increasingly rare among U.S. children.
b. influenced by genetics and environmental factors.
c. less common in U.S. children than in Japanese children.
d. a result of parental neglect.

Organize It!

Making lists is a fun and useful way to categorize information in your mind. After making each list, think of ways to memorize it so that you have immediate recall. Singing a list, dancing while you recite it, or simply saying it in a rhythmic pattern as you are walking, driving, or jogging allows your brain to store the information in easily retrievable form. Try it!

1. List the three principles that help school-aged children understand conservation.

   1.
   2.
   3.

2. List and describe Piaget's two stages of moral development.

   1.

   2.

3. List and briefly describe Howard Gardner's eight intelligences.

   1.

   2.

   3.

   4.

   5.

   6.

   7.

   8.

4. List and describe two intelligence tests for schoolchildren.

   1.

   2.

5. List four of the most common mnemonic aids.

   1.
   2.
   3.
   4.

6. List and briefly describe Sternberg's three components of intelligence.

   1.

   2.

   3.

Short Essay Questions

These short essay questions are based on the Checkpoints in the chapter. Answer each question as completely and succinctly as possible.

1. On the basis of the descriptions in the chapter, which approach to second-language education do you favor? Support your position with research.

2. Is intelligence related to how well a person adapts to the dominant culture, or should intelligence tests be designed to take a minority culture into account?

3. According to Piaget's theory of moral development, more mature moral judgments consider intent, not just the seriousness of the offense. Do you agree that intent is an important factor in morality? In what ways does the criminal justice system reflect this view?

4. Based on what you have read about Theodore Roosevelt's childhood and later adult life, what can you say about the importance of maintaining physical fitness in school-aged children? What suggestions can you make for motivating all children to stay physically fit?

5. In view of childhood malnutrition's long-term effects on physical, social, and cognitive development, what can and should various sectors of society—government agencies, community groups, and private organizations—do to combat it?

Critical Thinking Questions

These questions may be used in small group discussions or as extra-credit reports.

1. Should the government force parents to make their children wear helmets when riding bicycles, scooters, and skateboards?

2. On which of Piaget's two levels of moral development does our criminal justice system work? Support your answer with examples.

3. Should IQ test scores be used to determine who gets into programs for special education and gifted education? Why or why not? What would some alternative assessment techniques be?

4. What is a reasonable amount of homework per class for one evening? One week?

5. Should stimulants be used to treat ADHD? Who should diagnose a child with ADHD?

6. Should gifted children get special educational attention? Why or why not?

Answer Keys

True/False Self-Test

1.	F	p. 309	GP 1		14.	F	p. 317	GP 3
2.	F	p. 310	GP 1		15.	T	p. 320	GP 3
3.	T	p. 310	GP 1		16.	T	p. 320	GP 3
4.	T	p. 312	GP 1		17.	F	p. 321	GP 4
5.	T	p. 311	GP 1		18.	T	p. 321	GP 4
6.	F	p. 311	GP 1		19.	F	p. 322	GP 4
7.	T	p. 313	GP 1		20.	T	p. 322	GP 4
8.	F	p. 312	GP 1		21.	F	p. 324	GP 5
9.	T	p. 313	GP 1		22.	T	p. 325	GP 5
10.	T	p. 315	GP 2		23.	T	p. 328	GP 5
11.	F	p. 315	GP 2		24.	T	p. 325	GP 5
12.	T	p. 314	GP 2		25.	F	p. 339	GP 8
13.	T	p. 316	GP 2					

Multiple-Choice Self-Test

1.	b	p. 340	GP 8		14.	b	p. 330	GP 6
2.	c	p. 344	GP 9		15.	b	p. 344	GP 9
3.	b	p. 343	GP 9		16.	b	p. 341	GP 8
4.	a	p. 344	GP 9		17.	a	p. 338	GP 7
5.	c	p. 345	GP 9		18.	d	p. 330	GP 6
6.	a	p. 343	GP 9		19.	c	p. 320	GP 3
7.	c	p. 318	GP 3		20.	b	p. 316	GP 2
8.	b	p. 318	GP 3		21.	d	p. 317	GP 3
9.	d	p. 319	GP 3		22.	a	p. 313	GP 1
10.	c	p. 321	GP 4		23.	b	p. 310	GP 1
11.	c	p. 322	GP 4		24.	a	p. 310	GP 1
12.	a	p. 318	GP 3		25.	b	p. 311	GP 1
13.	c	p. 340	GP 8					

Organize It!

1.	p. 319	GP 3
2.	p. 320	GP 3
3.	p. 327	GP 5
4.	p. 325	GP 5
5.	p. 322	GP 4
6.	p. 328	GP 5

Short Essay Questions

1.	pp. 338-339	GP 8
2.	p. 326	GP 5
3.	p. 320	GP 3
4.	p. 313	GP 1
5.	p. 311	GP 1

CHAPTER 10: PSYCHOSOCIAL DEVELOPMENT IN MIDDLE CHILDHOOD

This chapter introduces school-age children in the context of self-esteem, emotional growth, family atmosphere and structure, peer group friendships, and mental health.

Guideposts for Study

1. How do school-age children develop a realistic self-concept, and what contributes to self-esteem?

2. How do school-age children show emotional growth?

3. How do parent-child relationships change in middle childhood?

4. What are the effects of parents' work and of poverty on family atmosphere?

5. What impact does family structure have on children's development?

6. How do siblings influence and get along with one another?

7. How do relationships with peers change in middle childhood, and what influences popularity and choice of friends?

8. What are the most common forms of aggressive behavior in middle childhood, and what influences contribute to it?

9. What emotional disorders may develop in childhood, and how are they treated?

10. How do the stresses of modern life affect children, and why are some children more resilient than others?

Detailed Chapter Outline with Key Terms

I. THE DEVELOPING SELF
    A. Representational Systems: A Neo-Piagetian View
       • **Representational systems**: The third stage in development of self-definition, characterized by breadth, balance, and integration and assessment of various aspects of the self.
       • *Real self:* Your knowledge of who you really are.
       • *Ideal self:* Knowledge of who you would like to be or think you should be.
    B. Self-Esteem
       • **Industry versus inferiority**: Erikson's fourth stage of psychosocial development, in which children must learn the productive skills their culture requires or else face feelings of inferiority.
       • *Competence:* A view of the self as able to master skills and complete tasks.
    C. Emotional Growth

II. THE CHILD IN THE FAMILY

- *Atmosphere:* In reference to the family environment, the general demeanor of the family, including personalities, presence or absence of support, monetary status, and conflicts.
- *Structure:* The composition of a family, such as single versus two parents, only child or several children, adopted children, stepfamilies, and other nontraditional families.

A. Family Atmosphere
1. Parenting Issues: Coregulation and Discipline
   Coregulation: Transitional stage in the control of behavior in which parents exercise general supervision and children exercise moment-to-moment self-regulation.
2. Effects of Parents' Work
3. Poverty and Parenting

B. Family Structure
1. Adoptive Families
   Open adoption: Type of adoption in which the parities share information or have direct contact.
2. When Parents Divorce
   - *Joint custody:* Custody of a minor child shared by both parents.
   - *Legal:* Type of joint custody in which parents share the right and responsibility to make decisions regarding the child's welfare.
   - *Physical:* Type of joint custody in which parents have the child or children live with each of them part of the time.
3. Living in a One-Parent Family
4. Living in a Stepfamily
5. Living with Gay or Lesbian Parents

C. Sibling Relationships

III. THE CHILD IN THE PEER GROUP

A. Positive and Negative Influences of Peer Relations
   Prejudice: Unfavorable attitude toward members of certain groups outside one's own, especially racial or ethnic groups.

B. Popularity

C. Friendship

D. Aggression and Bullying
   - **Hostile aggression**: Aggression aimed at hurting its target.
   - *Instrumental aggression:* Aggression aimed at achieving an objective.
   - *Overt aggression:* Physical force or verbal threats.
   - *Relational aggression:* Social aggression, such as insulting someone or spreading rumors about that person.
1. Aggression and Social Information Processing
   - *Reactive aggressor:* Another term for hostile aggression on the part of an individual.
   - *Hostile attribution bias, or hostile attribution of intent:* When a child sees other children as trying to hurt him or her and strikes out angrily in retaliation or self-defense.
   - *Proactive aggression:* Another term for instrumental aggression.
2. Does Televised Violence Lead to Aggression?
3. Bullies and Victims
   Bullying: Aggression deliberately and persistently directed against a particular target, or victim, typically one who is weak, vulnerable, and defenseless.

IV. MENTAL HEALTH

Mental health: The emotional health of a person.

A. Common Emotional Disorders

- *Anxiety disorders:* Disorders having to do with excessive fear or anxiety.
- *Mood disorders:* Disorders having to do with emotional imbalances, such as sadness or depression.
- *Disruptive conduct disorders:* Disorders having to do with undesirable behavior, such as aggression or defiance, stealing, and other antisocial behavior.

1. Disruptive Behavior Disorders
   - **Oppositional defiant disorder (ODD):** Pattern of behavior, persisting into middle childhood, marked by negativity, hostility, and defiance.
   - **Conduct disorder (CD):** Repetitive, persistent pattern of aggressive, antisocial behavior violating societal norms or the rights of others.

2. School Phobia and Other Anxiety Disorders
   - **School phobia:** Unrealistic fear of going to school; may be a form of *separation anxiety disorder* or *social phobia*.
   - **Separation anxiety disorder:** Condition involving excessive, prolonged anxiety concerning separation from home or from people to whom a child is attached.
   - **Social phobia:** Extreme fear and/or avoidance of social situations.
   - **Generalized anxiety disorder:** Anxiety not focused on any single target.
   - **Obsessive-compulsive disorder (OCD):** Anxiety aroused by repetitive, intrusive thoughts, images, or impulses, often leading to ritualistic behaviors.

3. **Childhood Depression:** Mood disorder characterized by such symptoms as a prolonged sense of friendlessness, inability to have fun or concentrate, fatigue, extreme activity or apathy, feelings of worthlessness, weight change, physical complaints, and thoughts of death or suicide.

B. Treatment Techniques

- **Individual psychotherapy:** Psychological treatment in which a therapist sees a troubled person one-on-one.
- **Family therapy:** Psychological treatment in which a therapist sees the whole family together to analyze patterns of family functioning.
- **Behavior therapy:** Therapeutic approach using principles of learning theory to encourage desired behaviors or eliminate undesired ones; also called *behavior modification*.
- **Play therapy:** Therapeutic approach in which a child plays freely while a therapist observes and occasionally comments, asks questions, or makes suggestions.
- **Art therapy:** Therapeutic approach that allows a child to express troubled feelings without words, using a variety of art materials and media.
- **Drug therapy:** Administration of drugs to treat emotional disorders.
- *Placebos:* Substances with no active ingredients.
- *Selective serotonin reuptake inhibitors (SSRIs):* Drugs shown to be effective in treating obsessive-compulsive, depressive, and anxiety disorders.

C. Stress and Resilience: Protective Factors

- **Stress:** Response to physical or psychological demands.
- **Stressors:** Stress-producing experiences.

1. Stresses of Modern Life
2. Coping with Stress: The Resilient Child
   - **Resilient children**: Children who weather adverse circumstances, function well despite challenges or threats, or bounce back from traumatic events.
   - **Protective factors**: Influences that reduce the impact of early stress and tend to predict positive outcomes.
     - *Family relationships:* A factor that, when positive, can be a protective influence in helping children and adolescents overcome stress.
     - *Cognitive functioning:* A factor that, when at a high level, can be a protective influence in helping children and adolescents overcome stress.
     - *The child's personality:* An adaptable, friendly, and competent personality can be a positive influence in dealing with stress.
     - *Reduced risk:* Referring to exposure of the child to only one risk factor, such as poverty or mental illness, which allows a child to better overcome stress.
     - *Compensating experiences:* Referring to a supportive school environment or successful experiences in areas such as studies, sports, music, or with other persons, which can help make up for a destructive home life.

True/False Self-Test

Place a T or an F in the appropriate space. These questions are taken from the chapter content, tables, key terms, Guideposts for Study, and Checkpoints.

1. _____ The cognitive growth that takes place during middle childhood enables children to develop in emotional understanding and control.

2. _____ The self-concept becomes less realistic during middle childhood.

3. _____ According to Erikson, the chief source of self-esteem is children's view of their productive competence.

4. _____ School-age children have internalized shame and pride.

5. _____ School-age children spend less time with their parents, but relationships with parents continue to be important.

6. _____ Coregulation is an intermediate stage in the transfer of control from parent to child.

7. _____ Homes with employed mothers tend to be less structured and less egalitarian than homes with stay-at-home mothers.

8. _____ Boys in lower-class families tend to do less well if their mothers work.

9. ____ Parents living in poverty may not be able to provide effective discipline.

10. ____ Maternal employment has a positive influence on children's school achievement in low-income families.

11. ____ Adopted children are less well adjusted than are naturally born children.

12. ____ Open adoption strongly affects children's adjustment and parents' satisfaction.

13. ____ One of the most important effects of family structure is in its impact on family atmosphere.

14. ____ Unwed motherhood creates fewer single-parent families than does divorce.

15. ____ Children tend to do better in traditional intact families than in nontraditional families.

16. ____ Girls adjust to stepfathers more readily than do boys.

17. ____ Boys tend to have more trouble than do girls in adjusting to divorce.

18. ____ Boys adjust better than do girls to the mother's remarriage.

19. ____ Despite public concern about children living with homosexual parents, studies have found no ill effects.

20. ____ Siblings in nonindustrialized societies teach their younger siblings more than do those in industrialized societies.

21. ____ Peer groups can have negative and positive effects on a child's development.

22. ____ Siblings have less structured roles and responsibilities in nonindustrialized countries.

23. ____ Relationships with parents do not affect sibling relationships.

24. ____ The peer group becomes more important in middle childhood.

25. ____ Resilient children are less able than others to withstand the negative effects of stress.

Multiple-Choice Self-Test

Circle the letter of the best answer. These questions are based on many aspects of the chapter content, in no particular order.

1. Broad, inclusive self-concepts that integrate different aspects of the self are known as
   a. social strata.
   b. representational systems.
   c. self-concept.
   d. None of the above.

2. Harter's research suggests that
   a. the "virtue" that develops with being able to master skills and complete tasks is competence.
   b. today's U.S. school-age children judge themselves more by good looks and popularity than by skills.
   c. Neither a nor b.
   d. Both a and b.

3. Child development is most strongly influenced by
   a. television.
   b. the church.
   c. home atmosphere.
   d. discipline outside the home.

4. The stage in which parents and children share power is known as
   a. adolescence.
   b. coregulation.
   c. conflict.
   d. strategic.

5. Through family conflict, children learn about
   a. rules and standards of behavior.
   b. winning arguments.
   c. manipulation.
   d. None of the above.

6. McLloyd's research on the effects of poverty on *adults* includes
   a. anxiety.
   b. depression.
   c. decreased responsiveness to children.
   d. All of the above.

7. The ethnic group that has been consistently far less likely to put their babies up for adoption is
   a. Latino women.
   b. Black women.
   c. White women.
   d. Asian women.

8. A typical reaction to violence in middle childhood is
   a. acting out and self-destructive behavior.
   b. identification with the aggressor.
   c. bed-wetting.
   d. aggressiveness.

9. According to Erikson, a major determinant of self-esteem is
   a. children's view of their capacity for productive work.
   b. appearance.
   c. athletic ability.
   d. popularity.

10. One important aspect of emotional growth is
    a. control of negative emotions.
    b. learning the difference between having an emotion and expressing it.
    c. learning how other people react to a display of emotions.
    d. All of the above.

11. Parents who acknowledge their children's feelings of distress encourage
a. dependency.
b. empathy and prosocial development.
c. independence.
d. suppression of emotions.

12. Shame and pride develop by age
a. 5 or 6.
b. 7 or 8.
c. 9 or 10.
d. 10 or 11.

13. Prosocial children tend to
a. act appropriately in social situations.
b. be relatively free from negative emotion.
c. cope with problems constructively.
d. All of the above.

14. During the period of coregulation, parents rely on
a. direct management of the child.
b. minimal contact with the child.
c. discussion with the child.
d. the school.

15. The processes by which parents and children resolve conflicts may be
a. more important than specific outcomes.
b. full of violence.
c. less important than the outcomes.
d. full of anger.

16. As children become preadolescents
a. discipline becomes easier.
b. the quality of family problem-solving often deteriorates.
c. they require less autonomy.
d. they become more positive in their negotiations.

17. The impact of a mother's work on school-age children depends on
a. the child's age.
b. how she feels about her work.
c. if her mate is supportive.
d. All of the above.

18. School-age children of employed mothers
a. are encouraged to be more independent.
b. live in less structured homes.
c. have fewer household responsibilities.
d. have less egalitarian attitudes about gender roles.

19. Families under economic stress are
a. more likely to have good cooperation with regard to parenting.
b. less likely to monitor children's activities.
c. more likely to monitor children's activities.
d. likely to have resilient children.

20. Research has found the following regarding joint custody:
a. There can be a few advantages in some cases.
b. Children enjoy it.
c. Most parents are cheerful about it.
d. Most parents prefer it.

21. One-parent families are the result of
a. divorce.
b. death.
c. unwed parenthood.
d. All of the above.

22. Sibling care is
a. common in nonindustrialized countries.
b. uncommon worldwide.
c. not beneficial.
d. None of the above.

23. In middle childhood, the peer group is
a. more important than in early childhood,
b. a factor in gauging abilities,
c. important in teaching children how to get along with others,
d. All of the above,

24. A negative influence of the peer group is
a. less self-efficacy.
b. testing values.
c. a tendency to reinforce prejudice.
d. unrealistic self-image.

25. Stage three of Selman's stages of friendship is characterized by
a. momentary playmateship.
b. one-way assistance.
c. possessiveness and exclusivity.
d. two-way fair-weather cooperation.

Organize It!

Making lists is a fun and useful way to categorize information in your mind. After making each list, think of ways to memorize it so that you have immediate recall. Singing a list, dancing while you recite it, or simply saying it in a rhythmic pattern as you are walking, driving, or jogging allows your brain to store the information in easily retrievable form. Try it!

1. List and describe four indicators of emotional growth in middle childhood.

    1.

    2.

    3.

    4.

2. Briefly list and describe three gender differences in response to maternal employment.

    1.

    2.

    3.

3. List and briefly describe eight common emotional disorders of childhood.

    1.

    2.

    3.

    4.

5.

6.

7.

8.

4. List and briefly describe Selman's four stages of friendship.

   1.

   2.

   3.

   4.

5. List and briefly describe five protective factors that have been identified for resilient children.

   1.

   2.

   3.

   4.

   5.

Short Essay Questions

These short essay questions are based on the Checkpoints in the chapter. Answer each question as completely and succinctly as possible.

1. Briefly summarize the factors that influence a child's adjustment to divorce.

2. Discuss the idea that children from traditional families are better adjusted than are children from nontraditional families.

3. How do the stresses of modern life affect children, and what enables resilient children to withstand them?

4. Summarize the most common forms of aggressive behavior in middle childhood, and discuss the influences that specifically contribute to aggressive behaviors.

5. Describe the changes that take place in the parent-child relationship in middle childhood.

Critical Thinking Questions

These questions may be used in small group discussions or as extra-credit reports.

1. If you were infertile, would you decide to adopt a child? Why or why not? Consider in your answer the age of the child you would want as well as the racial and cultural characteristics you would find important in your decision.

2. Is it a good idea to stay married until young children are grown and then get a divorce? Or should you divorce when the problems begin?

3. What do you think causes the violent outbreaks in middle childhood and young adolescence that have been in the news during the past several years? What are some contributing factors?

Answer Keys

True/False Self-Test

1. T   p. 353   GP 2
2. F   p. 351   GP 1
3. T   p. 352   GP 1
4. T   p. 353   GP 2
5. T   p. 354   GP 3
6. T   p. 355   GP 3
7. F   p. 356   GP 4
8. F   p. 356   GP 4
9. T   p. 357   GP 4
10. T   p. 356   GP 4
11. F   p. 359   GP 5
12. F   p. 360   GP 5
13. T   p. 358   GP 5
14. F   p. 363   GP 5
15. T   p. 361   GP 5
16. F   p. 364   GP 5
17. T   p. 360   GP 5
18. T   p. 364   GP 5
19. T   p. 364   GP 5
20. T   p. 365   GP 6
21. T   p. 366   GP 7
22. F   p. 356   GP 6
23. F   p. 365   GP 6
24. T   p. 366   GP 7
25. F   p. 378   GP 10

Multiple-Choice Self-Test

1. b   p. 351   GP 1
2. b   p. 352   GP 1
3. c   p. 355   GP 3
4. b   p. 355   GP 3
5. a   p. 355   GP 3
6. d   p. 357   GP 4
7. b   p. 359   GP 5
8. d   p. 372   GP 8
9. a   p. 352   GP 1
10. d   p. 353   GP 2
11. b   p. 354   GP 2
12. b   p. 353   GP 2
13. d   p. 353   GP 2
14. c   p. 355   GP 3
15. a   p. 355   GP 3
16. b   p. 356   GP 3
17. d   p. 356   GP 4
18. a   p. 356   GP 4
19. b   p. 357   GP 4
20. a   p. 361   GP 5
21. d   p. 363   GP 5
22. a   p. 365   GP 6
23. d   p. 366   GP 7
24. c   p. 366   GP 7
25. c   p. 369   GP 7

Organize It!

1. p. 353   GP 2
2. p. 356   GP 4
3. pp. 374-375   GP 9
4. p. 369   GP 7
5. p. 379   GP 10

Short Essay Questions

1. p. 360   GP 5
2. p. 361   GP 5
3. p. 377   GP 10
4. p. 370   GP 8
5. pp. 354-356   GP 3

PART 5: ADOLESCENCE

CHAPTER 11: PHYSICAL AND COGNITIVE DEVELOPMENT IN ADOLESCENCE

Chapter 11, which opens Part 5 of the text, introduces the student to the period of adolescence. Physical growth and other changes are rapid and profound as reproductive maturity occurs. Major health risks arise from behavioral issues, such as eating disorders and drug abuse. The ability to think abstractly and to use scientific reasoning develops at this time. Immature thinking persists in some attitudes, and education becomes focused on preparation for college or vocations.

Guideposts for Study

1. What is adolescence, when does it begin and end, and what opportunities and risks does it entail?

2. What physical changes do adolescents experience, and how do these changes affect them psychologically?

3. What are some common health problems in adolescence, and how can they be prevented?

4. How does adolescents' thinking and use of language differ from that of younger children?

5. On what basis do adolescents make moral judgments?

6. What influences affect school success, and why do some students drop out?

7. What factors affect educational and vocational planning and preparation?

Detailed Chapter Outline with Key Terms

I. ADOLESCENCE: A DEVELOPMENTAL TRANSITION
   - **Adolescence**: Developmental transition between childhood and adulthood entailing major physical, cognitive, and psychosocial changes.
   - **Puberty**: Process by which a person attains sexual maturity and reproductive ability.
   - *Pubescence:* Term meaning puberty.

PHYSICAL DEVELOPMENT
II. PUBERTY: THE END OF CHILDHOOD
   A. How Puberty Begins
   B. Timing, Sequence, and Signs of Maturation
      Secular trend: Trend that can be seen only by observing several generations, such as the trend toward earlier attainment of adult height and sexual maturity, which began a century ago.
      1. **The Adolescent Growth Spurt**: Sharp increase in height and weight that precedes sexual maturity.

2. Primary and Secondary Sex Characteristics
   - **Primary sex characteristics**: Organs directly related to reproduction, which enlarge and mature during adolescence.
   - **Secondary sex characteristics**: Physiological signs of sexual maturation, such as breast development and body hair growth, that do not involve sex organs.
   - *Areolae:* The pigmented areas surrounding the nipples, which enlarge during puberty.
3. Signs of Sexual Maturity: Sperm Production and Menstruation
   - *Nocturnal emission:* An involuntary ejaculation of semen (commonly referred to as a *wet dream*) that happens at night in males.
   - **Spermarche**: Boy's first ejaculation.
   - *Menstruation:* The monthly shedding of tissue from the lining of the womb.
   - **Menarche**: Girl's first menstruation.
   - *Pheromones:* Odorous chemicals that attract mates in animals and possibly in humans.

III. PHYSICAL AND MENTAL HEALTH
A. Physical Fitness
B. Sleep Needs
   - *Circadian timing system:* The natural sleep-wake cycle of the brain, lasting 24 hours.
   - *Melatonin:* A hormone secreted by the pineal gland, which promotes sleep.
C. Nutrition and Eating Disorders
   1. Obesity
   2. Body Image and Eating Disorders
      - **Body image**: Descriptive and evaluative beliefs about one's appearance.
      - **Anorexia nervosa**: Eating disorder characterized by self-starvation.
      - **Bulimia nervosa**: Eating disorder in which a person regularly eats huge quantities of food and then purges the body by taking laxatives, inducing vomiting, fasting, or exercising excessively.
      - *Binge eating disorder:* Frequent bingeing without subsequent fasting, exercise, or vomiting.
D. Use and Abuse of Drugs
   1. Risk Factors for Drug Abuse
      - Poor impulse control and sensation-seeking
      - Family influences
      - Difficult temperament
      - Early and persistent behavior problems
      - Academic failure and lack of commitment to education
      - Peer rejection
      - Associating with drug users
      - Alienation and rebelliousness
      - Favorable attitudes toward drug use
      - Early initiation into drug use
   2. **Gateway Drugs**: Drugs such as alcohol, tobacco, and marijuana, the use of which tends to lead to use of more addictive drugs.
E. Depression

F. Death in Adolescence
   1. Deaths from Vehicle Accidents and Firearms
   2. Suicide

COGNITIVE DEVELOPMENT
IV. ASPECTS OF COGNITIVE MATURATION
   A. Piaget's Stage of **Formal Operations**: Piaget's final stage of cognitive development, characterized by the ability to think abstractly.
      1. **Hypothetical-deductive reasoning**: Ability believed by Piaget to accompany the state of formal operations, to develop, consider, and test hypotheses.
      2. Evaluating Piaget's Theory
         Metacognition: Awareness and monitoring of one's own mental processes and strategies.
   B. Language Development
      Social perspective-taking: The ability to understand another person's point of view and level of knowledge and to speak accordingly.
   C. Elkind: Immature Characteristics of Adolescent Thought
      Six Characteristics of Immature Adolescent Thought:
      1. Idealism and Criticalness
      2. Argumentativeness
      3. Indecisiveness
      4. Apparent Hypocrisy
      5. Self-consciousness
      6. Specialness and Invulnerability
      • **Imaginary audience**: Elkind's term for an observer who exists only in an adolescent's mind and is as concerned with the adolescent's thoughts and actions as the adolescent is.
      • **Personal fable**: Elkind's term for the conviction that one is special, unique, and not subject to the rules that govern the rest of the world.
   D. Moral Reasoning: Kohlberg's Theory
      1. Kohlberg's Levels and Stages
         • Level I: **Preconventional morality**: First level, in which control is external.
         • Level II: **Conventional morality (or morality of conventional role conformity)**: Second level, in which standards of authority figures are internalized.
         • Level III: **Postconventional morality (or morality of autonomous moral principles)**: Third level, in which people follow internally held moral principles and can decide among conflicting moral standards.
      2. Evaluating Kohlberg's Theory
         a. Family Influences
         b. Validity for Women and Girls
         c. Cross-cultural Validity
         Female genital mutilation: Female circumcision.

V. EDUCATIONAL AND VOCATIONAL ISSUES
   A. Influences on School Achievement
      1. Self-Efficacy Beliefs and Academic Motivation

> *Self-efficacy:* Belief in one's own mastery of situations, such as mastery of academic material.
2. Use of Time
3. Socioeconomic Status and the Family Environment
4. Parental Involvement and Parenting Styles
   - *Authoritative parents:* Those who are warm, involved, and encourage their adolescents to be independent while maintaining reasonable control and discipline.
   - *Authoritarian parents:* Those who are controlling without warmth, rigid, overly punitive, and discourage inquiry.
   - *Permissive parents:* Those who seem not to care about adolescent grades and make no rules, and who are relatively uninvolved with their adolescents.
5. School Factors
B. Dropping Out of High School
   Active engagement: Involvement in schooling.
C. Educational and Vocational Preparation
   1. Influences on Students' Aspirations
   2. Guiding Students Not Bound for College
   3. Should High School Students Work Part Time?

True/False Self-Test

Place a T or an F in the appropriate space. These questions are taken from the chapter content, tables, key terms, Guideposts for Study, and Checkpoints.

1. ____ The concept of adolescence is a social construction.

2. ____ The beginning and the end of adolescence is clearly marked in Western societies.

3. ____ Puberty is triggered by hormonal changes, which may affect moods and behavior.

4. ____ Risky behavior patterns do not emerge until late adolescence.

5. ____ Puberty begins earlier in boys than in girls.

6. ____ During puberty, both boys and girls undergo an adolescent growth spurt.

7. ____ Girls who mature early tend to adjust less easily than early maturing boys.

8. ____ Adolescents are more likely than young children to get regular medical care.

9. ____ For the most part, the adolescent years are relatively healthy.

10. ____ The principal signs of sexual maturity are production of sperm for males and menstruation for females.

11. ___ Most high school students engage in vigorous physical activity.

12. ___ Many adolescents do not get enough sleep because the high school schedule is out of sync with their circadian timing system.

13. ___ Substance abuse is less common among adolescents today than in recent years.

14. ___ Anorexia and bulimia affect mostly girls.

15. ___ The three leading causes of death among adolescents are accidents, homicide, and suicide.

16. ___ Outcomes for bulimia tend to be better than for anorexia.

17. ___ Alcohol, cocaine, and heroin are the gateway drugs popular with adolescents.

18. ___ Adolescence is a time of development of abstract thought, according to Piaget.

19. ___ The ability to think abstractly has emotional implications.

20. ___ Many late adolescents and adults seem incapable of abstract thought as Piaget defined it.

21. ___ The personal fable and imaginary audience suggested by Elkind disappear in late adolescence.

22. ___ Kohlberg has described 10 levels of moral reasoning.

23. ___ According to Kohlberg, some people never reach the third level of moral reasoning.

24. ___ Neither Piaget nor Kohlberg considered parents important to children's moral development.

25. ___ According to Gilligan, women may see morality in terms of responsibility to show care and avoid harm.

Multiple-Choice Self-Test

Circle the letter of the best answer. These questions are based on many aspects of the chapter content, in no particular order.

1. Puberty begins
a. in the sixth grade.
b. in high school.
c. with a sharp increase in the production of sex hormones.
d. None of the above.

2. Leptin is a hormone that is needed to
a. keep mice healthy.
b. stimulate the hypothalamus.
c. keep girls immature.
d. keep boys physically active.

3. Secretion of the sex hormones
a. partially depends on reaching a critical weight level.
b. has nothing to do with weight.
c. is culturally dependent.
d. is climate regulated.

4. Alcohol, marijuana, and tobacco are called gateway drugs because
a. teens are usually introduced to the drugs by their peers.
b. their use often leads to use of more addictive substances.
c. their use typically leads to destructive behaviors.
d. teens who use them are teetering on the fringes of society.

5. Hormones are more strongly associated with moods in
a. younger girls.
b. older girls.
c. older boys.
d. younger boys.

6. The range for onset of puberty in both boys and girls is about
a. 4 years.
b. 3 years.
c. 7 years.
d. 10 years.

7. Puberty begins earlier for
a. girls.
b. boys.
c. neither sex.
d. boys who are raised in the countryside.

8. With respect to formal operational thought,
a. research has demonstrated that normal adolescents and adults rely primarily on this type of thinking.
b. the role of the situation in influencing adolescents' thinking has been well documented.
c. it can be clearly delineated from concrete operational thought.
d. Piaget's analysis of its development may not have given enough credit to experiences and wisdom.

9. The secular trend that began about 100 years ago in Japan, the United States, and western Europe includes
a. a lowering of the age when puberty begins.
b. a raising of the age when puberty begins.
c. increased height in males only.
d. decreased weight in females only.

10. In less developed countries, the average age of sexual maturity is
a. earlier than in developed countries.
b. later than in developed countries.
c. the same as in developed countries.
d. dependent on social class.

11. Which of the following is NOT a behavior that Elkind attributes to adolescence?
a. argumentativeness
b. respect for authority figures
c. apparent hypocrisy
d. assumption of invulnerability

12. African American girls tend to enter puberty
a. earlier than white girls.
b. later than white girls.
c. at the same time as white girls.
d. at age 18.

13. The adolescent growth spurt usually lasts
a. 10 years.
b. 6 years.
c. 2 years.
d. 5 years.

14. Kohlberg's theory of moral development
a. finds that children whose parents use humor, praise, and ask their children's opinions show greater progress through the stages.
b. finds that parental input and support are critical elements of developing a high sense of morality.
c. is oriented toward values that are more important to women than to men.
d. has demonstrated that people around the world progress into all three levels.

15. Muscular growth peaks for boys at age
a. 16.
b. 12 1/2.
c. 14 1/2.
d. 20.

16. Muscular growth peaks for girls at age
a. 16.
b. 12 1/2.
c. 14 1/2.
d. 20.

17. In a national survey, almost _____ of students reported seriously considering suicide during the past year.
a. 10 percent
b. 50 percent
c. 25 percent
d. 90 percent

18. The primary sex characteristics are
a. the organs necessary for reproduction.
b. readily apparent in girls.
c. breasts in females.
d. growth of facial hair in males

19. _____ seems to help young people from disadvantaged neighborhoods do well in school.
a. Innate intelligence
b. Academic tracking
c. Authoritarian parenting
d. Social capital

20. In males, the principal sign of sexual maturity is
a. facial hair.
b. chest hair.
c. deepened voice.
d. sperm production.

21. Perhaps the most important factor in whether a student will finish school is
a. parenting style.
b. active engagement.
c. school resources.
d. socioeconomic status.

22. Which factors are associated with early pubertal development in girls?
a. absent father
b. cold, distant father
c. genetic influences
d. All of the above.

23. Most adolescents
a. are reasonably healthy.
b. don't get enough sleep.
c. don't exercise enough.
d. All of the above.

24. In the morning, most teenagers are
a. alert.
b. not alert.
c. happy and energetic.
d. ready to study.

25. After puberty, secretion of this hormone takes place later at night.
a. estrogen
b. serotonin
c. melatonin
d. testosterone

Organize It!

Making lists is a fun and useful way to categorize information in your mind. After making each list, think of ways to memorize it so that you have immediate recall. Singing a list, dancing while you recite it, or simply saying it in a rhythmic pattern as you are walking, driving, or jogging allows your brain to store the information in easily retrievable form. Try it!

1. List the three most common mineral deficiencies in adolescence.

    1.

    2.

    3.

2. List four signs of anorexia nervosa and four signs of bulimia nervosa.

    Anorexia
    1.
    2.
    3.
    4.

    Bulimia
    1.
    2.
    3.
    4.

3. List four secondary sex characteristics each for boys and girls.

    Boys
    1.
    2.
    3.
    4.

    Girls
    1.
    2.
    3.
    4.

4. List and briefly describe Elkind's six immature characteristics of adolescent thought.

1.

2.

3.

4.

5.

6.

Short Essay Questions

These short essay questions are based on the Checkpoints in the chapter. Answer each question as completely and succinctly as possible.

1. Kohlberg's theory of assessing moral development by evaluating participants' reactions to moral dilemmas is widely used. Does this seem like the most appropriate method? Why or why not? Can you suggest an alternative measure?

2. What are some educational practices that can help high school students do better?

3. What are some reasons for and against high school students working part-time?

4. Should marijuana be legal, like alcohol? Why or why not? Should there be tighter restrictions on cigarette advertising? If so, what kinds of restrictions would you favor?

Critical Thinking Questions

These questions may be used in small group discussions or as extra-credit reports.

1. How might early maturation be different for girls than for boys? Late maturation?

2. Why are eating disorders so prevalent in Western cultures? What might be some ways to reduce the prevalence of eating disorders?

3. Regarding Kohlberg's method of assessing moral development, do you see any problems? What might be an alternative method of assessment?

4. What might be some ways that parents and educators could encourage students to finish high school?

Answer Keys

True/False Self-Test

1. T	p. 387	GP 1	
2. F	p. 387	GP 1	
3. T	p. 389	GP 2	
4. F	p. 388	GP 1	
5. F	p. 389	GP 2	
6. T	p. 390	GP 2	
7. T	p. 392	GP 2	
8. F	p. 394	GP 3	
9. T	p. 393	GP 3	
10. T	p. 392	GP 2	
11. F	p. 394	GP 3	
12. T	p. 395	GP 3	
13. T	p. 398	GP 3	

14. T	p. 396	GP 3
15. T	p. 400	GP 3
16. T	p. 397	GP 3
17. F	p. 399	GP 3
18. T	p. 402	GP 4
19. T	p. 402	GP 4
20. T	p. 404	GP 4
21. F	p. 407	GP 4
22. F	p. 408	GP 5
23. T	p. 408	GP 5
24. T	p. 410	GP 5
25. T	p. 411	GP 5

Multiple-Choice Self-Test

1. c	p. 389	GP 2
2. b	p. 389	GP 2
3. a	p. 389	GP 2
4. b	p. 399	GP 3
5. d	p. 389	GP 2
6. c	p. 389	GP 2
7. a	p. 389	GP 2
8. d	p. 405	GP 4
9. a	p. 389	GP 2
10. b	p. 389	GP 2
11. b	p. 405	GP 4
12. a	p. 390	GP 2
13. c	p. 390	GP 2

14. a	p. 408	GP 5
15. c	p. 390	GP 2
16. b	p. 390	GP 2
17. c	p. 401	GP 3
18. a	p. 391	GP 2
19. d	p. 413	GP 6
20. d	p. 389	GP 2
21. b	p. 416	GP 6
22. d	p. 392	GP 2
23. d	p. 393	GP 3
24. b	p. 395	GP 3
25. c	p. 395	GP 3

Organize It!

1.	p. 395	GP 3
2.	pp. 396-397	GP 3
3.	p. 391	GP 2
4.	pp. 405-406	GP 4

Short Essay Questions

1.	pp. 408-409	GP 5
2.	p. 415	GP 6
3.	p. 418	GP 7
4.	p. 418	GP 3

CHAPTER 12: PSYCHOSOCIAL DEVELOPMENT IN ADOLESCENCE

This chapter focuses on the search for identity in adolescence, sexuality, and relationships with family, peers, and adult society. The views of Erikson, Marcia, and Elkind are explored. Focus boxes examine the topics of preventing teen pregnancy and the youth violence epidemic in the United States.

Guideposts for Study

1. How do adolescents form an identity?

2. What determines sexual orientation?

3. What sexual practices are common among adolescents, and what leads some to engage in risky sexual behavior?

4. How common are sexually transmitted diseases and teenage pregnancy, and what are the usual outcomes?

5. How typical is "adolescent rebellion"?

6. How do adolescents relate to parents, siblings, and peers?

7. What are the root causes of antisocial behavior and juvenile delinquency, and what can be done to reduce these and other risks of adolescence?

Detailed Chapter Outline and Key Terms

I. THE SEARCH FOR IDENTITY
Identity: According to Erikson, a coherent conception of the self, made up of goals, values, and beliefs to which a person is solidly committed.
A. Erikson: Identity versus Identity Confusion
- **Identity versus identity confusion**: Erikson's fifth crisis of psychosocial development, in which an adolescent seeks to develop a coherent sense of self, including the role she or he is to play in society. Also called *identity versus role confusion*.
- *Industry versus inferiority:* Erikson's crisis of middle childhood, in which children acquire the skills needed for success in their culture.
- *Psychological moratorium:* In Erikson's theory, a "time-out" period that is provided by adolescence.
- *Fidelity:* In Erikson's theory, the virtue attained in the fifth crisis, involving sustained loyalty, faith, and/or a sense of belonging to loved ones.
B. Marcia: Identity Status—Crisis and Commitment
- **Identity statuses**: States of ego development that depend on the presence or absence of crisis and commitment.
- *Identity-status interviews:* Semi-structured interviews lasting approximately 30 minutes, during which a person's identity status is determined.

- **Crisis**: A period of conscious decision making related to identity formation.
- **Commitment**: Personal investment in an occupation or system of beliefs.
- **Identity achievement**: Identity status that is characterized by a commitment to choices made following a crisis, a period spent in exploring alternatives.
- **Foreclosure**: Identity status in which a person who has not spent time considering alternatives (i.e., has not been in crisis) is committed to other people's plans for his or her life.
- **Moratorium**: Identity status in which a person is currently considering alternatives (in crisis) and seems headed for commitment.
- **Identity diffusion**: Identity status that is characterized by absence of commitment and lack of serious consideration of alternatives.

C. Gender Differences in Identity Formation
D. Ethnic Factors in Identity Formation
Four Stages of Ethnic Identity:
1. *Diffuse:* Little or no exploration of ethnic identity, no clear understanding of issues involved.
2. *Foreclosed:* Little or no exploration of ethnic identity, but has positive or negative feelings about it from attitudes absorbed at home.
3. *Moratorium:* Has begun to explore ethnic identity but is confused about what it means.
4. *Achieved:* Has explored ethnic identity and understands and accepts it.

II. SEXUALITY
A. Sexual Orientation
- **Sexual orientation**: Focus of consistent sexual, romantic, and affectionate interest, either heterosexual, homosexual, or bisexual.
- *Heterosexual:* Attracted to persons of the opposite sex.
- *Homosexual:* Attracted to persons of the same sex.
- *Bisexual:* Attracted to persons of either sex.

B. Sexual Behavior
1. Heterosexual Activity
2. Homosexual Identity and Behavior
C. Sexual Risk Taking
Sexually transmitted diseases (STDs): Diseases spread by sexual contact.
1. Early Sexual Activity
2. Contraceptive Use
3. Where Do Teenagers Get Information about Sex?
D. Sexually Transmitted Diseases (STDs)
E. Teenage Pregnancy and Childbearing

III. RELATIONSHIPS WITH FAMILY, PEERS, AND ADULT SOCIETY
A. Is Adolescent Rebellion a Myth?
Adolescent rebellion: Pattern of emotional turmoil, characteristic of a minority of adolescents, which may involve conflict with family, alienation from adult society, reckless behavior, and rejection of adult values.
B. Changing Time Use and Changing Relationships

C. Adolescents and Parents
   1. Conversation, Autonomy, and Conflict
   2. Parenting Styles
   3. Family Structure and Mothers' Employment
   4. Economic Stress
D. Adolescents and Siblings
E. Adolescents and Peers
   1. Popularity
      • *Peer status groups:* Status of popularity or lack of popularity among schoolchildren, determined by asking children to name the classmates they like most and least.
      • *Popular:* Children who received many positive nominations.
      • *Rejected:* Children who received many negative nominations.
      • *Neglected:* Children who received few nominations, either negative or positive type.
      • *Controversial:* Children who received many positive and negative nominations.
      • *Average:* Children who did not receive an unusual number of either kind of nomination.
   2. Friendships
F. Adolescents in Trouble: Antisocial Behavior and Juvenile Delinquency
   1. Becoming a Delinquent: How Influences Interact
   2. Preventing and Treating Delinquency

True/False Self-Test

Place a T or an F in the appropriate space. These questions are taken from the chapter content, tables, key terms, Guideposts for Study, and Checkpoints.

1. _____ Erikson has described the psychosocial crisis of adolescence as industry versus inferiority.

2. _____ A central concern during adolescence is the search for the right marriage partner.

3. _____ Foreclosure is one of James Marcia's four identity statuses.

4. _____ Ethnicity is an unimportant part of identity.

5. _____ Adolescents who accept the plans of others as their goals are in foreclosure status.

6. _____ Erikson believed that identity and intimacy develop together for women.

7. _____ Sexual orientation appears to be influenced by peer group pressure.

8. _____ Sexual attitudes and behaviors are more liberal than in the past.

9. _____ Adolescents who are at greatest risk for sexually transmitted diseases are those who become sexually active late.

10. ___ Sexually transmitted diseases have become far more prevalent since the 1960s.

11. ___ Teenage pregnancy and birth rates are climbing in the United States.

12. ___ Conflict with parents tends to be more frequent in early adolescence and more intense in middle adolescence.

13. ___ Conflict in Asian and European cultures is more likely with mothers than with fathers.

14. ___ Authoritative parenting is most often associated with positive outcomes.

15. ___ Economic stress does not affect relationships in two-parent families.

16. ___ Most juvenile delinquents grow up to be law-abiding citizens.

17. ___ Relationships with siblings tend to become more equal and more distant during adolescence.

18. ___ In three out of four assaults or murders by young people, the perpetrators are members of gangs.

19. ___ Violence and antisocial behavior have roots in childhood.

20. ___ Children who are raised in a rejecting or coercive atmosphere or in an overly permissive or chaotic one tend to show aggressive behavior, and the hostility they evoke in others increases their own aggression.

21. ___ Adolescents are more likely to turn violent if they have witnessed or have been victims of violence, such as physical abuse or neighborhood fights.

22. ___ Peer interactions can stimulate moral growth if the peer climate is positive.

23. ___ STDs are more likely to develop undetected in men than in women.

24. ___ Friendships become more intimate and supportive in adolescence, especially among girls.

25. ___ In Marcia's terminology, commitment is a personal investment in an occupation or system of beliefs.

Multiple-Choice Self-Test

Circle the letter of the best answer. These questions are based on many aspects of the chapter content, in no particular order.

1. The chief task of adolescence, according to Erikson, is
   a. trust vs. mistrust.
   b. identity vs. identity confusion.
   c. autonomy vs. shame and doubt.
   d. industry vs. guilt.

2. According to Erikson, adolescents form their identity by
   a. modeling themselves after other people.
   b. following their parents' wishes.
   c. getting an education.
   d. modifying and synthesizing earlier identifications.

3. Cliquishness and intolerance of differences are
   a. abnormal and extreme reactions.
   b. hallmarks of autism.
   c. seen mainly in Asian girls.
   d. normal adolescent defenses against identity confusion.

4. Identity forms as young people resolve the following:
   a. choice of an occupation
   b. adoption of values to believe in and live by
   c. development of a satisfying sexual identity
   d. All of the above.

5. Erikson's theory
   a. describes male identity development as the norm.
   b. describes female identity development as the norm.
   c. describes males as achieving identity through intimacy.
   d. is invalid today.

6. An adolescent who has made commitments, not as a result of a crisis, but by accepting someone else's plans for his or her life, is in
   a. moratorium.
   b. foreclosure.
   c. identity achievement.
   d. identity diffusion.

7. An adolescent who is unsure, unhappy, lonely, has no commitments to serious goals, and has only superficial friendships is in
   a. identity diffusion.
   b. moratorium.
   c. foreclosure.
   d. identity achievement.

8. Most research supports Erikson's view that, for women,
   a. identity and intimacy are unrelated.
   b. intimacy and identity develop together.
   c. more time is spent in identity diffusion.
   d. more time is spent in foreclosure.

9. During adolescence, self-esteem develops largely
   a. in the context of relationships with parents.
   b. in the context of relationships with peers.
   c. as a result of employment.
   d. as a function of academic excellence.

10. Identity formation is especially complicated for
    a. young people in minority groups.
    b. girls.
    c. boys.
    d. All of the above.

11. In the stages of ethnic identity, a girl who has begun to explore her ethnicity but is confused about what it means is in which stage?
a. diffuse
b. achieved
c. foreclosed
d. moratorium

12. The urgent awareness of _____ is an important aspect of identity formation.
a. self-esteen
b. gender
c. ethnicity
d. sexuality

13. Homosexuality is
a. considered a mental illness.
b. a consequence of poor parental supervision.
c. the result of imbalanced hormones.
d. no longer considered a mental disorder.

14. Sexual orientation
a. may be at least partially genetic.
b. may be influenced by a complex prenatal process.
c. may be influenced by biological, psychological, and social influences.
d. All of the above.

15. The sexual evolution has
a. brought more acceptance of homosexuality.
b. reduced tolerance of homosexuality.
c. not affected attitudes about homosexuality.
d. brought more tension and confusion.

16. The likelihood of early sexual activity is influenced by
a. early entrance into puberty.
b. poor school performance.
c. poverty.
d. All of the above.

17. The best safeguard for sexually active teens is

a. regular use of condoms.
b. regular church attendance.
c. private school.
d. home schooling.

18. Adolescents who do not use contraceptives, or who use them irregularly or ineffectively,
a. tend to be in their early teens.
b. tend to be in their late teens.
c. usually have high self-esteem.
d. are very experienced with sex.

19. Teenagers in the "high-risk group"
a. tend to have low grades.
b. are usually frequent drinkers.
c. tend to have been abused by parents.
d. All of the above.

20. Many teenagers obtain their unrealistic information about sex from
a. school classes.
b. the media.
c. peers.
d. parents.

21. Teenage pregnancy rates in the United States are
a. the lowest in six decades.
b. many times higher than in other industrialized countries.
c. the same as in Sweden.
d. lower than most industrialized countries.

22. Abstinence-only sex education programs
a. do not lead to more sexual activity.
b. increase sexual activity among preteens.
c. do not delay sexual activity.
d. are highly successful

23. The most prevalent STD is
a. human papilloma virus.
b. chlamydia.
c. AIDS.
d. genital herpes virus.

24. Full-fledged teenage rebellion is
a. a normal result of hormonal changes.
b. normal.
c. uncommon even in Western societies.
d. None of the above.

25. "Storm and stress" is
a. universal.
b. not universal.
c. common to American teenagers.
d. mainly biological in source.

Organize It!

Making lists is a fun and useful way to categorize information in your mind. After making each list, think of ways to memorize it so that you have immediate recall. Singing a list, dancing while you recite it, or simply saying it in a rhythmic pattern as you are walking, driving, or jogging allows your brain to store the information in easily retrievable form. Try it!

1. List Marcia's four types of identity status.

    1.
    2.
    3.
    4.

2. List seven factors associated with the timing of first intercourse (see Table 12-3).

    1.
    2.
    3.
    4.
    5.
    6.
    7.

3. List the eight most common sexually transmitted diseases (see Table 12-4).

    1.
    2.
    3
    4.
    5.
    6.
    7.
    8.

4. List the three major issues involved in identity formation, according to Erikson.

    1.
    2.
    3.

Short Essay Questions

These short essay questions are based on the Checkpoints in the chapter. Answer each question as completely and succinctly as possible.

1. Discuss the five peer status groups and the likelihood for each of future adjustment problems.

2. Discuss theories and research regarding origins of sexual orientation.

3. Summarize trends in teenage pregnancy and birth rate. Include in your discussion the problems and outcomes of teenage pregnancy and your suggestions for preventing it.

4. Identify age and cultural differences in how young people spend their time, and discuss their significance.

5. Discuss important features of girls' and boys' friendships in adolescence.

Critical Thinking Questions

These questions may be used in small group discussions or as extra-credit reports.

1. Which of Marcia's identity statuses do you think you fit into as an adolescent? Has your identity status changed since then? If so, how?

2. If you learned that your son or daughter was homosexual rather than heterosexual, how do you think you would feel? What would you say or do?

3. If you have siblings, how are your relationships with them different now from what they were when you were adolescents?

4. Should the media be held responsible for the prevalence of violence portrayed in the various formats (e.g., television, movies)? What can parents do to help prevent violence in their adolescent children?

Answer Keys

True/False Self-Test

1. F	p. 425	GP 1
2. F	p. 425	GP 1
3. T	p. 427	GP 1
4. F	p. 429	GP 1
5. T	p. 428	GP 1
6. T	p. 428	GP 1
7. F	p. 430	GP 2
8. T	p. 431	GP 3
9. F	p. 433	GP 3
10. T	p. 436	GP 4
11. F	p. 439	GP 4
12. T	p. 442	GP 6
13. T	p. 442	GP 6

14. T	p. 442	GP 6
15. F	p. 445	GP 6
16. T	p. 449	GP 7
17. T	p. 445	GP 6
18. T	p. 450	GP 7
19. T	p. 450	GP 7
20. T	p. 451	GP 7
21. T	p. 451	GP 7
22. T	p. 452	GP 7
23. F	p. 437	GP 3
24. T	p. 448	GP 6
25. T	p. 427	GP 1

Multiple-Choice Self-Test

1. b	p. 425	GP 1
2. d	p. 425	GP 1
3. d	p. 425	GP 1
4. d	p. 426	GP 1
5. a	p. 426	GP 1
6. b	p. 428	GP 1
7. a	p. 428	GP 1
8. b	p. 428	GP 1
9. b	p. 429	GP 1
10. a	p. 429	GP 1
11. d	p. 430	GP 1
12. d	p. 430	GP 2
13. d	p. 430	GP 2

14. d	p. 431	GP 2
15. a	p. 432	GP 2
16. d	p. 433	GP 2
17. a	p. 434	GP 2
18. a	p. 434	GP 2
19. d	p. 433	GP 2
20. b	p. 435	GP 2
21. a	p. 438	GP 4
22. c	p. 435	GP 3
23. a	p. 436	GP 4
24. c	p. 440	GP 5
25. b	p. 440	GP 5

Organize It!

1.	pp. 427-428	GP 1
2.	p. 434	GP 3
3.	p. 438	GP 4
4.	p. 426	GP 1

Short Essay Questions

1.	pp. 430-431	GP 6
2.	p. 439	GP 2
3.	pp. 440-441	GP 4
4.	pp. 464-465	GP 6
5.	p. 448	GP 6

PART 6: YOUNG ADULTHOOD

CHAPTER 13: PHYSICAL AND COGNITIVE DEVELOPMENT IN YOUNG ADULTHOOD

This chapter introduces Part 6 of the text. The chapter explores physical development, cognitive development, moral development, education, and work. The focus boxes examine assisted fertility and the development of faith across the life span.

Guideposts for Study

1. In what physical condition is the typical young adult, and what factors affect health and well-being?

2. What are some sexual and reproductive issues at this time of life?

3. What is distinctive about adult thought and intelligence?

4. How does moral reasoning develop?

5. How do higher education and work affect cognitive development?

6. How can continuing education help adults meet workplace demands?

Detailed Chapter Outline with Key Terms

PHYSICAL DEVELOPMENT
I. HEALTH AND PHYSICAL CONDITION
   A. Health Status
   B. Genetic Influences on Health
   C. Behavioral Influences on Health and Fitness
      1. Nutrition and Cholesterol
      2. Obesity
         - **Obesity**: Extreme overweight, often measured in adults by a body mass index of 30 or more or by more than 25 percent body fat in men and more than 30 percent in women.
         - *Body mass index (BMI):* The number of kilograms of weight per square meter of height.
         - *Leptin:* A protein found in the brain that is related to appetite.
      3. Physical Activity
      4. Smoking
      5. Alcohol
      Alcoholism: Chronic disease involving dependence on use of alcohol, causing interference with normal functioning and fulfillment of obligations.
      6. Drug Use

D. Indirect Influences on Health and Fitness
   1. Socioeconomic Status and Race/Ethnicity
   2. Gender
   3. Relationships and Health

II. SEXUAL AND REPRODUCTIVE ISSUES
   A. **Premenstrual syndrome (PMS)**: Disorder producing symptoms of physical discomfort and emotional tension during the one to two weeks before a menstrual period.
   B. Sexually Transmitted Diseases (STDs)
      1. **Infertility**: Inability to conceive after 12 to 18 months of trying.
      2. Assisted Reproduction
         • *In vitro fertilization (IVF):* Fertilization outside the mother's body, usually in a gel-filled laboratory dish.
         • *Intracytoplasmic sperm injection (ICSI):* Injection of a single sperm directly into the egg cell.
         • *Artificial insemination:* The injection of sperm into a woman's vagina, cervix, or uterus.
         • *Donor insemination:* Artificial insemination using the sperm of a donor.
         • *Ovum transfer:* An egg (*donor egg*) from another woman is fertilized in vitro and then inserted into the prospective mother's uterus.
         • *Gamete intrafallopian transfer (GIFT):* Egg and sperm are inserted into the fallopian tube.
         • *Zygote intrafallopian transfer (ZIFT):* A fertilized egg is inserted into the fallopian tube.
         • *Surrogate motherhood:* A fertile woman is impregnated by the prospective father, usually by artificial insemination, and the woman carries the baby to term and gives the child to the father and his mate.

COGNITIVE DEVELOPMENT
III. PERSPECTIVES ON ADULT COGNITION
   A. Beyond Piaget: The Shift to Postformal Thought
   Postformal thought: Mature type of thinking, which relies on subjective experience and intuition as well as logic and is useful in dealing with ambiguity, uncertainty, inconsistency, contradiction, imperfection, and compromise.
   Four Criteria of Postformal Thought:
   1. *Shifting gears:* Ability to shift back and forth between the abstract and the practical.
   2. *Multiple causality, multiple solutions:* Awareness that most problems have more than one cause and more than one solution, with some solutions more likely to work than others.
   3. *Pragmatism:* Ability to choose the best of several possible solutions and to recognize the criteria for choosing.
   4. *Awareness of a paradox:* Recognition that a problem or solution involves inherent conflict.

B. Schaie: A Life-Span Model of Cognitive Development
Schaie's Seven Stages:
  1. **Acquisitive stage**: Children and adolescents learn information and skills largely for their own sake or as preparation for participation in society.
  2. **Achieving stage**: Young adults use knowledge to gain competence and independence.
  3. **Responsible stage**: Middle-aged people are concerned with long-range goals and practical problems related to their responsibility for others.
  4. **Executive stage**: Middle-aged people responsible for societal systems deal with complex relationships on several levels.
  5. **Reorganizational stage**: Adults entering retirement reorganize their lives around nonwork-related activities.
  6. **Reintegrative stage**: Older adults choose to focus limited energy on tasks that have meaning to them.
  7. **Legacy-creating stage**: Very old people prepare for death by recording their life stories, distributing possessions, and the like.
C. Sternberg: Insight and Know-How
  - **Experiential element**: In Sternberg's triarchic theory, the insightful aspect of intelligence, which determines how effectively people approach both novel and familiar tasks.
  - **Contextual element**: In Sternberg's triarchic theory, the practical aspect of intelligence, which determines how effectively people deal with their environment.
  - **Componential element**: In Sternberg's triarchic theory, the analytic aspect of intelligence, which determines how efficiently people process information and solve problems.
  - **Tacit knowledge**: In Sternberg's terminology, information that is not formally taught or openly expressed but is necessary to get ahead.
    ➢ *Self-management:* Part of tacit knowledge, knowing how to motivate oneself and organize time and energy.
    ➢ *Management of tasks:* Part of tacit knowledge, knowing how to do particular tasks.
    ➢ *Management of others:* Part of tacit knowledge, knowing when to reward or criticize subordinates.
D. Emotional Intelligence
  Emotional intelligence: In Salovey's and Mayer's terminology, ability to understand and regulate emotions; an important component of effective, intelligent behavior.
  - *Self-awareness:* A competency relying on emotional intelligence (EI), in which a person is aware of emotions and is self-confident and an accurate assessor of self.
  - *Self-management:* A competency relying on emotional intelligence (EI), in which a person has self-control, adaptability, and a drive to achieve among other qualities.
  - *Social awareness:* A competency relying on emotional intelligence (EI), in which a person has empathy and is oriented toward helping others.
  - *Relationship management:* A competency relying on emotional intelligence (EI), in which a person can develop others, exert influence, communicate effectively, and be a good leader.

IV. MORAL DEVELOPMENT
Culture and Moral Development
A. The Seventh Stage
B. Gender and Moral Development

V. EDUCATION AND WORK
A. The Transition to College

Distance learning: A type of learning in which the instructor and student are separated by space, and sometimes, by time.

1. Cognitive Growth in College
   - *Statistical and methodological reasoning:* The ability to generate patterns.
   - *Conditional reasoning:* Formal deductive logic.
   - *Verbal reasoning:* The ability to recognize arguments, evaluate evidence, and detect analogies.
   - *Commitment within relativism:* When a young adult is able to make his or her own judgments and choose his or her own beliefs and values despite uncertainty and the recognition of other valid possibilities.

B. Entering the World of Work
C. Cognitive Complexity of Work
   - **Substantive complexity**: Degree to which a person's work requires thought and independent judgment.
   - *Fronto-polar prefrontal cortex (FPPC):* The most frontward part of the frontal lobes, with a special role in problem solving and planning.
   - *Branching:* Ability to put an unfinished task "on hold" and shift attention to another task.
   - **Spillover hypothesis**: Hypothesis that a positive correlation exists between intellectuality of work and of leisure activities because of a carryover of learning from work to leisure.

D. Adult Education and Literacy

Literacy: In an adult, ability to use printed and written information to function in society, achieve goals, and develop knowledge and potential.

True/False Self-Test

Place a T or an F in the appropriate space. These questions are taken from the chapter content, tables, key terms, Guideposts for Study, and Checkpoints.

1. _____ The typical young adult is in good condition; physical and sensory abilities are usually excellent.

2. _____ Social relationships, especially marriage, tend to be associated with physical and mental health.

3. _____ Alcoholism is not a major health problem of young adults.

4. _____ Homicide is the leading cause of death for young adults.

5. ____ Men tend to live longer than women do, in part for biological reasons.

6. ____ Schaie has proposed five stages of age-related cognitive development based on social roles and objectives of learning.

7. ____ Emotional intelligence may play an important part in intelligent behavior and life success.

8. ____ According to Lawrence Kohlberg, moral development depends entirely on genetics.

9. ____ Experience may be interpreted differently in various cultural contexts.

10. ___ Carol Gilligan proposed that women have moral concerns and perspectives that are not tapped in Kohlberg's theory.

11. ___ Tests that measure componential knowledge are unrelated to traditional intelligence tests.

12. ___ According to Perry, college students' thinking tends to progress from flexibility to rigidity.

13. ___ Research has found a relationship between substantive complexity of work and cognitive growth.

14. ___ According to the spillover hypothesis, people who do more complex work tend to engage in more intellectually demanding leisure activities.

15. ___ Nearly 20 percent of U.S. couples experience infertility.

16. ___ Worldwide, women tend to earn less than men do, and they often do low-paid, low-status work.

17. ___ In developed countries, literacy is directly linked to occupational status and income.

18. ___ In developing countries, illiteracy is more common among men than women.

19. ___ An increasing number of older women are returning to school.

20. ___ Postformal thought is relativistic.

21. ___ Shifting gears, pragmatism, multiple causality, and awareness of paradox are all part of Sinnott's criteria of postformal thought.

22. ___ Schaie's acquisitive stage usually occurs in people in their late teens or early twenties.

23. ___ According to Kohlberg, the first level of moral reasoning is postconventional morality.

24. ___ In Chinese society, people follow Kohlberg's justice-guided morality.

25. ___ According to Gilligan, a woman's central moral dilemma is the conflict between her own needs and those of others.

Multiple-Choice Self-Test

Circle the letter of the best answer. These questions are based on many aspects of the chapter content, in no particular order.

1. Some investigators propose a distinctively adult stage of cognition beyond formal operations, known as
   a. pragmatism.
   b. abstraction.
   c. pessimism.
   d. postformal thought.

2. The most common cause of infertility in men is
   a. premature ejaculation.
   b. anxiety.
   c. low sperm count.
   d. shyness.

3. Hormones of the menstrual cycle have protective effects but can also cause health problems, notably
   a. blockage of the fallopian tubes.
   b. premenstrual syndrome.
   c. promiscuity.
   d. hypothyroidism.

4. The AIDS epidemic in the United States is
   a. coming under control.
   b. is unchanged since 1960.
   c. is out of control.
   d. None of the above.

5. Globally, most HIV-infected adults are
   a. homosexual.
   b. heterosexual.
   c. IV drug users.
   d. people who have received transfusions.

6. In 1995, the leading cause of death for 25- to 44-year-olds in the United States was
   a. accidents.
   b. AIDS.
   c. heart disease.
   d. cancer.

7. The second of Schaie's five cognitive stages is
   a. executive stage.
   b. achieving stage.
   c. acquisitive stage.
   d. mythic-faith stage.

8. According to Perry, college students' thinking tends to progress in which order?
   a. rigid, flexible, freely chosen commitments
   b. flexible, rigid, freely chosen commitments
   c. freely chosen commitments, rigid, flexible
   d. freely chosen commitments, flexible, rigid

9. Emotional intelligence
   a. as a distinct construct is controversial and hard to measure.
   b. may play an important part in intelligent behavior.
   c. may play an important role in life success.
   d. All of the above.

10. According to Sternberg's triarchic theory of intelligence, which elements become particularly important during adulthood?
a. acquisitive, achieving
b. contextual, experiential
c. responsible, reintegrative
d. All of the above.

11. Currently, the leading causes of death for Americans ages 20 to 34 in order are
a. suicide, AIDS, and cancer.
b. cancer, accidents, and homicide.
c. accidents, homicide, and suicide.
d. heart disease, suicide, and homicide.

12. Schaie's reintegrative stage of cognitive development typically occurs in
a. late adulthood.
b. early adulthood.
c. middle adulthood.
d. adolescence.

13. Postformal thinking is
a. black and white.
b. relativistic.
c. polarized.
d. rigid

14. Thought in adulthood often
a. is flexible, open, and adaptive.
b. draws on intuition and emotion.
c. applies the fruits of experience to ambiguous situations.
d. All of the above.

15. Shifting gears, multiple causality, multiple solutions, pragmatism, and awareness of paradox are all proposed criteria of postformal thought by
a. Schaie.
b. Piaget.
c. Sinnott.
d. Erikson.

16. Recognition that a problem or solution involves inherent conflict ("Doing this will give him what he wants, but it will only make him unhappy in the end.") is known as
a. pragmatism.
b. awareness of paradox.
c. shifting gears.
d. multiple causality, multiple solutions.

17. Arthur Ashe's decision not to reveal that he had AIDS was based in part on his concern for his family's privacy. This is an example of which of Schaie's stages of cognitive development?
a. acquisitive
b. achieving
c. responsible
d. executive

18. Self-management, management of tasks, and management of others are all part of
a. tacit knowledge.
b. crisis orientation.
c. emotional intelligence.
d. None of the above.

19. Fowler's theory has been criticized for
a. underestimating the maturity of a simple, solid, unquestioning faith.
b. findings that may represent people of above average intelligence and education.
c. overlooking the adaptive value of conventional religious belief for many older adults.
d. All of the above.

20. Gilligan's first level of moral development in women is
a. goodness as self-sacrifice.
b. orientation of individual survival.
c. goodness to truth.
d. morality of nonviolence.

21. A woman who assesses her decisions not on the basis of how others will react to them but on her intentions and the consequences of her actions is in which of Gilligan's levels of moral development?
a. level 1
b. level 2
c. level 3
d. None of the above.

22. With regard to postsecondary education, socioeconomic status
a. plays a major part in access.
b. has no impact on access.
c. is used to "weed out" potential students.
d. None of the above.

23. Nearly _____ of U.S. adults are illiterate.
a. half
b. one-fourth
c. one-fifth
d. three-quarters

24. In general, those holding bachelor's degrees make _____ as do high-school graduates.
a. nearly twice as much money
b. nearly half as much money
c. about the same amount of money
d. nearly three times as much money

25. According to Schaie, the stage in which middle-aged people responsible for societal systems deal with complex relationships on several levels is
a. the achieving stage.
b. the executive stage.
c. the response stage.
d. the emotional stage.

Organize It!

Making lists is a fun and useful way to categorize information in your mind. After making each list, think of ways to memorize it so that you have immediate recall. Singing a list, dancing while you recite it, or simply saying it in a rhythmic pattern as you are walking, driving, or jogging allows your brain to store the information in easily retrievable form. Try it!

1. List Schaie's five stages of cognitive development.

   1.
   2.
   3.
   4.
   5.

2. List Gilligan's three levels of women's moral development.

   1.
   2.
   3.

3. List Fowler's six stages of the development of faith.

1.
2.
3
4.
5.
6.

4. List and briefly describe six means of assisted reproduction.

1.

2.

3.

4.

5.

6.

Short Essay Questions

These short essay questions are based on the Checkpoints in the chapter. Answer each question as completely and succinctly as possible.

1. Discuss how relationships, especially marriage, affect mental and physical health.

2. Should surrogate parenthood be made illegal? If not, under what conditions should it be allowed?

3. Compare several theoretical views on adult cognition.

4. State Gilligan's original position on gender differences in moral development, and summarize research findings on the subject.

5. Tell how college, and working while in college, can affect cognitive development.

6. Explain the relationship between substantive complexity of work and cognitive development.

Critical Thinking Questions

These questions can be used in small group discussions or for extra-credit reports.

1. What kind of lifestyle changes would you need to make to live a healthier lifestyle?

2. If you or your partner were infertile, which of the methods of assisted reproduction might you try? Why or why not?

3. Think of the most intelligent person you know. How does this person relate to each of Sternberg's three components of intelligence?

4. Which, if either, do you consider to be higher moral priorities: justice and rights, or compassion and care?

5. Where do you fit in Fowler's stages of faith?

Answer Keys

True/False Self-Test

1. T	p. 459	GP 1		14. T	p. 486	GP 5
2. T	p. 468	GP 1		15. F	p. 470	GP 2
3. F	p. 464	GP 1		16. T	p. 485	GP 5
4. F	p. 459	GP 1		17. T	p. 487	GP 6
5. F	p. 467	GP 1		18. F	p. 487	GP 6
6. T	p. 474	GP 3		19. T	p. 482	GP 5
7. T	p. 477	GP 3		20. T	p. 473	GP 3
8. F	p. 478	GP 4		21. T	p. 473	GP 3
9. T	p. 479	GP 4		22. F	p. 474	GP 3
10. T	p. 480	GP 4		23. F	p. 478	GP 4
11. F	p. 476	GP 3		24. F	p. 479	GP 4
12. F	p. 485	GP 5		25. T	p. 480	GP 4
13. T	p. 486	GP 5				

Multiple-Choice Self-Test

1. d	p. 473	GP 3		14. d	p. 473	GP 3
2. c	p. 470	GP 2		15. c	p. 473	GP 3
3. b	p. 469	GP 2		16. b	p. 473	GP 3
4. a	p. 469	GP 2		17. c	p. 474	GP 3
5. b	p. 469	GP 2		18. a	p. 476	GP 3
6. b	p. 469	GP 2		19. d	p. 483	GP 4
7. b	p. 474	GP 3		20. b	p. 481	GP 4
8. a	p. 485	GP 5		21. b	p. 481	GP 4
9. d	p. 477	GP 3		22. a	p. 483	GP 5
10. b	p. 476	GP 3		23. a	p. 487	GP 6
11. c	p. 459	GP 1		24. a	p. 485	GP 5
12. a	p. 475	GP 3		25. b	p. 474	GP 3
13. b	p. 473	GP 3				

Organize It!

1.	pp. 474-475	GP 3
2.	pp. 480-481	GP 4
3.	pp. 482-483	GP 4
4.	pp. 470-471	GP 2

Short Essay Questions

1.	p. 468	GP 1
2.	p. 472	GP 2
3.	pp. 472-478	GP 3
4.	pp. 480-481	GP 4
5.	pp. 484-486	GP 5
6.	p. 486	GP 5

CHAPTER 14: PSYCHOSOCIAL DEVELOPMENT IN YOUNG ADULTHOOD

This chapter explores four theoretical approaches to psychosocial development in young adulthood and continues with a discussion of the foundations of intimate relationships, marital and nonmarital lifestyles, and family life. The two focus boxes discuss cultural conceptions of love and domestic violence.

Guideposts for Study

1. Does personality change during adulthood, and if so, how?

2. What is intimacy, and how is it expressed in friendship, love, and sexuality?

3. Why do some people remain single?

4. How do homosexuals deal with "coming out," and what is the nature of gay and lesbian relationships?

5. What are the pros and cons of cohabitation?

6. What do adults gain from marriage, what cultural patterns surround entrance into marriage, and why do some marriages succeed while others fail?

7. When do most adults become parents, and how does parenthood affect a marriage?

8. How do dual-earner couples divide responsibilities and deal with role conflicts?

9. Why have divorce rates risen, and how do adults adjust to divorce, remarriage, and stepparenthood?

Detailed Chapter Outline with Key Terms

I. PERSONALITY DEVELOPMENT: FOUR VIEWS
   - **Normative-stage models**: Theoretical models that describe psychosocial development in terms of a definite sequence of age-related changes.
   - **Timing-of-events model**: Theoretical model that describes adult psychosocial development as a response to the expected or unexpected occurrence and timing of important life events.
   - **Trait models**: Theoretical models that focus on mental, emotional, temperamental, and behavioral traits or attributes.
   - **Typological models**: Theoretical models that identify broad personality types or styles.
   A. Normative-Stage Models
   Stages: Successive periods in development.
      1. Erikson: Intimacy versus Isolation
         - **Intimacy versus isolation**: According to Erikson, the sixth stage of psychosocial development, in which young adults either make commitments to others or face a possible sense of isolation and consequent self-absorption.

- *Intimacies:* Contact of a sexual nature, which may take place in casual encounters.
- *Intimacy with a capital "I":* Intimacy that goes beyond mere sexuality.
- *Love:* In Erikson's theory, the virtue of the sixth stage; a mutual devotion between partners who have chosen to share their lives, have children, and help those children achieve their own healthy development.

2. Erikson's Heirs: Vaillant and Levinson
   - *Career consolidation:* In Vaillant's theory, stage of adult personality development in which men work hard at their careers and devote themselves to their families.
   - **Adaptive mechanisms**: Vaillant's term to describe four characteristic ways people adapt to life circumstances: *mature* (such as using humor or helping others), *immature* (such as developing aches and pains with no physical basis), *psychotic* (distorting or denying reality), and *neurotic* (repressing anxiety or developing irrational fears).
   - **Life structure**: In Levinson's theory, the underlying pattern of a person's life at a given time, built on whatever aspects of life the person finds most important.
   - *Dream:* In Levinson's theory, one's hopes about what one wishes to achieve in the future, part of the entry phase of young adulthood.

3. Evaluating Normative Stage Models

B. Timing-of-Events Model
   - **Normative life events**: In the timing-of-events model, commonly expected life experiences that occur at customary times. Also called *normative age-graded events*.
   - *On time:* Referring to events that happen when expected.
   - *Off time:* Referring to events that happen earlier or later than usual.
   - **Social clock**: Set of cultural norms or expectations for the times of life when certain important events, such as marriage, parenthood, entry into work, and retirement, should occur.

C. Trait Models: Costa and McCrae's Five Factors
   Five-factor model: Theoretical model, developed and tested by Costa and McCrae, based on the "Big Five" factors underlying clusters of related personality traits: neuroticism, extraversion, openness to experience, conscientiousness, and agreeableness.
   1. *Neuroticism:* A cluster of six negative traits indicating emotional instability: anxiety, hostility, depression, self-consciousness, impulsiveness, and vulnerability.
   2. *Extraversion:* A cluster of six facets: warmth, gregariousness, assertiveness, activity, excitement-seeking, and positive emotions.
   3. *Open to experience:* People high in this trait are willing to try new things and embrace new ideas.
   4. *Conscientiousness:* People high in this trait are achievers: competent, orderly, dutiful, deliberate, and disciplined.
   5. *Agreeable:* People who are trusting, straightforward, altruistic, compliant, modest, and easily swayed.

D. Typological Models
   - *Typological approach:* An approach to personality development that looks at personality as a functioning whole that affects and reflects attitudes, values, behavior, and social interactions.
   - **Ego-resiliency**: Adaptability under potential sources of stress.
   - **Ego-control**: Self-control.
   - *Ego-resilient:* Referring to people who are well adjusted, confident, and task-focused.

- *Overcontrolled:* Referring to people who are shy, quiet, anxious, and who withdraw from conflict.
- *Undercontrolled:* Referring to people who are active, energetic, impulsive, stubborn, and distractible.
- *Trajectories:* Long-term patterns of behavior.

E. Integrating Approaches to Personality Development
Six Basic Elements of Personality Theories:
1. *Basic tendencies:* Personality traits, physical health, appearance, gender, sexual orientation, intelligence, and artistic abilities.
2. *External influences:* Environmental influences.
3. *Characteristic adaptations:* Social roles, attitudes, interests, skills, activities, habits, and beliefs.
4. *Self-concept:* One's idea of self.
5. *Objective biography:* The events of a person's life.
6. *Dynamic processes:* Processes that promote change, such as learning.

II. FOUNDATIONS OF INTIMATE RELATIONSHIPS

Intimacy: Emotional and psychological closeness to another, often including but not limited to sexual contact, and including self-disclosure.
Self-disclosure: Revealing important information about oneself to another.

A. Friendship
B. Love
- **Triangular theory of love**: Sternberg's theory that patterns of love hinge on the balance among three elements: intimacy, passion, and commitment.
- *Passion:* The sexual desire component of love.
- *Commitment:* The decision to love and stay with the beloved.
- *The matching hypothesis:* The tendency of people to develop close relationships with people who are about equally attractive.

C. Sexuality: Issues and Attitudes
- *Reproductive:* Attitude concerning sex that sex is permissible only for reproductive purposes within marriage.
- *Recreational:* Attitude concerning sex that whatever feels good and doesn't hurt anyone is fine.
- *Relational:* Attitude that sex should be accompanied by love or affection, but not necessarily marriage.

III. NONMARITAL AND MARITAL LIFESTYLES

A. Single Life
B. Gay and Lesbian Relationships
Coming out: Process of openly disclosing one's homosexual orientation.
Four Stages of Coming Out:
1. Recognition of being homosexual.
2. Getting to know other homosexuals.
3. Telling family and friends.
4. Complete openness.

C. Cohabitation
  - **Cohabitation**: Status of a couple who live together and maintain a sexual relationship without being legally married.
  - *Consensual or informal union:* An unmarried couple living in a sexual relationship.
D. Marriage
  - *Polygyny:* A man's marriage to more than one woman at a time.
  - *Polyandry:* A woman's marriage to more than one man at a time.
  1. Entering Matrimony
  2. Sexual Activity after Marriage
  3. Factors in Marital Success or Failure

IV. PARENTHOOD
  A. Becoming Parents
  B. Parenthood as a Developmental Experience
  1. Men's and Women's Involvement in Parenthood
  2. How Parenthood Affects Marital Satisfaction
  C. How Dual-Earner Families Cope
  1. Benefits and Drawbacks of a Dual-Earner Lifestyle
  2. Division of Domestic Work and Effects on the Marriage

V. WHEN MARRIAGE ENDS
  A. Divorce
  1. Why Has Divorce Increased?
  2. Adjusting to Divorce
  Process: In divorce, a sequence of potentially stressful experiences that begin before physical separation and continue after it.
  B. Remarriage and Stepparenthood

True/False Self-Test

Place a T or an F in the appropriate space. These questions are taken from the chapter content, tables, key terms, Guideposts for Study, and Checkpoints.

1. _____ Openness to experience, neuroticism, and extraversion are some of the personality traits that do not change much after age 30, according to Costa and McCrae.

2. _____ In Erikson's theory, the crisis of young adulthood is intimacy versus isolation.

3. _____ Typological research focuses on age-related social and emotional changes emerging in successive periods marked by crises.

4. _____ In Levinson's theory, transitions or crises lead to reevaluation and modification of the life structure.

5. _____ The most important message of the normative-stage models is that adults continue to change, develop, and grow.

6. ____ Since the mid-twentieth century, Western societies have become more age-conscious.

7. ____ Intimacy includes a sense of belonging.

8. ____ The development of identity is the crucial task of young adulthood.

9. ____ People tend to be healthier physically if they have satisfying close relationships.

10. ____ Intimacy, passion, and commitment are the main components of Sternberg's triangular theory of love.

11. ____ Intimacy has no connection to physical and mental health.

12. ____ About 80 percent of Americans have traditional (reproductive) attitudes about sex.

13. ____ Most people no longer disapprove of homosexuality.

14. ____ Women's friendships tend to be more intimate than men's.

15. ____ People tend to choose partners like themselves and, according to the matching hypothesis, become more alike with time.

16. ____ Only 10 percent of adults say they have changed their sexual behavior because of AIDS.

17. ____ Today more adults postpone marriage or never marry.

18. ____ Gay men and lesbian women do not form enduring romantic relationships.

19. ____ Cohabitation has become common and is the norm in many countries.

20. ____ Couples who cohabit before marriage tend to have stronger marriages.

21. ____ Men benefit more than women from marriage.

22. ____ Age at marriage is a major predictor of whether a marriage will last.

23. ____ Women who give birth at a later age tend to make more money than those who give birth while young.

24. ____ Expectations and sharing of tasks can contribute to a marriage's deterioration or improvement.

25. ____ Most divorced people never remarry.

Multiple-Choice Self-Test

Circle the letter of the best answer. These questions are based on many aspects of the chapter content, in no particular order.

1. During the childraising years, marital satisfaction typically
   a. declines.
   b. increases.
   c. remains unchanged.
   d. greatly increases.

2. Couples who choose to remain childless do so on the basis of
   a. concern over the financial burdens of parenthood.
   b. a wish to enjoy an adult lifestyle.
   c. a desire to concentrate on careers.
   d. All of the above.

3. In the U.S. the rate of divorce
   a. is the highest in the world.
   b. is about 4 divorces per year for each 1,000 people.
   c. has tripled for women born between 1945 and 1954.
   d. All of the above.

4. Divorced men are
   a. more likely to remarry than are women.
   b. not likely to remarry.
   c. unusually happy.
   d. just as likely to remarry as are women.

5. Who among the following is likely to adjust better to divorce?
   a. older women
   b. those without children
   c. those with higher incomes
   d. All of the above.

6. For homosexuals, the process of coming out
   a. is very short.
   b. may last well into adulthood.
   c. is usually over by late adolescence.
   d. does not occur until midlife.

7. Frequency of sexual relations in a marriage
   a. declines with age.
   b. increases with years of marriage.
   c. is unpredictable.
   d. depends entirely on religious beliefs.

8. Marriage
   a. meets economic needs.
   b. meets sexual and reproductive needs.
   c. benefits men and women equally.
   d. All of the above.

9. Couples who cohabit before marriage
   a. tend to be happier.
   b. tend to have weaker marriages.
   c. tend to have stronger marriages.
   d. usually stay together forever.

10. A major predictor of whether a marriage will last is
   a. age at marriage.
   b. physical attractiveness.
   c. social status.
   d. job status.

11. In most cases, the burdens of a dual-earner lifestyle fall most heavily on
   a. the woman.
   b. the man.
   c. both the woman and the man.
   d. the person with the largest income.

12. In blended families, who has the most difficulty being a stepparent?
   a. stepfathers
   b. stepmothers
   c. both parents
   d. neither parent

13. Divorce in the U.S. is high because of
a. greater "expectability" of divorce.
b. women's greater financial independence.
c. reluctance to expose children to parental conflict.
d. All of the above.

14. According to Costa and McCrae, people who are trusting, straightforward, altruistic, compliant, modest, and easily swayed are
a. agreeable.
b. extraverts.
c. conscientious.
d. neurotic.

15. In Block's model, people who are active, energetic, compulsive, stubborn, and easily distracted are
a. overcontrolled.
b. undercontrolled.
c. ego-resilient.
d. type A personalities.

16. The normative-stage models are largely the work of
a. George Vaillant and Daniel Levinson.
b. Sigmund Freud.
c. Albert Bandura.
d. Carl Rogers.

17. In Levinson's view, a man who is building his first provisional life structure faces these two important tasks
a. finding a job and a home.
b. finding a wife and a home.
c. finding a dream and an occupation.
d. finding the right geographic location.

18. A characteristic of men's friendships is
a. sharing of information and activities.
b. sharing of confidences.
c. intimacy.
d. All of the above.

19. According to Sternberg, love that involves intimacy and passion, but lacks commitment is
a. empty love.
b. romantic love.
c. fatuous love.
d. consummate love.

20. According to Sternberg, love that involves passion, but lacks intimacy and commitment is
a. liking.
b. infatuation.
c. empty love.
d. consummate love.

21. Consummate love is
a. easier to reach than to hold on to.
b. "love at first sight."
c. the kind of love that leads to a whirlwind courtship.
d. found in long-term relationships that lack intimacy and passion.

22. The type of love in which intimacy and commitment are both present, but in which physical attraction has died down, leaving partners close and likely to stay together is
a. empty love.
b. companionate love.
c. consummate love.
d. liking.

23. College women are
a. happier overall than other women.
b. more likely to become rape victims than the general population.
c. less likely to become rape victims than the general population.
d. None of the above.

24. Gay and lesbian couples who live together
a. tend to be as committed as married couples.
b. tend to be less committed than married couples.
c. have unique commitment problems.
d. are overcommitted to each other.

25. Research has shown that couples who live together before marriage tend to have
a. unhappier marriages.
b. more risk of domestic violence.
c. less likelihood of divorce.
d. None of the above.

Organize It!

1. List the five factors in Costa and McCrae's trait model.

   1.
   2.
   3.
   4.
   5.

2. List two factors that are important elements of intimacy.

   1.
   2.

3. List the four stages of "coming out" for homosexuals.

   1.
   2.
   3.
   4.

4. List and describe Sternberg's eight patterns of loving (see Table 14-2).

   1.
   2.
   3.
   4.
   5.
   6.
   7.
   8.

Short Essay Questions

These short essay questions are based in part on the Checkpoints in the chapter. Answer each question as completely and succinctly as possible.

1. Summarize and compare five major theoretical approaches to adult personality development.

2. Summarize recent trends and gender differences in sexual attitudes and behavior.

3. Identify several benefits of marriage.

4. Compare men's and women's attitudes toward parenthood and parental responsibilities.

5. Discuss factors in adjustment to divorce.

Critical Thinking Questions

These questions may be used for extra credit or small-group discussion.

1. Which of the models presented in this chapter seems to most adequately describe your experience of psychosocial development? Why?

2. How might our ideas of love change in the future?

3. Should homosexuals be allowed to marry? To adopt children? Be covered by a partner's health care plan?

4. Is cohabitation before marriage a good idea or a bad idea? List your reasons.

5. Should divorce be harder to obtain in the United States than it presently is?

Answer Keys

True/False Self-Test

1.	T	p. 497	GP 1
2.	T	p. 494	GP 1
3.	F	p. 498	GP 1
4.	T	p. 495	GP 1
5.	T	p. 495	GP 1
6.	F	p. 496	GP 1
7.	T	p. 500	GP 2
8.	F	p. 500	GP 2
9.	T	p. 501	GP 2
10.	T	p. 501	GP 2
11.	F	p. 501	GP 2
12.	F	p. 503	GP 2
13.	F	p. 504	GP 2
14.	T	p. 501	GP 2
15.	T	p. 502	GP 2
16.	F	p. 503	GP 2
17.	T	p. 504	GP 3
18.	F	p. 506	GP 4
19.	T	p. 506	GP 5
20.	F	p. 507	GP 5
21.	F	p. 508	GP 6
22.	T	p. 510	GP 6
23	T	p. 513	GP 7
24.	T	p. 515	GP 7
25.	F	p. 518	GP 9

Multiple-Choice Self-Test

1.	a	p. 514	GP 7
2.	d	p. 512	GP 7
3.	d	p. 517	GP 9
4.	a	p. 518	GP 9
5.	d	p. 518	GP 9
6.	b	p. 505	GP 4
7.	a	p. 509	GP 6
8.	d	p. 508	GP 6
9.	b	p. 507	GP 5
10.	a	p. 510	GP 6
11.	a	p. 516	GP 8
12.	b	p. 519	GP 9
13.	d	p. 517	GP 9
14.	a	p. 497	GP 1
15.	b	p. 498	GP 1
16.	a	p. 494	GP 1
17.	c	p. 494	GP 1
18.	a	p. 501	GP 2
19.	b	p. 503	GP 2
20.	b	p. 503	GP 2
21.	a	p. 503	GP 2
22.	b	p. 503	GP 2
23.	b	p. 503	GP 2
24.	a	p. 506	GP 4
25.	a	p. 507	GP 5

Organize It!

1.	p. 496	GP 1
2.	p. 500	GP 2
3.	pp. 505-506	GP 4
4.	p. 503	GP 2

Short Essay Questions

1.	pp. 493-498	GP 1
2.	pp. 503-504	GP 2
3.	p. 508	GP 6
4.	p. 514	GP 7
5.	p. 518	GP 9

PART 7: MIDDLE ADULTHOOD

CHAPTER 15: PHYSICAL AND COGNITIVE DEVELOPMENT IN MIDDLE ADULTHOOD

Chapter 15 opens Part 7 with a discussion of middle age as a cultural construct. The sensory, psychomotor, structural, systemic, sexual, and reproductive changes are discussed in the first section, along with health concerns. The second section deals with cognition, creativity, and intelligence in middle age. Education and work conclude the chapter. The two focus boxes discuss menopause and moral leadership.

Guideposts for Study

1. What are the distinguishing features of middle age?

2. What physical changes generally occur during the middle years, and what is their psychological impact?

3. What factors affect health at midlife?

4. What cognitive gains and losses occur during middle age?

5. Do mature adults think differently than younger people do?

6. What accounts for creative achievement, and how does it change with age?

7. How have work patterns changed, and how does work contribute to cognitive development?

8. What is the value of education for mature learners?

Detailed Chapter Outline with Key Terms

I. MIDDLE AGE: A CULTURAL CONSTRUCT
   A. When Is Middle Age?
      Middle adulthood: The years between ages 40 and 65.
   B. The Meaning of Middle Age

PHYSICAL DEVELOPMENT
II. PHYSICAL CHANGES
   A. Sensory and Psychomotor Functioning
      Visual Problems Related to Age:
      • Near vision
      • Dynamic vision (reading moving signs)
      • Sensitivity to light
      • Visual search (for example, locating a sign)
      • Speed of processing

- **Presbyopia**: Farsightedness associated with aging, resulting when the lens of the eye becomes less elastic.
- **Myopia**: Nearsightedness.
- **Presbycusis**: Gradual loss of hearing, which accelerates after age 55, especially with regard to sounds at the upper frequencies.
- **Basal metabolism**: Use of energy to maintain vital functions.

B. Structural and Systemic Changes

Vital capacity: Amount of air that can be drawn in with a deep breath and expelled; may be a biological marker of aging.

C. Sexuality and Reproductive Functioning
   1. Menopause and Its Meaning
      - **Menopause**: Cessation of menstruation and of ability to bear children, typically around age 50.
      - **Perimenopause**: Period of several years during which a woman experiences physiological changes that bring on menopause; also called *climacteric*.
      a. Attitudes Toward Menopause
         Climacteric: In the early nineteenth century, referred to the period of life at which the vital forces begin to decline.
      b. Symptoms and Myths
   2. Changes in Male Sexuality
      Male climacteric: A period of physiological, emotional, and psychological change involving a man's reproductive system and other body systems.
   3. Sexual Activity
   4. Sexual Dysfunction
      - **Sexual dysfunction**: Persistent disturbance in sexual desire or sexual response.
      - **Erectile dysfunction**: Inability of a man to achieve or maintain an erect penis sufficient for satisfactory sexual performance. (Also called *impotence*.)
   5. Concern with Appearance and Attractiveness

III. HEALTH
   A. Health Concerns
   Hypertension: Chronically high blood pressure.
   B. Indirect Influences on Health: Socioeconomic Status
   C. Indirect Influences on Health: Race/Ethnicity
   D. Women's Health after Menopause
      1. Heart Disease
      2. Bone Loss and Osteoporosis
      Osteoporosis: Condition in which the bones become thin and brittle as a result of rapid calcium depletion.
      3. Breast Cancer and Mammography
      Mammography: Diagnostic x-ray examination of the breasts.
      4. Hysterectomy
      Hysterectomy: Surgical removal of the uterus.
      5. Hormone Replacement Therapy
         - **Hormone replacement therapy (HRT)**: Treatment with artificial estrogen, sometimes in combination with the hormone progesterone, to relieve or prevent symptoms caused by decline in estrogen levels after menopause.

- *Selective estrogen receptor modulators:* Nonhormonal chemicals that seem to have favorable effects on bone density and cholesterol levels without the risk of breast cancer.
D. Influence of Emotional States, Personality, and Stress
Neuroticism: Emotional instability.
1. Stress: Causes and Effects
Stressors: Stress-producing experiences.
2. Managing Stress
Adaptive defenses: Ways of adapting to stress that help a person make the best of a bad situation.
3. Occupational Stress
- *Karoshi:* Japanese word for "death from overwork."
- *Occupational stress:* Stress that is work-related.
- *Sexual harassment:* Psychological pressure created by unwelcome sexual overtures, particularly from a superior, which create a hostile or abusive environment.
4. Burnout
Burnout: Syndrome of emotional exhaustion and a sense that one can no longer accomplish anything on the job.
5. Unemployment

COGNITIVE DEVELOPMENT
IV. MEASURING COGNITIVE ABILITIES IN MIDDLE AGE
- **Fluid intelligence**: Type of intelligence, proposed by Horn and Cattell, which is applied to novel problems and is relatively independent of educational and cultural influences.
- **Crystallized intelligence**: Type of intelligence, proposed by Horn and Cattell, involving the ability to remember and use learned information; it is largely dependent on education and cultural background.

V. THE DISTINCTIVENESS OF ADULT COGNITION
A. The Role of Expertise
Encapsulation: In Hoyer's terminology, progressive dedication of information processing and fluid thinking to specific knowledge systems, making knowledge more readily accessible.
B. Integrative Thought
Integrative: The ability of mature adults to use logic, intuition, and emotion; conflicting facts and ideas; and new information with old information in combination.
C. Practical Problem Solving
- *Instrumental:* Kind of problem concerning everyday activities, such as reading a map.
- *Social:* Kind of problem concerning the differences among people of varying ages and backgrounds.

VI. CREATIVITY
- *Creative potential:* The talent for creativity that is present in a person, such as a child, but not yet realized in fact.
- *Creative performance:* What, and how much, a creative mind produces.

A. Creativity and Intelligence
- *Insightful:* In Sternberg's theory, the ability to think originally and creatively.
- *Analytic:* In Sternberg's theory, the ability to process information efficiently, as in problem-solving.
- *Practical:* In Sternberg's theory, the ability to size up a situation and decide what to do: adapt to it, change it, or get out of it.

B. Creativity and Age
Quality ratio: The proportion of major works to total output.

VII. WORK AND EDUCATION: ARE AGE-BASED ROLES OBSOLETE?
- **Age-differentiated**: Life structure in which primary roles—learning, working, and leisure—are based on age; typical in industrialized societies.
- **Age-integrated**: Life structure in which primary roles—learning, working, and leisure—are open to adults of all ages and can be interspersed throughout the life span.

A. Occupational Patterns and Paths
- *Stable:* Referring to a career pattern in which the individual stays with a single vocation and, often by midlife, reaches a position of power and responsibility.
- *Shifting:* Referring to a career pattern in which the individual continually reevaluates his or her abilities, expectations, and wants, often leading to a career change.

B. Work versus Early Retirement
C. Work and Cognitive Development
D. The Mature Learner

True/False Self-Test

Place a T or an F in the appropriate space. These questions are taken from the chapter content, tables, key terms, Guideposts for Study, and Checkpoints.

1. _____ From young adulthood through the middle years, sensory and motor changes are small, gradual, and almost imperceptible.

2. _____ The incidence of myopia and presbyopia increases through middle age.

3. _____ By the end of middle age, 1 out of 4 people has a significant hearing loss.

4. _____ Loss of endurance results from a sudden decrease in basal metabolism.

5. _____ Typically, middle-aged adults are better drivers than younger ones are.

6. _____ Middle-aged workers are more likely than younger workers to suffer disabling injuries on the job.

7. _____ Heart disease becomes more common beginning in the late forties or early fifties, especially among men.

8. ___ Some women experience menopause as early as 45.

9. ___ Sexual activity ends abruptly in midlife.

10. ___ The idea that menopause produces depression in most women is a myth.

11. ___ Men experience a gradual decline in testosterone levels after age 60.

12. ___ Low income has no impact on general health in midlife.

13. ___ An accumulation of minor, everyday stressors has less impact than major life changes on physical and psychological health.

14. ___ Fluid intelligence declines earlier than crystallized intelligence.

15. ___ Postformal thought seems to be useful in situations calling for integrative thinking.

16. ___ Hot flashes have been found to be rare or infrequent among Mayan, North African, Navajo, and some Indonesian women.

17. ___ Men have an experience comparable to menopause when their levels of testosterone take a sudden drop in midlife.

18. ___ Many children of middle-aged parents are vastly ignorant of their parents' sexual activity.

19. ___ Gradual loss of bone density is an abnormal sign of aging in midlife.

20. ___ The most troublesome physical effects of menopause are linked to reduced levels of estrogen.

21. ___ The death rates for middle-aged African Americans is half that of white Americans.

22. ___ Unemployment has been linked to heart attack, stroke, anxiety, and depression.

23. ___ Cognitively speaking, middle-aged people are in their prime.

24. ___ An important feature of postformal thought is its integrative nature.

25. ___ The traditional life structure in industrialized societies is age-integrated.

Multiple-Choice Self-Test

Circle the letter of the best answer. These questions are based on many aspects of the chapter content, in no particular order.

1. Poor health in midlife is associated with
   a. low income.
   b. African American ethnicity.
   c. male gender.
   d. All of the above.

2. Postmenopausal women are more susceptible to
   a. nervous breakdowns.
   b. divorce.
   c. heart disease.
   d. jaundice.

3. Occupational stress can be caused by
   a. work overload.
   b. high pressure.
   c. low control.
   d. All of the above.

4. Many men in midlife experience
   a. a decline in fertility.
   b. more freedom in their marriages.
   c. more divorce.
   d. depression.

5. Sexual activity in midlife
   a. is virtually nonexistent.
   b. is rare.
   c. diminishes only slightly and gradually.
   d. is unchanged from early adulthood.

6. The cessation of menstruation and of ability to bear children that typically occurs at around age 50 is known as
   a. climacteric.
   b. menopause.
   c. perimenopause.
   d. sterility.

7. A condition in which the bones become thin and brittle as a result of rapid calcium depletion is known as
   a. hypertension.
   b. climacteric.
   c. osteoporosis.
   d. vital capacity.

8. Farsightedness associated with aging, resulting when the lens of the eye becomes less elastic, is
   a. myopia.
   b. presbyopia.
   c. presbycuspis.
   d. HRT.

9. Life structure in which primary roles—learning, working, and leisure— are open to adults of all ages and can be interspersed throughout the life span is called
   a. age-integrated.
   b. age-differentiated.
   c. utopia.
   d. distance learning

10. In Hoyer's terminology, progressive dedication of information processing and fluid thinking to specific knowledge systems, making knowledge more readily accessible, is known as
    a. encapsulation.
    b. crystallized intelligence.
    c. fluid intelligence.
    d. creative performance.

11. Today the double standard of aging is
    a. waning.
    b. in place.
    c. escalating.
    d. nonexistent.

12. Most cases of osteoporosis occur in
a. women.
b. men.
c. in adolescents.
d. in early adulthood.

13. Bone loss can be slowed or even reversed with
a. nutrition.
b. exercise.
c. quitting smoking.
d. All of the above.

14. Hormone replacement therapy
a. prevents bone loss.
b. makes women more cheerful.
c. increases fertility in midlife.
d. causes increased sexual activity.

15. Tamoxifen and raloxifene are
a. selective estrogen receptor modulators.
b. cancer drugs.
c. fertility drugs.
d. None of the above.

16. The largest single underlying factor in the excessive mortality rate for African Americans is
a. cancer.
b. genetics.
c. poverty.
d. venereal disease.

17. The cumulative effects of stress show up
a. in late adulthood.
b. in adolescence.
c. in middle age.
d. in early adulthood.

18. According to Table 15-3, the two life events rated as the most stress producing are
a. marital separation and pregnancy.
b. death of a spouse and divorce.
c. personal injury and illness.
d. foreclosure of mortgage and sex difficulties.

19. According to Table 15-3, minor violations of law and changes in residence are regarded as
a. low stress.
b. moderate stress.
c. high stress.
d. None of the above.

20. A feeling of emotional exhaustion, inability to get anything done at work, and a sense of helplessness and loss of control are all symptoms of
a. schizophrenia.
b. burnout.
c. nervous breakdown.
d. hypertension.

Organize It!

1. List four physical changes of midlife.

   1.

   2.

   3.

   4.

2. List the six basic mental abilities that showed longitudinal change in people ages 25 to 67, according to Schaie (see Figure 15-4).

   1.
   2.
   3.
   4.
   5.
   6.

Short Essay Questions

These short essay questions are based on the Checkpoints in the chapter. Answer each question as completely and succinctly as possible.

1. Identify factors that can affect women's experience of menopause.

2. Summarize changes in sensory and motor functioning and body structure and systems that may begin in middle age.

3. Discuss the relationship between creative potential and creative performance, and name several qualities of creative achievers.

4. Tell how women's risk of heart disease and osteoporosis increases after menopause, and weigh the risks and benefits of, and alternatives to, hormone replacement therapy.

5. Discuss the excessive mortality of African Americans and cite factors that have been found to be linked to it.

Critical Thinking Questions

These questions can be used for extra credit or small-group discussions.

1. In your opinion, when does middle age begin? When does it end?

2. In your opinion, do middle-aged women show more concern about their appearance than middle-aged men? If so, in what ways do they show this concern?

3. What are the main sources of stress in your life?

4. If you needed surgery, would you rather go to a middle-aged doctor or a young doctor? Why?

5. In addition to those mentioned in the text, can you think of ways in which an age-integrated society would be different from an age-differentiated one?

6. Based on your own observations, do students of nontraditional age do better or worse in college than those who are younger? How do you explain your observation?

Answer Keys

True/False Self-Test

1. T	p. 529	GP 2		14. T	p. 552	GP 4
2. T	p. 530	GP 2		15. T	p. 554	GP 5
3. T	p. 530	GP 2		16. T	p. 535	GP 2
4. F	p. 531	GP 2		17. F	p. 534	GP 2
5. T	p. 531	GP 2		18. T	p. 536	GP 2
6. F	p. 531	GP 2		19. F	p. 541	GP 3
7. T	p. 532	GP 2		20. T	p. 543	GP 3
8. T	p. 532	GP 2		21. F	p. 540	GP 3
9. F	p. 532	GP 2		22. T	p. 549	GP 3
10. T	p. 533	GP 2		23. T	p. 550	GP 4
11. T	p. 534	GP 2		24. T	p. 554	GP 5
12. F	p. 540	GP 3		25. F	p. 558	GP 7
13. F	p. 545	GP 3				

Multiple-Choice Self-Test

1. d	p. 538	GP 3		11. a	p. 538	GP 2
2. c	p. 541	GP 3		12. a	p. 541	GP 3
3. d	p. 547	GP 3		13. d	p. 542	GP 3
4. a	p. 535	GP 2		14. a	p. 543	GP 3
5. c	p. 536	GP 2		15. a	p. 543	GP 3
6. b	p. 532	GP 2		16. c	p. 541	GP 3
7. c	p. 541	GP 3		17. c	p. 546	GP 3
8. b	p. 530	GP 2		18. b	p. 545	GP 3
9. a	p. 558	GP 7		19. a	p. 545	GP 3
10. a	p. 553	GP 5		20. b	p. 548	GP 3

Organize It!

1.	pp. 529-534	GP 2
2.	p. 550	GP 4

Short Essay Questions

1.	p. 533	GP 2
2.	pp. 529-534	GP 2
3.	pp. 556-557	GP 6
4.	pp. 541-544	GP 3
5.	pp. 540-541	GP 3

CHAPTER 16: PSYCHOSOCIAL DEVELOPMENT IN MIDDLE ADULTHOOD

This chapter explores classic theoretical approaches to midlife change, identity development, midlife crisis, and changes in relationships. Marriage, divorce, relationships with children, and aging parents are discussed in the second section. The two focus boxes discuss the possibility of a society without middle age and preventing caregiver burnout.

Guideposts for Study

1. How do developmental scientists approach the study of psychosocial development in middle adulthood?

2. What do classic theorists have to say about psychosocial change in middle age?

3. What issues concerning the self come to the fore during middle adulthood?

4. What role do social relationships play in the lives of middle-aged people?

5. Do marriages typically become happier or unhappier during the middle years?

6. How common is divorce at this time of life?

7. How do gay and lesbian relationships compare with heterosexual ones?

8. How do friendships fare during middle age?

9. How do parent-child relationships change as children approach and reach adulthood?

10. How do middle-aged people get along with parents and siblings?

11. How has grandparenthood changed, and what roles do grandparents play?

Detailed Chapter Outline with Key Terms

I. LOOKING AT THE LIFE COURSE IN MIDDLE AGE
Middle adulthood: The 25-year span between the ages of 40 and 65.

II. CHANGE AT MIDLIFE: CLASSIC THEORETICAL APPROACHES
Self-actualization: Full realization of human potential.
   A. Normative-Stage Models
      1. Carl G. Jung: Individuation and Transcendence
      Individuation: Emergence of the true self through balancing or integration of conflicting parts of the personality.
      2. Erik Erikson: Generativity versus Stagnation
      • **Generativity versus stagnation**: The seventh critical alternative of psychosocial development, in which the middle-aged adult develops a concern with establishing, guiding, and influencing the next generation or else experiences stagnation (a sense of inactivity or lifelessness).

- **Generativity**: Concern of mature adults for establishing, guiding, and influencing the next generation.
- *Care:* The virtue of the seventh crisis in Erikson's theory, a widening commitment to take care of the persons, the products, and the ideas one has learned to care for.

Kotre's Four Forms of Generativity:
1. *Biological:* Conceiving and bearing children.
2. *Parental:* Nurturing and raising children.
3. *Technical:* Teaching skills to apprentices.
4. *Cultural:* Transmitting cultural values and institutions.
   - *Communal:* The expression of generativity involving nurturance of others.
   - *Agentic:* The expression of generativity involving personal contributions.
3. Jung's and Erikson's Legacy: Valliant and Levinson
   Interiority: In Neugarten's terminology, a concern with inner life (introversion or introspection), which usually appears in middle age.
B. Timing of Events: The Social Clock

III. THE SELF AT MIDLIFE: ISSUES AND THEMES
A. Is There a Midlife Crisis?
- **Midlife crisis**: In some normative-crisis models, stressful life period precipitated by review and reevaluation of one's past, typically occurring in early to middle forties.
- **Midlife review**: Introspective examination that often occurs in middle age, leading to reappraisal and revision of values and priorities.
- *Developmental deadlines:* Time constraints on one's ability to accomplish certain things, like having a baby.
- *Ego-resiliency:* The ability to adapt flexibly and resourcefully to potential sources of stress.
B. Identity Development
1. Susan Krauss Whitbourne: Identity as a Process
   - **Identity process model**: Whitbourne's model of identity development based on processes of assimilation and accommodation.
   - **Identity assimilation**: Effort to fit new experience into an existing self-concept.
   - **Identity accommodation**: Adjusting the self-concept to fit new experience.
   - **Identity style**: Characteristic ways of confronting, interpreting, and responding to experience.
     - *Assimilative identity style:* A person who uses assimilation more than accommodation in adapting a self-concept.
     - *Accommodative identity style:* A person who uses accommodation more than assimilation in adapting a self-concept.
     - *Assimilate:* Take experiences into oneself without changing self.
     - *Accommodate:* Change oneself to fit new experiences.
     - *Balanced identity style:* Healthiest style, in which identity is flexible enough to change when warranted but not unstructured to the point that every new experience causes the person to question fundamental assumptions about self.

2. Generativity, Identity, and Age
   Life-course perspective on generativity: The idea that generativity, rather than being only a midlife stage of development, can be affected at any point in time by such things as social expectations, social roles, gender, education, race, ethnicity, and cohort concerns, as well as the timing and sequence of life events.
3. Narrative Psychology: Identity as a Life Story
   * *Narrative psychology:* Field that views the development of the self as a continuous process of constructing one's own life story.
   * *Generativity script:* Life story in which generativity plays a key role, and which gives the life story a happy ending.
   * *Commitment story:* Life story of highly generative adults typified by selfless dedication to social improvement and helping others.
4. Gender Identity
   * **Gender crossover:** In Gutmannn's terminology, reversal of gender roles after the end of active parenting.
   * *Androgyny:* Integration of both "masculine" and "feminine" traits.

C. Psychological Well-Being and Positive Mental Health
   Positive: Referring to mental health, a sense of psychological well-being and a healthy sense of self.
   1. Carol Ryff: Multiple Dimensions of Well-Being
      Six Dimensions of Well-Being:
      1. Self-acceptance
      2. Positive relations with others
      3. Autonomy
      4. Environmental mastery
      5. Purpose in life
      6. Personal growth
   2. Generativity as a Factor in Psychosocial Adjustment
   3. Is Middle Age a Woman's Prime of Life?

IV. CHANGES IN RELATIONSHIPS AT MIDLIFE
A. Theories of Social Contact
   * **Social convoy theory:** Theory of aging, proposed by Kahn and Antonucci, which holds that people move through life surrounded by concentric circles of intimate relationships or varying degrees of closeness, on which people rely for assistance, well-being, and social support.
   * *Social convoys:* Circles of close friends and family members on whom people can rely for assistance, well-being, and social support, and to whom they offer reciprocal care.
   * **Socioemotional selectivity theory:** Theory, proposed by Carstensen, that people select social contacts throughout life on the basis of the changing relative importance of social interaction as a source of information, as an aid in developing and maintaining a self-concept, and as a source of emotional well-being.
B. Relationships and Quality of Life

V. CONSENSUAL RELATIONSHIPS
A. Marriage
B. Midlife Divorce

- **Marital capital**: Financial and emotional benefits built up during a long-standing marriage, which tend to hold a couple together.
- **Empty nest**: Transitional phase of parenting following the last child's leaving the parents' home.

C. Gay and Lesbian Relationships

D. Friendships

VI. RELATIONSHIPS WITH MATURING CHILDREN

A. Adolescent Children: Issues for Parents

B. When Children Leave: The Empty Nest

C. Parenting Grown Children
- *Tight-knit:* Intergenerational families in which the members live physically close and are emotionally close.
- *Sociable:* Intergenerational families in which there is less emotional affinity or commitment, although the members live physically close to one another.
- *Obligatory:* Intergenerational families in which there is a lot of interaction but little emotional attachment.
- *Detached:* Intergenerational families in which members are geographically and emotionally far away from each other.
- *Intimate but distant:* Intergenerational families in which members live far away from each other or spend little time with each other, but retain warm feelings.

D. Prolonged Parenting: The "Cluttered Nest"

Revolving door syndrome: Tendency for young adults to return to their parent's home while getting on their feet or in times of financial, marital, or other trouble. (Also called the *boomerang phenomenon.*)

VII. OTHER KINSHIP TIES

A. Relationships with Aging Parents
   1. Contact and Mutual Help
   - **Filial maturity**: Stage of life, proposed by Marcoen and others, in which middle-aged children, as the outcome of a filial crisis, learn to accept and meet their parents' need to depend on them.
   - **Filial crisis**: In Marcoen's terminology, normative development of middle age, in which adults learn to balance love and duty to their parents with autonomy within a two-way relationship.
   2. Becoming a Caregiver for Aging Parents
   - **Sandwich generation**: Middle-aged adults squeezed by competing needs to raise or launch children and to care for elderly parents.
   - **Caregiver burnout**: Condition of physical, mental, and emotional exhaustion affecting adults who care for aged persons.

B. Relationships with Siblings

C. Grandparenthood
   1. The Grandparent's Role
   2. Grandparenting After Divorce and Remarriage
   3. Raising Grandchildren

Kinship care: Care of children living without parents in the home of grandparents or other relatives, with or without a change of legal custody.

True/False Self-Test

Place a T or an F in the appropriate space. Statements are based on Guideposts for Study, tables, and chapter content.

1. ____ Developmentalists view midlife psychosocial development objectively in terms of pathways and trajectories.

2. ____ Although some theorists, such as Freud and Costa and McCrae, held that personality is essentially formed by midlife, there is growing consensus that midlife development shows change as well as stability.

3. ____ Classic theories of midlife psychosocial development include normative-crisis models and the timing-of-events model.

4. ____ Erikson's seventh psychosocial crisis is guilt versus stagnation.

5. ____ The virtue of Erikson's seventh crisis is care.

6. ____ People no longer expect and assess their lives by the social clock.

7. ____ The "sandwich generation" is caught between competing needs to care for aging parents as well as their own children.

8. ____ Research supports the concept of a universal midlife crisis.

9. ____ Key psychosocial issues in midlife include identity development, psychological well-being, and gender identity.

10. ____ Vaillant and Levinson found no major midlife shifts in men.

11. ____ Generativity can be expressed through parenting and grandparenting.

12. ____ In midlife, identity development is no longer a central aspect of adulthood.

13. ____ Much research, including Helson's longitudinal studies, suggests that for women, the fifties are a prime time of life.

14. ____ Identity style can predict adaptation to the onset of aging.

15. ____ Research generally does not support Gutmann's hypothesis of gender crossover.

16. ____ Relationships at midlife have very little effect on physical and mental health, as they did in young adulthood.

17. ____ Research on the quality of marriage suggests a decline in marital satisfaction during the childrearing years.

18. ___ Research using Ryff's model has found that midlife is generally a period of poor mental health and declining socioeconomic status.

19. ___ According to narrative psychology, identity development is a continuous process of constructing a life story.

20. ___ Social convoys never change.

21. ___ Gay men who do not "come out" until midlife often go through a prolonged search for identity.

22. ___ During the first 20 to 24 years of marriage, couples become progressively more satisfied and happy.

23. ___ The years of marital decline are those in which parental and work responsibilities are greatest.

24. ___ Middle-aged sons are most likely to care for their aging parents.

25. ___ Women are more negatively affected by divorce at any age than are men.

Multiple-Choice Self-Test

Circle the letter of the best answer. These questions are based on many aspects of the chapter content, in no particular order.

1. The phenomenon of young adults, especially men, returning to their parents' homes, sometimes more than once, or delaying leaving the parents home, is called
a. the sandwich generation.
b. generativity.
c. the revolving door syndrome.
d. None of the above.

2. Costa and McCrae held that
a. personality is essentially formed by midlife.
b. men and women in midlife undergo individuation.
c. people in midlife are introspective and questioning.
d. interiority is essential in midlife.

3. A normative midlife crisis is
a. supported by research.
b. nonexistent.
c. not supported by research.
d. normal for females.

4. Compared to heterosexual couples, gay and lesbian couples
a. tend to have more egalitarian relationships.
b. experience very few problems in balancing family and career commitment.
c. are very different in most respects.
d. None of the above.

5. Carl Jung's two tasks of individuation are
a. giving up the image of youth and acknowledging mortality.
b. leaving material wealth and growing spiritually.
c. lessening of gender differentiation and interiority.
d. None of the above.

6. The individual life course is affected by
a. interaction with others.
b. cohort and gender.
c. socioeconomic status.
d. All of the above.

7. Relationships between middle-aged adults and their parents are
a. usually distant and superficial.
b. often strained.
c. usually characterized by a strong bond of affection.
d. very competitive.

8. The "emptying of the nest" may be most stressful for
a. mothers who have failed to prepare for the event .
b. fathers who have not been involved in childrearing.
c. Both a and b.
d. Neither a nor b.

9. Caregiving is a source of considerable stress for
a. everyone.
b. the sandwich generation.
c. the revolving door generation.
d. people in their thirties especially.

10. A characteristic trait of ego-resiliency is
a. the tendency to initiate humor.
b. emotional blandness.
c. denial of unpleasant thoughts and experiences.
d. relating to all roles in the same way.

11. The view of identity as "an organizing schema through which the individual's experiences are interpreted" is the theoretical model of
a. Costa and McCrae.
b. David Elkind.
c. Susan Krauss Whitbourne.
d. Piaget.

12. Ryff's scale of well-being includes
a. twelve stages.
b. six dimensions.
c. four levels.
d. ten steps.

13. Gutmann's view of traditional gender roles includes the idea that
a. gender roles evolved to ensure the security and well-being of growing children.
b. gender roles are too rigid to be useful in modern times.
c. women are stronger than men.
d. men are more vulnerable than women, emotionally speaking.

14. Circles of close friends and family members who can be relied on for assistance, well-being, and social support are known as
a. cohort.
b. social convoys.
c. consensual relationships.
d. None of the above.

15. All of the following are suggested as effective ways to prevent caregiver burnout except
a. use of community support services, such as meal delivery and transportation.
b. use of respite care.
c. behavior training and/or psychotherapy.
d. pushing oneself to the edge of one's financial, emotional, and physical limits.

Organize It!

Making lists is a fun and useful way to categorize information in your mind. After making each list, think of ways to memorize it so that you have immediate recall. Singing a list, dancing while you recite it, or simply saying it in a rhythmic pattern as you are walking, driving, or jogging allows your brain to store the information in easily retrievable form. Try it!

1. List the six dimensions of well-being in Ryff's scale (see Table 16-3).

    1.

    2.

    3.

    4.

    5.

    6.

2. List five characteristics of ego-resilient adults (see Table 16-1).

    1.
    2.
    3.
    4.
    5.

3. List the five female and four male Gusii life stages (see Windows on the World box).

    Female
    1.
    2.
    3.
    4.
    5.

    Male
    1.
    2.
    3.
    4.

Short Essay Questions

These short essay questions are based on the Checkpoints in the chapter. Answer each question as completely and succinctly as possible.

1. Explain why, and under what circumstances, parents of adolescent children tend to go through a process of reappraisal or lessened well-being.

2. Summarize important changes that occur at midlife, according to Jung and Erikson, and tell how these ideas influenced other normative-crisis research.

3. Summarize Whitbourne's model of identity, and describe ways in which people with each of the three identity styles might deal with signs of aging.

4. Compare Jung's and Gutmannn's concepts of changes in gender identity at midlife, and assess their research support.

Critical Thinking Questions

These questions can be used as extra credit or in small-group discussions.

1. On the basis of your own observations, do you believe that adults' personalities change significantly during middle age? If so, do such changes seem to be related to maturation, or do they accompany important events, such as divorce, occupational change, or grandparenthood?

2. Did either of your parents seem to go through a midlife crisis? If you are middle-aged, did you go through a crisis? What issues, if any, made it a crisis?

3. From what you have observed, do men and women face similar or different kinds of challenges at midlife?

4. Think of a long-term married couple that you know and whom you think of as happily married. What are the characteristics of their marriage? Are they similar to those listed in the text?

5. What should be the "house rules" when adult children (with or without grandchildren) move back into their parents' home?

6. What are some things that might be done to improve nursing home care?

Answer Keys

True/False Self-Test

1.	T	p. 567	GP 1
2.	T	p. 568	GP 2
3.	T	p. 568	GP 2
4.	F	p. 569	GP 2
5.	T	p. 569	GP 2
6.	F	p. 571	GP 2
7.	T	p. 592	GP 10
8.	F	p. 572	GP 3
9.	T	p. 572	GP 3
10.	F	p. 569	GP 2
11.	T	p. 569	GP 2
12.	F	p. 572	GP 3
13.	T	p. 574	GP 3
14.	T	p. 577	GP 3
15.	T	p. 583	GP 3
16.	F	p. 584	GP 4
17.	T	p. 579	GP 5
18.	F	p. 576	GP 3
19.	T	p. 582	GP 3
20.	F	p. 586	GP 4
21.	T	p. 584	GP 7
22.	F	p. 585	GP 5
23.	T	p. 592	GP 5
24.	F	p. 585	GP 10
25.	T	p. 580	GP 6

Multiple-Choice Self-Test

1.	c	p. 589	GP 9
2.	a	p. 568	GP 2
3.	c	p. 572	GP 3
4.	a	p. 587	GP 7
5.	a	p. 569	GP 2
6.	d	p. 568	GP 1
7.	c	p. 590	GP 10
8.	c	p. 588	GP 10
9.	b	p. 592	GP 10
10.	a	p. 573	GP 3
11.	c	p. 573	GP 3
12.	b	p. 578	GP 3
13.	a	p. 577	GP 3
14.	b	p. 582	GP 4
15.	d	p. 593	GP 10

Organize It!

1.	p. 579	GP 3
2.	p. 573	GP 3
3.	p. 570	GP 2

Short Essay Questions

1.	p. 588	GP 9
2.	pp. 568-570	GP 2
3.	pp. 573-574	GP 3
4.	p. 577	GP 3

PART 8: LATE ADULTHOOD

CHAPTER 17: PHYSICAL AND COGNITIVE DEVELOPMENT IN LATE ADULTHOOD

This chapter opens Part 8 of the text with a discussion of images of aging today, physical development, longevity, and physical and mental health in the first section. The second section explores cognitive development, including intelligence and processing abilities, memory, wisdom, and lifelong learning. The focus boxes discuss centenarians and new environments for the aging population.

Guideposts for Study

1. How is today's older population changing?

2. How has life expectancy changed, and how does it vary?

3. What theories have been advanced for causes of aging, and what does research suggest about possibilities for extending the life span?

4. What physical changes occur during old age, and how do these changes vary among individuals?

5. What health problems are common in late adulthood, and what factors influence health at that time?

6. What mental and behavioral disorders do some older people experience?

7. What gains and losses in cognitive abilities tend to occur in late adulthood, and are there ways to improve older people's cognitive performance?

8. What educational opportunities can older adults pursue?

Detailed Chapter Outline with Key Terms

I. OLD AGE TODAY

Ageism: Prejudice or discrimination against a person (most commonly an older person) based on age.

A. The Graying of the Population

B. "Young Old, " "Old Old," and "Oldest Old"

- **Primary aging**: Gradual, inevitable process of bodily deterioration throughout the life span.
- **Secondary aging**: Aging processes that result from disease and bodily abuse and disuse and are often preventable.
- *Young old:* People ages 65 to 74, or those who are the healthy, active majority of older adults.
- *Old old:* People ages 75 to 84, or those who are frail, infirm, and in the minority of older people.

- *Oldest old:* People age 85 and older.
- **Functional age**: Measure of a person's ability to function effectively in his or her physical and social environment in comparison with others of the same chronological age.
- **Gerontology**: Study of the aged and the process of aging.
- **Geriatrics**: Branch of medicine concerned with processes of aging and age-related medical conditions.

PHYSICAL DEVELOPMENT
II. LONGEVITY AND AGING
- **Life expectancy**: Age to which a person in a particular cohort is statistically likely to live (given his or her current age and health status), on the basis of average longevity of a population.
- **Longevity**: Length of an individual's life.
- **Life span**: The longest period that members of a species can live.
A. Trends and Factors in Life Expectancy
   1. Regional and Ethnic Differences
   2. Gender Differences
B. Why People Age
   Senescence: Period of the life span marked by changes in physical functioning associated with aging; begins at different ages for different people.
   1. Genetic-Programming Theories
      - **Genetic-programming theories**: Theories that explain biological aging as resulting from a genetically determined developmental timetable.
      - **Hayflick limit**: Genetically controlled limit, proposed by Hayflick, on the number of times cells can divide in members of a species.
      - *Programmed senescence:* Theory of aging in which specific genes "switch off" before age-related losses, such as in vision or hearing, become evident.
      - *Hormonal changes:* Changes in the hormones used by the body, possibly caused by genetic malfunction and creating the effects of aging.
      - *Immune system:* The body's defense system against disease.
      - *Telomeres:* The protective tips of chromosomes, which shorten each time a cell divides.
      - *Telomerase:* An enzyme that enables sex chromosomes to repair their telomeres.
   2. Variable-Rate Theories
      - **Variable-rate theories**: Theories explaining biological aging as a result of processes that vary from person to person and are influenced by both the internal and the external environment; sometimes called *error theories.*
      - **Metabolism**: Conversion of food and oxygen into energy.
      - *Wear-and-tear theory:* Theory that the body ages as a result of accumulated damage to the system beyond the body's ability to repair it.
      - *Free-radical theory:* Theory that attributes aging to the harmful effects of *free radicals,* which react with and can damage cell membranes, cell proteins, fats, carbohydrates, and even DNA.
      - **Free radicals**: Highly unstable oxygen atoms or molecules formed during metabolism.
      - *Mitochondria:* Organisms contained in human cells that generate energy.

- *Rate-of-living theory:* Theory of aging that suggests that the body can do just so much work, and the faster it works, the faster it wears out.
- *Autoimmune theory:* Theory of aging that suggests that an aging immune system can become "confused" and release antibodies that attack the body's own cells.
- **Autoimmunity**: Tendency of an aging body to mistake its own tissues for foreign invaders and to attack and destroy them.

C. How Far Can the Life Span Be Extended?

Survival curves: Curves, plotted on a graph, showing percentages of a population that survive at each age level.

III. PHYSICAL CHANGES

A. Organic and Systemic Changes

Reserve capacity: Ability of body organs and systems to put forth four to ten times as much effort as usual under stress; also called *organ reserve*.

B. The Aging Brain
- *Neurons:* Nerve cells.
- *Cerebral cortex:* The part of the brain that handles most cognitive tasks.
- *Axons:* Connective nerve tissue that carries messages to other cells.
- *Dendrites:* Connective nerve tissue that receives messages from other cells.
- *Synapses:* Gap between neurons and across which nerve messages flow.

C. Sensory and Psychomotor Functioning

1. Vision
   - **Cataracts**: Cloudy or opaque areas in the lens of the eye, which cause blurred vision.
   - **Age-related macular degeneration**: Condition in which the center of the retina gradually loses its ability to discern fine details; leading cause of irreversible visual impairment in older adults.
   - **Glaucoma**: Irreversible damage to the optic nerve caused by increased pressure in the eye.

2. Hearing

   Presbycusis: Age-related reduction in the ability to hear high-pitched sounds.

3. Taste and Smell

4. Strength, Endurance, Balance, and Reaction Time
   - *Plasticity:* Modifiability of performance.
   - *Tai chi:* Traditional Chinese exercises.

D. Sexual Functioning

IV. PHYSICAL AND MENTAL HEALTH

A. Health Status and Health Care

1. Chronic Conditions and Disabilities
   - **Arthritis**: Group of disorders affecting the joints, causing pain and loss of movement.
   - *Osteoarthritis:* Degenerative joint disease.
   - *Rheumatoid arthritis:* Crippling disease that progressively destroys joint tissue.

B. Influences on Health
   1. Physical Activity
   2. Nutrition
      Periodontitis: Gum disease.
C. Mental and Behavioral Problems
   - **Dementia**: Deterioration in cognitive and behavioral functioning caused by physiological changes.
   - **Alzheimer's disease (AD)**: Progressive, degenerative brain disorder characterized by irreversible deterioration in memory, intelligence, awareness, and control of bodily functions, eventually leading to death.
   - **Parkinson's disease**: Progressive, irreversible degenerative neurological disorder, characterized by tremor, stiffness, slowed movement, and unstable posture.
   - *Dopamine:* Neurotransmitter found in the brain and associated with Parkinson disease.
   - **Multi-infarct dementia (MD)**: Irreversible dementia caused by a series of small strokes.
   1. Alzheimer's Disease
      a. Symptoms and Diagnosis
         - **Neurofibrillary tangles**: Twisted masses of protein fibers found in brains of persons with Alzheimer's disease.
         - **Amyloid plaque**: Waxy chunks of insoluble tissue found in the brain of persons with Alzheimer's disease.
         - *Beta amyloid:* Abnormal protein variant associated with amyloid plaque deposits.
      b. Causes and Risk Factors
         ApoE-4: A variant of a gene on chromosome 19 carried by about 30 percent of the U.S. population and an important risk factor for late-onset Alzheimer's disease.
      c. Treatment and Prevention
         Cholinesterase inhibitors: Drugs that slow or stabilize the symptoms of Alzheimer's for at least six months to a year.
   2. Reversible Conditions: Depression
      Selective serotonin reuptake inhibitors (SSRIs): Drugs that have an antidepressant effect.

COGNITIVE DEVELOPMENT
V. ASPECTS OF COGNITIVE DEVELOPMENT
   A. Intelligence and Processing Abilities
      1. Measuring Older Adults' Intelligence
         - **Wechsler Adult Intelligence Scale (WAIS)**: Intelligence test for adults, which yields verbal and performance scores as well as a combined score.
         - *Classic aging pattern:* Tendency for scores on nonverbal performance to become lower as a person gets older, whereas verbal scores remain relatively stable.
         - *Fluid and crystallized:* Referring to mental abilities, with the former depending largely on neurological status and the latter on accumulated knowledge.
         - **Dual-process model**: Model of cognitive functioning in late adulthood, proposed by Baltes, which identifies and seeks to measure two dimensions of intelligence: mechanics and pragmatics.

- **Mechanics of intelligence**: In Baltes's dual-process model, the abilities to process information and solve problems, irrespective of content; the area of cognition in which there is often an age-related decline.
- **Pragmatics of intelligence**: In Baltes's dual-process model, the dimension of intelligence that tends to grow with age and includes practical thinking, application of accumulated knowledge and skills, specialized expertise, professional productivity, and wisdom.
- **Selective optimization with compensation**: In Baltes's dual-process model, strategy for maintaining or enhancing overall cognitive functioning by using stronger abilities to compensate for those that have weakened.

2. Changes in Processing Abilities

Event-related potentials (ERPs): Fluctuations in the direction of the brain's electrical activity that can be measured with electrodes attached to the scalp.

3. The Seattle Longitudinal Study

Engagement hypothesis: Proposal that an active, engaged lifestyle that challenges cognitive skills predicts retention or growth of those skills in later life.

4. Competence in Everyday Tasks and Problem Solving

Instrumental activities of daily living (IADLs): Everyday activities, competence in which is considered a measure of the ability to live independently; these activities include managing finances, shopping for necessities, using the telephone, obtaining transportation, preparing meals, taking medication, and performing housekeeping tasks.

5. Can Older People Improve Their Cognitive Performance?

B. Memory: How Does It Change?

1. Short-Term Memory
- *Digit span forward:* Test of short-term memory in which a person is to repeat a sequence of numbers in the order in which the numbers were presented.
- *Digit span backward:* Test of short-term memory in which a person is to repeat a sequence of numbers in the reverse order in which the numbers were presented.
- **Sensory memory**: Initial, brief, temporary storage of sensory information.
- **Working memory**: Short-term storage of information being actively processed.
- *Rehearsal:* Repetition of information.
- *Reorganization:* Organizing information in a way that allows better retrieval of that information.
- *Elaboration:* Mentally expanding and elaborating on information to be remembered.

2. Long-Term Memory
- **Episodic memory**: Long-term memory of specific experiences or events, linked to time and place.
- **Semantic memory**: Long-term memory of general factual knowledge, social customs, and language.
- **Procedural memory**: Long-term memory of motor skills, habits, and ways of doing things, which can often be recalled without conscious effort; sometimes called *implicit memory.*
- **Priming**: Increase in ease of doing a task or remembering information as a result of a previous encounter with the task or information.

3. Why Do Some Aspects of Memory Decline?
   a. Problems in Encoding, Storage, and Retrieval
      - *Encoding:* Process by which information is prepared for long-term storage and later retrieval.
      - *Storage:* Retention of memories for future use.
      - *Retrieval:* Process by which information is accessed or recalled from memory storage.
   b. Neurological Change
      - *Hippocampus:* Area of the brain associated with formation of memory.
      - *Corpus callosum:* Neural connection between the left and right hemispheres.
      - *Prefrontal cortex:* Foremost part of the cerebral cortex, associated with planning and decision making.
      - *Source monitoring:* Awareness of where a memory originated.
4. Metamemory: The View from Within
   Metamemory in Adulthood (MIA): Questionnaire designed to measure various aspects of adults' metamemory, including beliefs about their own memory and selection and use of strategies for remembering.
5. Improving Memory in Older Adults
   Mnemonics: Techniques designed to help people remember.

C. Wisdom
   - *Cognitive:* Referring to a mental ability.
   - *Tacit knowledge:* In Sternberg's terminology, information that is not formally taught or openly expressed but is necessary to get ahead.
   - *Fundamental pragmatics of life:* Knowledge and judgment about life's conduct and meaning.

VI. LIFELONG LEARNING
   - **Lifelong learning:** Organized, sustained study by adults of all ages.
   - *Kominkans:* Community education centers in Japan.

True/False Self-Test

Place a T or an F in the appropriate space. These questions are taken from the chapter content, tables, key terms, Guideposts for Study, and Checkpoints.

1. _____ According to studies using metamemory in adulthood, older adults may overestimate their memory loss, perhaps because of stereotypes of aging memory.

2. _____ According to Baltes's study of wisdom, older adults show it as much or more than younger adults.

3. _____ Lifelong learning serves mainly as entertainment for older adults.

4. _____ Although the effects of primary aging may be beyond people's control, they can often avoid the effects of secondary aging.

5. ____ Specialists in gerontology refer to people 85 and older as "old."

6. ____ Survival curves do not support the idea of a definite limit to the human life span.

7. ____ Heart disease, cancer, and stroke are the three leading causes of death for people older than 65.

8. ____ White people tend to have greater longevity than do black people.

9. ____ Older men outnumber women 3 to 2.

10. ____ The brain seems to be able to grow new neurons and build new connections late in life.

11. ____ A common vision disorder for the elderly is macular degeneration.

12. ____ Major depressive disorder tends to be underdiagnosed in older adults.

13. ____ Crystallized intelligence increases into old age.

14. ____ The Seattle Longitudinal Study found that cognitive functioning in late adulthood is highly variable.

15. ____ The ability to solve interpersonal and emotionally charged problems declines sharply in late life.

Multiple-Choice Self-Test

Circle the letter of the best answer. These questions are based on many aspects of the chapter content, in no particular order.

1. The graying of the population is largely due to
a. high birth rates in the mid-20th century.
b. high immigration rates in the mid-20th century.
c. Neither of the above.
d. Both of the above.

2. Leonard Hayflick found that
a. human cells in the laboratory will divide no more than 50 times.
b. mouse genes will combine with human genes.
c. the onset of senescence is highly predictable.
d. None of the above.

3. Free-radical theory is an example of which kind of theory?
a. genetic-programming theory
b. variable-rate theory
c. operant conditioning
d. survival curve theory

4. Genetic-programming theory implies
a. the Yalta limit.
b. a genetically decreed maximum to the life span.
c. that there is no limit to the life span.
d. that life span can be expanded by cloning.

5. The theories that explain biological aging as a result of processes that vary from person to person and are influenced by both the internal and external environment are
a. biological theories.
b. free-radical theories.
c. autoimmune theories.
d. variable-rate theories.

6. Telomeres are
a. hormones that control aging.
b. the protective tips of chromosomes.
c. highly unstable atoms formed during metabolism.
d. random bits of RNA.

7. The theory that proposes that specific genes may "switch off" before age-related changes become evident is
a. immunological theory.
b. free-radical theory.
c. programmed senescence theory.
d. endocrine theory.

8. Free-radical theory
a. focuses on the harmful effects of free radicals.
b. focuses on the beneficial effects of free radicals.
c. focuses on the beneficial effects of oxygen.
d. None of the above.

9. Recent data on centenarians seems to
a. contradict the view that the upper limit for human life span is 110 to 120 years.
b. supports the idea of the running out of the cellular clock.
c. support the Hayflick limit.
d. None of the above.

10. Dietary restriction theories support the view that
a. diet has no effect on aging.
b. rate of metabolism is a crucial determinant of aging.
c. caloric restriction increases the production of free radicals.
d. dietary restriction weakens the immune system.

11. Hearing loss in older adults is most often caused by
a. noise exposure.
b. presbycusis.
c. smoking.
d. middle ear infections.

12. Cataracts occur in
a. more than half of people older than 65.
b. very few people older than 65.
c. smokers, mainly.
d. females, mainly.

13. The most prominent early symptom of Alzheimer's disease is
a. inability to use language.
b. failure to recognize family members.
c. inability to recall recent events or take in new information.
d. inability to eat without help.

14. Which of the following is NOT a symptom of Alzheimer's disease?
a. misplacing everyday items
b. forgetting simple words
c. rapid, dramatic mood swings and personality changes; loss of initiative
d. getting lost on one's own block

15. The diagnosis of Alzheimer's disease in a living person is
a. about 85 percent accurate.
b. made on the basis of physical tests.
c. made on the basis of neurological tests.
d. All of the above.

16. Symptoms of depression are
a. diagnosed less often in late life.
b. less common in older adults than in younger ones.
c. a natural part of aging.
d. a sign of weakness.

17. Cognitive deterioration is
a. inevitable.
b. irreversible.
c. related to disuse.
d. overestimated.

18. The Metamemory in Adulthood questionnaire looks at
a. beliefs about one's own memory.
b. selection of strategies for remembering.
c. use of strategies for remembering.
d. All of the above.

Organize It!

Making lists is a fun and useful way to categorize information in your mind. After making each list, think of ways to memorize it so that you have immediate recall. Singing a list, dancing while you recite it, or simply saying it in a rhythmic pattern as you are walking, driving, or jogging allows your brain to store the information in easily retrievable form. Try it!

1. List three main causes of dementia in older adults.

    1.

    2.

    3.

2. List four stereotypes that are misconceptions about aging.

    1.
    2.
    3.
    4.

3. List four aspects of memory that appear nearly as efficient in older adults as in younger people.

    1.
    2.
    3.
    4.

Short Essay Questions

These short essay questions are based in part on the Checkpoints in the chapter. Answer each question as completely and succinctly as possible.

1. Give examples of negative and positive stereotypes about aging.

2. Compare two kinds of theories of biological aging, their implications, and supporting evidence.

3. Give several reasons why older adults' intelligence tends to be underestimated.

4. Summarize the findings of the Seattle Longitudinal Study with regard to cognitive changes in old age.

Critical Thinking Questions

These questions can be used for extra credit or in small-group discussions.

1. What stereotypes about aging have you seen or heard in the media or in everyday life?

2. If it were possible, would you want to live forever?

3. If you could live as long as you wanted to, how long would you choose to live?

4. What are some ways you might try to maintain your cognitive abilities, such as memory and problem solving, well into old age?

Answer Keys

True/False Self-Test

1. T	p. 639	GP 7
2. T	p. 640	GP 7
3. F	p. 641	GP 8
4. T	p. 609	GP 1
5. F	p. 609	GP 1
6. F	p. 615	GP 3
7. T	p. 610	GP 2
8. T	p. 612	GP 2

9. F	p. 612	GP 2
10. T	p. 619	GP 4
11. T	p. 620	GP 4
12. T	p. 630	GP 6
13. T	p. 632	GP 7
14. T	p. 633	GP 7
15. F	p. 635	GP 7

Multiple-Choice Self-Test

1. d	p. 608	GP 1
2. a	p. 613	GP 3
3. b	p. 614	GP 3
4. b	p. 613	GP 3
5. d	p. 614	GP 3
6. b	p. 614	GP 3
7. c	p. 613	GP 3
8. a	p. 614	GP 3
9. a	p. 615	GP 3

10. b	p. 617	GP 3
11. b	p. 621	GP 4
12. a	p. 620	GP 4
13. c	p. 627	GP 6
14. a	p. 627	GP 6
15. d	p. 627	GP 6
16. a	p. 630	GP 6
17. c	p. 634	GP 7
18. d	p. 639	GP 7

Organize It!

1.	p. 626	GP 6
2.	p. 607	GP 1
3.	pp. 636-637	GP 7

Short Essay Questions

1.	p. 607	GP 1
2.	pp. 613-615	GP 3
3.	p. 631	GP 7
4.	pp. 633-634	GP 7

CHAPTER 18: PSYCHOSOCIAL DEVELOPMENT IN LATE ADULTHOOD

This chapter explores the stability of personality traits, normative issues and tasks, and coping models of "successful aging," as well as personal and consensual relationships in late life. The final section of the chapter deals with nonmarital kinship ties. The two focus boxes examine the question of whether longevity and health may be related to personality and a glimpse of aging in Japan.

Guideposts for Study

1. What happens to personality in old age?

2. What special issues or tasks do older people need to deal with?

3. How do older adults cope?

4. Is there such a thing as successful aging? If so, how can it be defined and measured?

5. What are some issues regarding work and retirement in late life, and how do older adults handle time and money?

6. What options for living arrangements do older adults have?

7. How do personal relationships change in old age, and what is their effect on well-being?

8. What are the characteristics of long-term marriages in late life, and what impact do divorce, remarriage, and widowhood have at this time?

9. How do unmarried older people and those in gay and lesbian relationships fare?

10. How does friendship change in old age?

11. How do older adults get along with—or without—grown children and with siblings, and how do they adjust to great-grandparenthood?

Detailed Chapter Outline with Key Terms

I. THEORY AND RESEARCH ON PSYCHOSOCIAL DEVELOPMENT
Successful or optimal aging: Terms referring to the aging process in adults who are relatively healthy, competent, and in control of their lives, and who experience late adulthood as a positive stage of life.
  A. Stability of Personality Traits
   - *Extraverted:* Outgoing and socially oriented personality.
   - *Neurotic:* Moody, touchy, anxious, and restless personality.
  B. Normative Issues and Tasks
   - **Ego integrity versus despair**: According to Erikson, the eighth and final critical crisis of psychosocial development, in which people in late adulthood either achieve a sense of integrity of the self by accepting the lives they have lived, and thus accept death, or yield to despair that their lives cannot be relived.

- *Wisdom:* The virtue in Erikson's eighth stage, an informed and detached concern with life in the face of death.

C. Models of Coping

Coping: Adaptive thinking or behavior aimed at reducing or relieving stress that arises from harmful, threatening, or challenging conditions.

1. George Vaillant: Factors in Emotional Health
   Adaptive defenses: Mature defenses, in Vaillant's theory, such as altruism, humor, suppression, anticipation, and sublimation.

2. Cognitive-Appraisal Model
   - **Cognitive-appraisal model:** Model of coping, proposed by Lazarus and Folkman, which holds that, on the basis of continuous appraisal of their relationship with the environment, people choose appropriate coping strategies to deal with situations that tax their normal resources.
   - **Problem-focused coping:** In the cognitive-appraisal model, coping strategy directed toward eliminating, managing, or improving a stressful situation.
   - **Emotion-focused coping:** In the cognitive-appraisal model, coping strategy directed toward managing the emotional response to a stressful situation to lessen its physical or psychological impact; sometimes called *palliative coping.*
   - **Ambiguous loss:** A loss that is not clearly defined or does not bring closure.

3. Religion and Well-Being in Late Life

D. Models of "Successful" or "Optimal" Aging
1. Disengagement Theory versus Activity Theory
   - **Disengagement theory:** Theory of aging, proposed by Cumming and Henry, which holds that successful aging is characterized by mutual withdrawal between the older person and society.
   - **Activity theory:** Theory of aging, proposed by Neugarten and others, which holds that in order to age successfully a person must remain as active as possible.
   - *Engagement hypothesis:* Proposal that an active, engaged lifestyle that challenges cognitive skills predicts retention or growth of those skills in later life.

2. **Continuity Theory:** Theory of aging, described by Atchley, which holds that in order to age successfully people must maintain a balance of continuity and change in both the internal and external structures of their lives.

3. The Role of Productivity

4. Selective Optimization with Compensation
   Selective optimization with compensation: In Baltes's dual-process model, strategy for maintaining or enhancing overall cognitive functioning by using stronger abilities to compensate for those that have weakened.

II. LIFESTYLE AND SOCIAL ISSUES RELATED TO AGING

A. Work, Retirement, and Leisure
1. Trends in Late-Life Work and Retirement
2. How Does Age Affect Job Performance and Attitudes Toward Work?
3. How Do Older Adults Fare Financially?
4. Life After Retirement
   - **Family-focused lifestyle:** Pattern of retirement activity that revolves around family, home, and companions.

- **Balanced investment**: Pattern of retirement activity allocated among family, work, and leisure.
- **Serious leisure**: Leisure activity requiring skill, attention, and commitment.
B. Living Arrangements
  1. Aging in Place—and Other Options
  2. Living Alone
  3. Living with Adult Children
  4. Living in Institutions
  5. Alternative Housing Options
  Assisted living: Living in a facility that enables the older person to maintain privacy, dignity, autonomy, and a sense of control over their own homelike space, while giving them easy access to needed personal and health care services.
C. Mistreatment of the Elderly
  Elder abuse: Maltreatment or neglect of dependent older persons, or violation of their personal rights.
  Five Categories of Elder Abuse:
  1. Physical violence (intended to cause injury)
  2. Psychological or emotional abuse (insults, threats)
  3. Material exploitation (misappropriation of money or property)
  4. Neglect (failure to meet a dependent older person's needs)
  5. Violating personal rights (such as the right to privacy or to make health decisions)

III. PERSONAL RELATIONSHIPS IN LATE LIFE
A. Social Contact
  - *Social convoy theory:* Theory of aging proposed by Kahn and Antonucci, which holds that people move through life surrounded by concentric circles of intimate relationships or varying degrees of closeness, on which people rely for assistance, well-being, and social support.
  - *Socioemotional selectivity theory:* Theory proposed by Carstensen that people select social contacts throughout life on the basis of the changing relative importance of social interaction as a source of information, as an aid in developing and maintaining a self-concept, and as a source of emotional well-being.
  1. Relationships and Health
  2. The Multigenerational Family
     - *Lineal:* Family style in which the emphasis is on intergenerational obligations, with power and authority lodged in the older generation.
     - *Collateral:* Family style in which the emphasis is on egalitarian relationships, with flexible household structures.

IV. CONSENSUAL RELATIONSHIPS
A. Long-Term Marriage
B. Divorce and Remarriage
C. Widowhood
D. Single Life
E. Gay and Lesbian Relationships
  Status: A way of viewing homosexuality as a characteristic of the self.
F. Friendships

V. NONMARITAL KINSHIP TIES
  A. Relationships with Adult Children—or Their Absence
  B. Relationships with Siblings
  C. Becoming Great-Grandparents

True-False Self-Test

Place a T or an F in the appropriate space. These questions are taken from the chapter content, tables, key terms, Guideposts for Study, and Checkpoints.

1. ___ According to Erikson, the crowning achievement of late adulthood is a sense of ego integrity.

2. ___ Wisdom, according to Erikson, is accepting the life one has lived with no regrets.

3. ___ According to Erikson, people who do not have acceptance are overwhelmed by despair.

4. ___ According to Vaillant's research, people in old age continue to adapt, much as they have adapted throughout their lives.

5. ___ Problem-focused coping focuses on eliminating, managing, or improving a stressful condition.

6. ___ One problem-focused strategy is to divert attention away from the problem.

7. ___ Apparently, with age, people develop less flexible coping strategies.

8. ___ Problem-focused coping seems to have a less positive effect on the well-being of older adults.

9. ___ Older adults have a more difficult time regulating their emotions than do younger people.

10. ___ Elderly white people are more involved with religious activity than are older African Americans.

11. ___ Religious involvement has a mostly positive impact on physical and mental health and longevity.

12. ___ People with the most or highest religious commitment tend to have the highest self-esteem.

13. ___ Researchers disagree on how to define and measure "successful aging."

14. ___ According to disengagement theory, aging normally brings a gradual reduction in social involvement and greater preoccupation with the self.

15. ___ Disengagement theory was one of the first influential theories in gerontology.

16. ___ Disengagement theory has received widespread research support.

17. ___ Compulsory retirement is an unwritten law that keeps the job market open for younger people.

18. ___ By 2025, Japan will have twice as many children as older adults.

Multiple-Choice Self-Test

Circle the letter of the best answer. These questions are based on many aspects of the chapter content, in no particular order.

1. In the United States, the number of people older than 65 years of age who live in institutions is
a. a small percentage.
b. growing steadily.
c. about 50 percent.
d. about 75 percent.

2. Older adults tend to
a. grow more depressed.
b. have more negative emotions.
c. grow more content and satisfied with life.
d. None of the above.

3. "Granny dumping" is
a. a form of elder abuse.
b. common in the United States.
c. a term referring to the abandonment of elderly persons in emergency rooms by caregivers who have reached the end of their rope.
d. All of the above.

4. Elder abuse
a. should be recognized as a form of domestic violence.
b. is uncommon.
c. is rare.
d. does not exist in the United States.

5. According to social convoy theory, changes in social contact typically affect
a. selectivity about friendships.
b. the chances of marriage.
c. a person's outer, less intimate social circles.
d. emotional needs.

6. Hispanic and Asian American cultures traditionally emphasize
a. collateral, egalitarian relationships.
b. lineal, intergenerational obligations.
c. highly flexible household structures.
d. None of the above.

7. Marriage in late life is
a. more common for men.
b. more common for older black men.
c. rare.
d. less likely to succeed than marriage in early adulthood.

8. Older, never-married people are
a. more likely than older divorced or widowed people to prefer single life.
b. less likely to be lonely.
c. a small percentage of the U.S. population.
d. All of the above.

9. Older people who are close to their sisters

a. feel better about life and worry less about aging.
b. feel more anxiety and worry more about aging.
c. are not different from those who have no siblings.
d. are not as satisfied as those who are close to their brothers.

10. Conflict and overt sibling rivalry

a. decrease by old age.
b. increase by old age.
c. do not change in old age.
d. are most common among brothers in old age.

Organize It!

1. List the six categories of elder abuse.

1.
2.
3.
4.
5.
6.

2. List the eight forms of group living arrangements suggested for older adults (see Table 18-1).

1.
2.
3.
4.
5.
6.
7.
8.

3. List 5 of the 18 United Nations Principles for Older Persons (see Table 18-2).

1.

2.

3.

4.

5.

Short Essay Questions

These short essay questions are based on the Checkpoints in the chapter. Answer each question as completely and succinctly as possible.

1. Compare two ways in which researchers try to measure successful or optimal aging, and point out drawbacks of each method.

2. Contrast disengagement theory, activity theory, continuity theory, and productive aging.

3. Identify several values great-grandparents find in their role.

Critical Thinking Questions

These questions can be used as extra credit or in small-group discussions.

1. What type of coping do you think you tend to use more: problem-focused coping or emotion-focused coping? What type of coping do your parents use? Your grandparents? In what kinds of situations does each type seem most efficient?

2. What is your definition of successful aging?

3. When do you expect to retire (if ever), and what do you want to do when you are retired?

4. If you were to become unable to care for yourself when old, what type of living arrangement would you want to have?

Answer Keys

True/False Self-Test

1.	T	p. 649	GP 2
2.	T	p. 650	GP 2
3.	T	p. 650	GP 2
4.	T	p. 650	GP 3
5.	T	p. 651	GP 3
6.	F	p. 652	GP 3
7.	F	p. 652	GP 3
8.	F	p. 652	GP 3
9.	F	p. 652	GP 3
10.	F	p. 653	GP 3
11.	T	p. 653	GP 3
12.	T	p. 653	GP 3
13.	T	p. 653	GP 4
14.	T	p. 654	GP 4
15.	T	p. 654	GP 4
16.	F	p. 654	GP 4
17.	F	p. 657	GP 5
18.	F	p. 657	GP 5

Multiple-Choice Self-Test

1.	a	p. 605	GP 6
2.	c	p. 649	GP 1
3.	d	p. 667	GP 6
4.	a	p. 669	GP 6
5.	c	p. 669	GP 7
6.	b	p. 670	GP 7
7.	a	p. 672	GP 8
8.	d	p. 672	GP 9
9.	a	p. 677	GP 11
10.	a	p. 676	GP 11

Organize It!

1.	p. 667	GP 6
2.	p. 667	GP 6
3.	p. 668	GP 6

Short Essay Questions

1.	pp. 653-654	GP 4
2.	pp. 654-656	GP 4
3.	p. 677	GP 11

PART 9: THE END OF LIFE

CHAPTER 19: DEALING WITH DEATH AND BEREAVEMENT

This chapter looks at the issues we all face as we approach the end of life. Some of the topics covered in this chapter are care of the dying, grief patterns, dealing with death at every stage of the life span, special losses such as those of a child or parent, suicide and assisted suicide, and finding meaning and purpose in life and death.

Guideposts for Study

1. How do attitudes and customs concerning death differ across cultures?

2. What are the implications of the "mortality revolution," and how does it affect care of the dying?

3. How do people change as they confront their own deaths?

4. Is there a normal pattern of grieving?

5. How do attitudes and understandings about death and bereavement differ across the life span?

6. What special challenges are involved in surviving a spouse, a parent, or a child, or in mourning a miscarriage?

7. How common is suicide?

8. Why are attitudes toward euthanasia ("mercy killing") and assisted suicide changing, and what concerns do these practices raise?

9. How can people overcome fear of dying and come to terms with death?

Detailed Chapter Outline with Key Terms

I. THE MANY FACES OF DEATH
   A. The Cultural Context
   - *Shiva:* Jewish custom in which mourners vent their feelings and share memories of the deceased.
   - *Mummification:* Early form of embalming to preserve a body so the soul can return to it.
   B. The Mortality Revolution
   Thanatology: Study of death and dying.
   C. Care of the Dying
   - **Hospice care**: Warm, personal, patient- and family-centered care for a person with a terminal illness.
   - **Palliative care**: Care aimed at relieving pain and suffering and allowing the terminally ill to die in peace, comfort, and dignity.

II. FACING DEATH AND LOSS: PSYCHOLOGICAL ISSUES

A. Confronting One's Own Death

Kübler-Ross's Five Stages of Coming to Terms with Death:

1. Denial (refusal to accept the reality of what is happening)
2. Anger
3. Bargaining for extra time
4. Depression
5. Acceptance

B. Patterns of Grieving

- **Bereavement**: Feeling of loss caused by death of someone to whom one feels close and the process of adjustment to the loss.
- **Grief**: Emotional response experienced in the early phases of bereavement.
- **Grief work**: Common pattern of working out psychological issues connected with grief, in which the bereaved person accepts the loss, releases the bond with the deceased, and rebuilds a life without that person.

  The Three Stages of Grief Work:
  1. Shock and disbelief
  2. Preoccupation with the memory of the dead person
  3. Resolution
- *Ambiguous:* Referring to a death that is unclear, such as a report of someone missing in action and presumed dead.
- **Grief therapy**: Treatment to help the bereaved cope with loss.

III. DEATH AND BEREAVEMENT ACROSS THE LIFE SPAN

A. Childhood and Adolescence

- *Irreversible:* Child's understanding that death is permanent and cannot be undone.
- *Universal and inevitable:* Child's understanding that all living things must die.
- *Nonfunctional:* Child's understanding that all life functions end at death.

B. Adulthood

- *Integrity versus despair:* According to Erikson, the eighth and final critical crisis of psychosocial development, in which people in late adulthood either achieve a sense of integrity of the self by accepting the lives they have lived, and thus accept death, or yield to despair that their lives cannot be relived.
- *Life review:* Reminiscence about one's life in order to see its significance.

IV. SPECIAL LOSSES

A. Surviving a Spouse

B. Losing a Parent in Adulthood

C. Losing a Child

D. Mourning a Miscarriage

Mizuko kuyo: Buddhist rite of apology and remembrance for miscarried children (*mizuko* means "water child," the Japanese word for a miscarried child).

V. MEDICAL, LEGAL, AND ETHICAL ISSUES: THE "RIGHT TO DIE"

   A. Suicide

   B. Aid in Dying

- **Active euthanasia**: Deliberate action taken to shorten the life of a terminally ill person in order to end suffering or to allow the death with dignity; also called *mercy killing.*
- **Passive euthanasia**: Deliberate withholding or discontinuation of life-prolonging treatment of a terminally ill person in order to end suffering or allow death with dignity.
- *Voluntary:* In referring to euthanasia, whether it is done at the direct request or to carry out the expressed wishes of the person whose death results.
- **Assisted suicide**: Suicide in which a physician or someone else helps a person take his or her own life.

    1. Advanced Directives

- **Advanced directive ("living will")**: Document specifying the type of care wanted by the will maker in the event of terminal illness.
- *Persistent vegetative state:* State in which, while technically alive, the person has no awareness and only rudimentary brain functioning.
- **Durable power of attorney**: Legal instrument that appoints an individual to make decisions in the event of another person's incapacitation.
- *Medical durable power of attorney:* Legal instrument that appoints an individual to make decisions about health care in the event of another person's incapacitation.

    2. Attitudes Toward Euthanasia and Assisted Suicide

    3. Efforts to Legalize Physician Aid in Dying

    4. End-of-Life Options

VI. FINDING MEANING AND PURPOSE IN LIFE AND DEATH

   A. Reviewing a Life

   Life review: Reminiscence about one's life in order to see its significance.

   B. Development: A Lifelong Process

True/False Self-Test

Place a T or and F in the appropriate space. Statements are basd on Guideposts for Study, tables, and other chapter content.

1. ___ Death and loss are universal experiences and have no cultural context.

2. ___ A traditional Jewish custom is never to leave a dying person alone.

3. ___ The three leading causes of death are heart disease, cancer, and strokes.

4. ___ The focus of hospice care is on preventing death.

5. ___ Kübler-Ross outlined five stages in coming to terms with death.

6. ___ Grief work is the typical pattern of three stages of dealing with loss.

7. ___ The second stage of grief work is shock and disbelief.

8. ___ Not all people who suffer a loss show signs of depression.

9. ___ Children understand that death is irreversible by age 3.

10. ___ People who feel that their lives have been meaningful may be better able to face death.

11. ___ Widowhood is the same for men as it is for women.

12. ___ The death of a second parent is usually not as painful as the death of the first parent.

13. ___ Suicide rates began declining in the late 1990s.

14. ___ Passive euthanasia is also known as mercy killing.

15. ___ Advance directives help many patients in comas or persistent vegetative states.

16. ___ In the United States, assisted suicide is illegal in almost all states.

17. ___ As the population ages, the issue of aid in dying will become more pressing.

18. ___ A life review is a process of reminiscence that helps a person see the importance of his or her life.

19. ___ Dying can be a developmental experience.

20. ___ Those who recall mostly negative events during the life review develop ego integrity.

Multiple-Choice Self-Test

Circle the letter of the best answer. These questions are based on many aspects of the chapter content.

1. Customs regarding disposal and remembrance of the dead
   a. are universal and unchanging.
   b. vary from culture to culture.
   c. are always governed by secular laws.
   d. None of the above.

2. Embalming actually goes back to the practice of
   a. sitting shiva.
   b. premature burial.
   c. mummification.
   d. cremation.

3. In the 1900s, the top causes of death in the United States were
a. diseases that affected mostly elderly people.
b. heart disease, cancer, and strokes.
c. diseases that affected mostly middle-aged people.
d. diseases that affected mostly children and young adults.

4. Care that focuses on relief of pain and suffering and allowing the person to die with dignity is known as
a. palliative care.
b. hospital care.
c. terminal care.
d. thanatos care.

5. In the _____ stage of coming to terms with death, a person refuses to accept the reality of what is happening.
a. denial
b. anger
c. bargaining
d. depression

6. The last stage of coming to terms with death is
a. anger.
b. acceptance.
c. bargaining.
d. depression.

7. The emotional response experienced in the early phases of loss of a loved one is called
a. bereavement.
b. grief work.
c. grief.
d. shock.

8. When memories of the dead person bring fond feelings mingled with sadness, the person is said to have reached the _____ stage of grief work.
a. first
b. second
c. third
d. fourth

9. Acceptance may be particularly difficult if the loss is
a. ambiguous.
b. sudden.
c. slow and drawn out.
d. unexpected.

10. Which of the following is NOT one of the concepts about death that children reach at about the age of 5 or 7?
a. death is irreversible
b. death is universal
c. a dead person is nonfunctional
d. they themselves will not die

11. Which of the following may make a loss more difficult for a child?
a. The child had a troubled relationship with the person who died.
b. The surviving parent depends too much on the child.
c. The death was unexpected.
d. All of the above.

12. In _____, people realize more keenly than before that they are going to die.
a. young adulthood
b. middle age
c. late adulthood
d. adolescence

13. Which of the following is TRUE concerning widowhood?
a. Men are more likely to be widowed than women.
b. Women tend to be widowed at an older age than are men.
c. One-third of women lose their husbands by age 65.
d. One-third of men lose their wives by age 65.

14. The death of a parent for an adult child can
a. be a maturing experience.
b. bring changes in other relationships.
c. free an adult child to spend more time and energy on other relationships.
d. All of the above.

15. The loss of a child may draw couples closer together if
a. the marriage was strong already.
b. the marriage was failing.
c. there were unresolved issues concerning the death of the child.
d. the parents were emotionally prepared for the event.

16. In the United States,
a. suicide rates lower with age.
b. suicide rates are higher among women than among men.
c. men are four times as likely to succeed in committing suicide as are women.
d. men make more attempts at suicide.

17. Deliberately withholding or discontinuing treatment that might extend the life of a terminally ill patient is called
a. active euthanasia.
b. passive euthanasia.
c. assisted suicide.
d. advanced directive euthanasia.

18. Assisted suicide is
a. legal in most states.
b. opposed by the AMA as being contrary to the physician's oath to do no harm.
c. legal in about half of the states.
d. None of the above.

19. A life review
a. can occur at any time.
b. has special meaning in old age.
c. can foster a sense of integrity.
d. All of the above.

20. Dying
a. can be a developmental experience.
b. is always unwelcome.
c. is never a "good death."
d. None of the above.

Organize It!

1. List the seven illness-related concerns for patients nearing death (see Table 19-1) and their associated questions and interventions.

   1.

   2.

   3.

4.

5.

6.

7.

2. List the stages of death and dying in Kübler-Ross's theory.

1.

2.

3.

4.

5.

3. List the three stages of grief work.

1.

2.

3.

Short Essay Questions

These short essay questions are based on the Checkpoints in the chapter. Answer each questions as completely and succinctly as possible.

1. Give some examples of crosscultural differences in customs and attitudes related to death.

2. Briefly discuss how people of different ages cope with death and bereavement.

3. Discuss the ways in which an adult's loss of a spouse or parent can be a maturing experience.

4. Discuss the ethical, practical, and legal issues involved in advance directives, euthanasia, and assisted suicide.

Critical Thinking Questions

These questions can be used for extra credit or small-group discussion.

1. If you have experienced a loss, especially an ambiguous one, how did you cope with it? What coping methods did you use?

2. What advice could you give a friend about what to say and what not to say to a person who is in mourning?

3. In your opinion, is the intentional ending of one's own life ever justified?

4. Would you ever donate an organ? To whom would you consider donating: a family member, a friend, a stranger?

5. Should assisted suicide be legalized? Why or why not?

Answer Keys

True/False Self-Test

1. F	p. 685	GP 1	
2. T	p. 686	GP 1	
3. T	p. 686	GP 2	
4. F	p. 687	GP 2	
5. T	p. 689	GP 3	
6. T	p. 690	GP 4	
7. F	p. 690	GP 4	
8. T	p. 691	GP 4	
9. F	p. 692	GP 5	
10. T	p. 694	GP 5	
11. F	p. 695	GP 6	
12. F	p. 696	GP 6	
13. T	p. 698	GP 7	
14. F	p. 700	GP 8	
15. F	p. 700	GP 8	
16. T	p. 702	GP 8	
17. T	p. 703	GP 8	
18. T	p. 704	GP 9	
19. T	p. 704	GP 9	
20. F	p. 704	GP 9	

Multiple-Choice Self-Test

1. b	p. 685	GP 1	
2. c	p. 686	GP 1	
3. d	p. 686	GP 2	
4. a	p. 687	GP 2	
5. a	p. 689	GP 3	
6. b	p. 689	GP 3	
7. c	p. 690	GP 4	
8. c	p. 690	GP 4	
9. a	p. 692	GP 4	
10. d	p. 692	GP 5	
11. d	p. 693	GP 5	
12. b	p. 694	GP 5	
13. c	p. 694	GP 6	
14. d	p. 696	GP 6	
15. a	p. 697	GP 6	
16. c	p. 699	GP 7	
17. b	p. 700	GP 8	
18. b	p. 700	GP 8	
19. d	p. 704	GP 9	
20. d	p. 704	GP 9	

Organize It!

1.	p. 688	GP 2
2.	p. 689	GP 3
3.	p. 690	GP 4

Short Essay Questions

1.	pp. 685-686	GP 2
2.	pp. 692-694	GP 5
3.	p. 696	GP 6
4.	pp. 700-703	GP 7